Spain Phras
Spanish

Castilian Spanish is the main language of Spain.

The term Castilian Spanish can be used in English for the specific dialects of Spanish spoken in north and central Spain. Sometimes it is more loosely used to denote the Spanish spoken in all of Spain as compared to Spanish spoken in Latin America; however, there are several different dialects of Spanish as well as other official languages in Spain.

Now, the Castilian Spanish of Spain is as British English is for those in England. Just as Portuguese in Portugal is as for those of Portuguese from Brazil. The country of origin keeps its dialects and its own sounds intact, but over longer periods of time some changes occur (just compare Shakespeare to modern British parlance for example). As for the explorers who brought their languages to the new world, the customs of the people and their own tribal languages had an effect to the languages brought by the explorers. Some things were probably entirely new to the Spaniards and instead of making up new words for it, they often just used the indigenous American word for it. Also, whenever a language is taught to a large group of people, some may end up learning it less than perfect and some of those idiosyncrasies found their way into some regional forms of Latin American Spanish. Some minor differences in grammar may also be attributable to different social realities (the disappearance of "vosotros" in Latin America may be because of that). So now, you have people from Latin America or the New World speaking different from those in Spain, England or Portugal.

So we wish to retain the original usage of this phrasebook relating to the whole regions of Spain where Castellano is spoken in its "original" form apart from the Spanish from Latin America. Particularly you shall notice all those 'th' sounds with the tongue sticking out between the teeth. Like for example the ci, ce, the d and the z get those 'th' sounds. The 'j' and the 'ge' and 'gi' gets guttural.

Pronunciation guide

This pronunciation usage is related to Castellano or the official language spoken in Spain. You will be understood if you travel from Latin America to Spain. There will be a few differences in sounds or words but you'll shall notice it here in this phrasebook. You shall notice the differences in sounds when it comes to Castilian Spanish.

Stress

Words that end in S, N or a vowel are stressed on the next to last syllable. For example:

estudiante (ehs-too-thee-AHN-teh), perros (PER-rohs), profesora (proh-feh-SOH-rah), repitan (reh-PEE-tahn),

Words that end in all other consonants (not S or N) are stressed on the last syllable. For example:

borrador (bohr-rah-DOHR), reloj (reh-LOHKH), pared (pah-REHTH), español (ehs-pah-NYOHL),

Words that do not obey the first two rules require an written accent mark on the stressed syllable. For example:

escribió (ehs-cree-BYOH), policía (poh-lee-THEE-ah), lección (lehk-THYON), lápiz (LAH-peeth),

Vowels

In Spanish, the vowels remain constant and it is the consonants that vary: Castilian Spanish-speakers use the "theta" sound for Ci, Ce, D and Z - it sounds like the "th" in the word "tooth". So in Madrid, the word zapatos sounds like `thah-PAH-tos'.

a
like 'a' in "father"
e
like 'e' in "pet" (at times this sound may be long as the 'e' in "bled")
i

like 'ee' in "speed"

o

like 'o' in "order"

u

like 'oo' in "goose

y

like 'y' in "simply ' (this letter by itself represents 'and')

Consonants

b

like 'b' in "boy"

ca

like 'ca' in "café"

ce

like 'the' in "there" [theh] /the tongue ought to be between both teeth/

ci

like 'the' in "thesis" [thee]

co

like 'co' in "cork" [kɔh]

cu

like 'coo' in "cook" [koo]

ch

like 'ch' in "church"

d

its more palatalized than the English 'd' at the beginning of a word and between vowels and at the end of a word its pronounced as 'th' as in "this" and at times it becomes silent.

f

like 'f' in "fish"

ga

like 'ga' in "gargle" [gah]

ge, gi

have a guttural sound like the 'ch' in "loch" or the 'ck' in "block" [kheh, khee].

go

like 'go' in "going" [goh]

gu

like 'goo' in "good" [goo]

gua

like 'gua' in "Nicaragua" [gwah]

güe

like 'gwe' in "Gwen" [gweh]

gue

like 'ge' in "get" [geh]

gui

like 'gee' in "geek" [gee]

güi

like 'gwi'

h

this letter is silent and its not pronounced

j

this sound is always guttural and a throaty sound like the 'ck' in "block" [kh]

k

like 'k' in "keep" hardly ever used except in (basque) proper names and loanwords

l

like 'l' in "lime"

ll

like 'y' in "yes" (Also pronounced like 'ly' in "homely" or "amply." Though still used in a few parts of Spain, this form is dying out.)

m

like 'm' in "monkey"

n

like 'n' in "nice"

ñ

like 'ny' in "canyon"

p

like 'p' in "post"

que

like 'ke' in "kept" [keh]

qui

like 'kee' in "keep" [kee]

r

trilled

rr

strongly trilled

s

like 's' in "son"

t

like 't' in "tent"

v

like 'b' in "base"

w

only used in foreign words like Walter

x

like 's' in "saw"

y

by itself is like 'y' in "possibly" and 'y' in "yes"

z

like 'th' in "think"

Common diphthongs

ai, ay

like side, eye

au

like found, cow

ea

like empty + art

eo

like end + obey

ei, ey

like pay

eu

like end + look

ia

like igloo + arrive

ie

like meek + end
io
like leek + open
oi, oy
like boy
ua
like walk
ue
like wet
ui
like week
uo
like won't

Phrase list

Basics

Hello.
¡Hola! (OH-lah)
How are you?
¿Cómo está usted? (KOH-moh ehs-TAH oos-TEHTH?)
I'm fine, thank you.
Estoy bien, gracias. (ehs-TOY BEE-ehn, grah-THEE-ahs)
What is your name?
¿Cómo se llama usted? (KOH-moh seh YAH-mah oos-TEHTH?)
My name is _____ .
Me llamo_____ . (meh YAH-moh)
Nice to meet you.
Mucho gusto. (MOO-choh GOOS-toh)
I'd like to introduce you to....
Me gustaría presentarle a.... (meh goos-tah-RYAH preh-sehn-TAHR-leh ah)
How old are you?
¿Cuántos años tiene usted? (KWAHN-tohs AH-nyohs TYEH-neh oos-TEHTH?)
I'm....years old.
Tengo....años. (TEHN-goh....AH-nyohs)

Please.

Por favor. (pohr fah-BOHR)

Thank you.

Gracias. (GRAH-thyahs)

Many thanks!

¡Muchas gracias! (moo-CHAHS grah-THYAHS)

You're welcome.

De nada. (theh NAH-thah)

Yes.

Sí. (SEE)

No.

No. (noh)

Excuse me. (getting attention)

Con permiso./Disculpe. (kohn pehr-MEE-soh/this-KOOL-peh)

Excuse me. (begging pardon)

Perdone./Perdóneme. (pehr-THOH-neh/pehr-THOH-neh-meh)

I'm sorry.

Lo siento. (loh SYEHN-toh)

Goodbye,

Adiós. (ah-THYOHS)

Good morning!

¡Buenos días! (BWEH-nohs THEE-ahs)

Good afternoon!

¡Buenas tardes! (BWEH-nahs TAHR-thehs)

Good evening!/Good night!

¡Buenas noches! (BWEH-nahs NOH-chehs)

Mrs.

Señora. (seh-NYOH-rah)

Mr./Sir.

Señor. (seh-NYOHR)

Miss.

Señorita. (seh-nyoh-REE-thah)

Language Barrier

Do you speak English? (formal)

¿Habla usted inglés? (AH-blah oos-TEHTH een-GLEHS?)

Does anyone here speaks English?

¿Alguien aquí habla el inglés? (ahl-GEE-ehn ah-KEE AH-blah ehl een-GLEHS?)

I speak a little.....

Hablo un poco..... (AH-bloh oon POH-koh)

I understand.

Entiendo. (ehn-TYEHN-thoh)

I don't understand.

No entiendo. (noh ehn-TYEHN-thoh)

Could you speak more slowly, please?

¿Podría Usted hablar más lento, por favor? (poh-DRYAH oos-TEHTH ah-BLAHR MAHS LEHN-toh, pohr fah-BOHR?)

Could you repeat that, please?

¿Podría usted repetir eso, por favor? (poh-DRYAH oos-TEHTH reh-peh-TEER EH-soh, pohr fah-BOHR?)

Could you show me in my dictionary/phrasebook?

¿Podría usted mostrarme en mi diccionario/libro de frases? (poh-DRYAH oos-TEHTH mohs-TRAHR-meh ehn mee deek-thyoh-NAH-ryoh/ LEE-broh theh frah-SEHS?)

Problems

Leave me alone.

Déjeme solo/la. (THEH-kheh-meh SOH-loh/lah)

Don't touch me!

¡No me tóque! (noh meh TOH-keh)

I'll call the police.

Llamaré la policía. (yah-mah-REH lah poh-lee-THYAH)

Police!

¡Policía! (poh-lee-THYAH)

Stop! Thief!

¡Párese! ¡Ladrón/na! (PAH-reh-seh lah-THROHN/nah)

I need your help.

Necesito su ayuda. (neh-theh-SEE-toh soo ah-YOO-thah)

It's an emergency.

Esto es una emergencia. (EHS-toh ehs OO-nah eh-mehr-KHEHN-thyah)

I'm lost.

Estoy perdido/dah. (ehs-TOY pehr-THEE-thoh/thah)

I lost my bag.

Perdí mi bolso. (pehr-THEE mee BOHL-soh)

I lost my wallet.

Perdí mi cartera/billetera. (pehr-THEE mee kahr-TEH-rah/bee-yeh-TEH-rah)

I'm sick.

Estoy enfermo/ma. (ehs-TOY ehn-FEHR-moh/mah)

I've been injured.

Estoy herido/da. (ehs-TOY eh-REE-thoh/thah)

I need a doctor.

Necesito a un doctor. (neh-theh-SEE-toh ah oon thohk-TOHR)

Can I use your phone?

¿Puedo usar su teléfono? (PWEH-thoh oo-SAHR soo teh-LEH-foh-noh)

Where are the toilets?

¿Dónde están los servicios? (THOHN-theh ehs-TAHN lohs sehr-VEE-thyohs)

At the Airport

Where is customs?

¿Dónde está aduanas? (THOHN-theh ehs-TAH ah-DWAH-nahs)

Where is passport control?

¿Dónde está el control de pasaportes? (THOHN-theh ehs-TAH ehl kohn-TROHL theh pah-sah-POHR-tehs)

Do you have anything to declare?

¿Tiene algo para declarar? (TYEH-neh AHL-goh PAH-rah theh-KLAH-rahr)

I have nothing to declare.

No tengo nada para declarar. (noh TEHN-goh NAH-dah PAH-rah theh-klah-RAHR)

I have something to declare.

Tengo algo para declarar. (TEHN-goh AHL-goh PAH-rah theh-klah-RAHR)

Where is the baggage claim area?

¿Dónde está el área para el reclamo de equipaje? (THOHN-theh ehs-TAH ehl AH-reh-ah PAH-rah ehl reh-KLAH-moh theh eh-KEE-pah-kheh)

Where are the international departures?

¿Dónde están las salidas internacionales? (THOHN-theh ehs-TAHN lahs sah-LEE-dahs een-tehr-nah-THYOH-nah-lehs)

Where are the arrivals?

¿Dónde están las llegadas? (THOHN-theh ehs-TAHN lahs yeh-GAH-thahs)

Where is gate_____?

¿Dónde está la puerta_____? (THOHN-theh ehs-TAH lah PWEHR-tah....)

Where is the information center?

¿Dónde está el centro de información? (THOHN-theh ehs-TAH ehl THEHN-troh theh een-fohr-mah-THYOHN)

Numbers

0
zero (THEH-roh)
1
uno/na (OO-noh/nah)
2
dos (thohs)
3
tres (trehs)
4
cuatro (KWAH-troh)
5
cinco (THEEN-koh)
6
seis (says)
7
siete (SYEH-teh)
8
ocho (OO-choh)
9
nueve (NWEH-beh)
10
diez (thyehth)
11
once (OHN-theh)

12

doce (DOH-theh)

13

trece (TREH-theh)

14

catorce (kah-TOHR-theh)

15

quince (KEEN-theh)

16

dieciséis (thyeh-thee-SAYS)

17

diecisiete (thyeh-thee-SYEH-teh)

18

dieciocho (thyeh-thee-OH-choh)

19

diecinueve (thyeh-thee-NWEH-beh)

20

veinte (BAYN-teh)

21

veintiuno (bayn-tee-OO-noh)

22

veintidós (bayn-tee-THOHS)

23

veintitrés (bayn-tee-TREHS)

30

treinta (TRAYN-tah)

40

cuarenta (kwah-REHN-tah)

50

cincuenta (theen-KWEHN-tah)

60

sesenta (seh-SEHN-tah)

70

setenta (seh-TEHN-tah)

80

ochenta (oh-CHEHN-tah)

90

noventa (noh-BEHN-tah)

100

cien (thyehn)

200

doscientos (thohs-THYEHN-tohs)

300

trescientos (trehs-THYEHN-tohs)

1000

mil/un mil (meel/oon meel)

2000

dos mil (thohs meel)

1,000,000

un millón (oon mee-YOHN)

1,000,000,000

mil millones (meel mee-YOH-nehs) in UK, mil millones (meel mee-YOH-nehs) in USA

1,000,000,000,000

un billón (oon bee-YOHN) in UK, un billón (oon bee-YOHN) in USA

number _____ (train, bus, etc.)

numero_____ (noo-MEH-roh)

half

mitad (mee-TAHTH)

less

menos (meh-NOHS)

more

más (MAHS)

Time

now

ahora (ah-OH-rah)

later

más tarde (MAHS TAHR-theh)

before

antes (ahn-TEHS)

morning

mañana (mah-NYAH-nah)

afternoon/evening

tarde (TAHR-theh)

night

noche (NOH-cheh)

day

día (THYAH)

dawn

alba/amanecer (AHL-bah/ah-mah-neh-THEHR)

sunset

puesta del sol (PWEHS-tah thehl sohl)

sunrise

salida del sol (sah-LEE-thah thehl sohl)

tommorrow

mañana (mah-NYAH-nah)

yesterday

ayer (ahh-YEARR)

Clock time

one o'clock AM

a la una de la mañana. (ah lah OO-nah theh lah mah-NYAH-nah)

two o'clock AM

a las dos de la mañana. (ah lahs thohs theh lah mah-NYAH-nah)

at noon

en mediodía. (ehn meh-thyoh-THYAH)

one o'clock PM

a la una de la tarde. (ah lah OO-nah theh lah TAHR-theh)

two o'clock PM

a las dos de la tarde. (ah lahs thohs theh lah TAHR-theh)

at midnight

en medianoche (ehn meh-thyah-NOH-cheh)

Duration

How long shall it be?

¿Cuánto de largo será? (KWAHN-toh theh LAHR-goh seh-RAH?)

How long is the duration?

¿Cuánto de largo es la duración? (KWAHN-toh theh LAHR-goh ehs lah thoo-rah-THYOHN?)

Will I/Will we have to wait that long?

¿Tengo que/Nosotros(as) tenemos que esperar esto mucho tiempo? (TEHN-goh keh/noh-SOH-trohs(ahs) teh-NEH-mohs keh ehs-PEH-rahr MOO-choh TYEHM-poh?)

_____ minute(s)

_____minuto(os) (mee-NOO-toh(ohs))

_____ hour(s)

_____hora(as) (KHOH-rah(ahs))

_____ day(s)

_____día(as) (thyah(ahs))

_____ week(s)

_____semana(as) (seh-MAH-nah(ahs))

_____ month(s)

_____mes(ses) (mehs(sehs))

_____ year(s)

_____año(os) (AH-nyoh(ohs))

Seasons

winter

invierno (een-BYEHR-noh)

spring

primavera (pree-mah-BEH-rah)

summer

verano (beh-RAH-noh)

autumn

otoño (oh-TOH-nyoh)

Days

today
hoy (oy)
yesterday
ayer (ah-YEHR)
tomorrow
mañana (mah-NYAH-nah)
this week
esta semana (EHS-tah seh-MAH-nah)
last week
la semana pasada (lah seh-MAH-nah pah-SAH-thah)
next week
la próxima semana (lah PROHK-see-mah seh-MAH-mah)
Sunday
domingo (doh-MEEN-goh)
Monday
lunes (LOO-nehs)
Tuesday
martes (MAHR-tehs)
Wednesday
miércoles (MYEHR-koh-lehs)
Thursday
jueves (KHWEH-behs)
Friday
viernes (BYEHR-nehs)
Saturday
sábado (SAH-bah-doh)

Months

January
enero (eh-NEH-roh)
February
febrero (feh-BREH-roh)
March
marzo (MAHR-thoh)
April

abril (ah-BREEL)
May
mayo (MAH-yoh)
June
junio (KHOO-nyoh)
July
julio (KHOO-lyoh)
August
agosto (ah-GOHS-toh)
September
septiembre (sehp-TYEHM-breh)
October
octubre (ohk-TOO-breh)
November
noviembre (noh-BYEHM-breh)
December
diciembre (thee-THYEHM-breh)

Writing time and date

As in most of Europe, the 24 hour clock is used. So you'll find train and other public schedules in the 24 hour clock form eg. 13:00am/pm. When telling time in Spanish, it is expressed by Es la for 1:00 only. And Son las for 2:00, 3:00, 4:00 and so on.

Colors

black
negro (NEH-groh)
white
blanco (BLAHN-koh)
gray
gris (grees)
red
rojo (ROH-khoh)
blue

azul (ah-THOOL)

yellow

amarillo (ah-mah-REE-yoh)

green

verde (BEHR-theh)

orange

anaranjado (ah-nah-rahn-KHAH-doh)

purple

morado (moh-RAH-thoh)

brown

marrón (mahr-ROHN)

pink

rosado (roh-SAH-thoh)

gold

dorado (thoh-RAH-thoh)

silver

plateado (plah-teh-AH-thoh)

Transportation

car

auto (OW-toh), coche (KOH-cheh)

taxi

taxi (TAHK-see)

bus

autobus (ow-TOH-boos)

van

furgón (foor-GOHN)

truck

camión (kah-MYOHN)

trolley

trolebús (troh-leh-BOOS)

tram

tranvía (trahn-VYAH)

train

tren (trehn)

subway
metro (MEH-troh)
ship
barco (BAHR-koh)
boat
bote (BOH-teh)
helicopter
helicóptero (eh-lee-KOHP-teh-roh)
airplane
avión (ah-BYOHN), aeroplano (ah-eh-roh-PLAH-noh)
airline
aerolínea (ah-eh-rah-LEE-neh-ah)
bicycle
bicicleta (bee-thee-KLEH-tah)
motorcycle
moto (MOH-toh), motocicleta (moh-toh-thee-KLEH-tah)
carriage
carruaje (kahr-RWAH-kheh)

Directions

How do I get to _____ ?
¿Cómo puedo llegar a_____? (KOH-moh PWEH-thoh YEH-gahr ah....?)
...the train station?
...la estación de tren? (lah ehs-tah-THYOHN theh trehn?)
...the bus station?
...la estación de autobuses? (lah ehs-tah-THYOHN theh ow-toh-BOO-sehs?)
...the airport?
...el aeropuerto? (ehl ah-eh-roh-PWEHR-toh?)
...downtown?
...el centro de la ciudad? (ehl THEHN-troh deh lah thyoo-THAHD)
...the youth hostel?
...el albergue juvenil? (ehl ahl-BEHR-geh khoo-beh-NEEL?)
...the _____ hotel?
...el_____hotel? (ehl...oh-TEHL?)
...the American/Canadian/Australian/British consulate?

...el consulado Americano/Canadiense/Australiano/Británico? (ehl kohn-soo-LAH-thoh ah-meh-ree-KAH-noh/kah-nah-THYEHN-seh/ows-trah-LYAH-noh/bree-TAH-nee-koh?)

Where are there a lot of...

¿Dónde hay un montón de... (THOHN-theh eye oon mohn-TOHN theh...)

...hotels?

...hoteles? (oh-TEH-lehs?)

...restaurants?

...restaurantes? (rehs-tow-RAHN-tehs?)

...bars?

...bares? (BAH-rehs)

...sites to see?

...sitios para ver? (SEE-tyohs PAH-rah vehr?)

Can you show me on the map?

¿Me puede mostrar en el mapa? (meh PWEH-theh mohs-TRAHR ehn ehl MAH-pah?)

street

calle/vía (KAH-yeh/BYAH)

avenue

avenida/rúa (ah-beh-NEE-thah/RWAH)

road

carretera/ruta (kahr-reh-TEH-rah/ROO-tah)

boulevard

bulevar (boo-LEH-bahr)

highway

autovía/autopista (ow-toh-BYAH/ow-toh-PEES-tah)

Turn left.

Gire a la izquierda. (KHEE-reh ah lah eeth-KYEHR-thah)

Turn right.

Gire a la derecha. (KHEE-reh ah lah theh-REH-chah)

left

izquierdo/da (eeth-KYEHR-doh/dah)

right

derecho/cha (deh-REH-choh/chah)

straight ahead

al recto (ahl REHK-toh)

towards the _____

hacia el _____ (AH-thyah ehl....)

past the _____

pasando la_____ (pah-SAHN-doh lah....)

before the _____

antes de la _____ (AHN-tehs deh lah.....)

Watch for the _____.

Esté atento al/los_____. (ehs-TEH ah-TEHN-toh ahl/los...)

intersection

intersección (een-tehr-sehk-THYOHN)

north

norte (NOHR-teh)

south

sur (soor)

east

este (EHS-teh)

west

oeste (oh-EHS-teh)

uphill

cuesta arriba (KWEHS-tah ahr-REE-bah)

downhill

cuesta abajo. (KWEHS-tah ah-BAH-khoh)

Car

Where can I rent a car?

¿Dónde puedo alquilar un coche? (THOHN-theh PWEH-thoh ahl-kee-LAHR oon KOH-cheh?)

How much is it daily/weekly?

¿Cuánto es diario/semanal? (KWAHN-toh ehs THYAH-ryoh/seh-mah-NAHL?)

Do you provide road maps?

¿Ofrece mapas de carreteras? (oh-FREH-theh MAH-pahs theh kahr-reh-TEH-rahs?)

Does that include insurance/mileage?

¿Eso incluye seguro/kilometraje? (EH-soh een-KLOO-yeh seh-GOO-roh/kee-loh-meh-TRAH-kheh?)

Where's the next petrol station?

¿Dónde está la próxima gasolinera? (THOHN-theh ehs-TAH lah PROHK-see-mah gah-soh-lee-NEH-rah?)

How long can I park here?

¿Cuánto tiempo puedo estacionarme aquí? (KWAHN-toh TYEHM-poh PWEH-thoh ehs-tah-thych-NAHR-meh ah-KEE?)

Does this street/road/highway lead to....?

¿Esta calle/carretera/autopista llega a....? (EHS-tah KAH-yeh/kahr-reh-TEH-rah/ow-toh-PEES-tah YEH-gah ah....?)

I need a mechanic.

Necesito un mecánico. (neh-theh-SEE-toh oon meh-KAH-nee-koh)

Bus and train

How much is a ticket to _____?

¿Cuánto cuesta un boleto a _____? (KWAHN-toh KWEHS-tah oon boh-LEH-toh ah...)

One ticket to _____, please.

Un boleto para _____, por favor. (oon boh-LEH-toh PAH-rah...., pohr fah-BOHR)

Where does this train/bus go?

¿Dónde va este tren/autobús? (THOHN-theh bah EHS-teh trehn/ow-toh-BOOS)

Where is the train/bus to _____?

¿Dónde está el tren/autobús a _____? (THOHN-theh ehs-TAH ehl trehn/ow-toh-BOOS ah.....)

Does this train/bus stop in _____?

¿Este tren/autobús hace parada en _____? (EHS-teh trehn/ow-toh-BOOS AH-seh pah-RAH-thah ehn....)

When does the train/bus for _____ leave?

Cuando sale el tren/autobus para _____ salen? (KWAHN-thoh SAH-leh ehl trehn/ow-TOH-boos PAH-rah...SAH-lehn?)

When will this train/bus arrive in _____?

¿Cuándo este tren/autobús llega a _____? (KWAHN-thoh EHS-teh trehn/ow-toh-BOOS YEH-gah ah....)

Taxi

Taxi!

¡Taxi! (TAHK-see)

Take me to _____, please.

Lléveme a _____, por favor. (YEH-beh-meh ah...., pohr fah-BOHR)

How much does it cost to get to _____?

¿Cuánto es el costo para llegar a _____? (KWAHN-toh ehs ehl KOHS-toh PAH-rah yeh-GAHR ah)

Take me there, please.

Lléveme ahí, por favor. (YEH-beh-meh ah-EE, pohr fah-BOHR)

Stop here, please.

Pare aquí, por favor. (PAH-reh ah-KEE, pohr fah-BOHR)

Lodging

Do you have any rooms available?

¿Se dispone de habitaciones libres? (seh thees-POH-neh theh ah-bee-tah-THYOH-nehs LEE-brehs)

How much is a room for one person/two people?

¿Cuánto cuesta una habitación para una persona/dos personas? (KWAHN-toh KWEHS-tah OO-nah ah-bee-tah-THYOHN PAH-rah oo-NAH pehr-SOH-nah/thohs pehr-SOH-nahs)

Does the room come with...

La habitación viene con... (lah ah-bee-tah-THYOHN BYEH-neh kohn...)

...bedsheets?

...sábanas? (SAH-bah-nahs)

...a bathroom?

...un cuarto de baño? (oon KWAHR-toh theh bah-NYOH)

...a telephone?

...un teléfono? (oon teh-LEH-foh-noh)

...a TV?

...un televisión? (oon teh-leh-vee-SYOHN)

May I see the room first?

¿Puedo ver la habitación primero? (PWEH-thoh behr lah ah-bee-tah-THYOHN pree-MEH-roh)

Do you have anything quieter?

¿Tiene algo más tranquilo? (TYEH-neh AHL-goh MAHS trahn-KEE-loh)

...bigger?

...más grande? (MAHS GRAHN-theh)

...cleaner?

...más limpio? (MAHS LEEM-pyoh)

...cheaper?

...más barato? (MAHS bah-RAH-toh)

OK, I'll take it.

Okay, lo cojo. (oh-KAY, loh KOH-khoh)

I will stay for _____ night(s).

Me quedaré por _____ noche(s). (meh keh-thah-REH pohr....NOH-cheh(s))

Can you suggest another hotel?

¿Puede sugerir otro hotel? (PWEH-theh soo-kheh-REER OH-troh oh-TEHL)

Do you have a safe?

¿Tiene usted una caja de seguro? (TYEH-neh oos-TEHD OO-nah KAH-khah theh seh-GOO-roh)

...lockers?

...armario? (ahr-MAH-ryoh)

Is breakfast/supper included?

¿Está el desayuno/la cena incluida? (ehs-TAH el theh-sah-YOO-noh/lah THEH-nah een-kloo-EE-dah)

What time is breakfast/supper?

¿A qué hora es el desayuno/la cena? (ah KEH OH-rah ehs ehl theh-sah-YOO-noh/lah THEH-nah)

Please clean my room.

Por favor, limpie mi cuarto. (pohr fah-BOHR, LEEM-pyeh mee KWAHR-toh)

Can you wake me at _____?

¿Me puede despertar a _____? (meh PWEH-theh thehs-PEHR-tahr ah....)

I want to check out.

Quiero desocupar mi habitación. (KYEH-roh theh-soh-koo-PAHR mee ah-bee-tah-THYOHN)

Money

Do you accept American/Australian/Canadian dollars?

¿Aceptan dólares americano/australiano/canadiense? (ah-THEHP-tahn THOH-lah-rehs ah-meh-ree-KAH-noh/ows-trah-LYAH-noh/kah-nah-THYEHN-seh)

Do you accept British pounds?

¿Aceptan libras esterlinas británicas? (ah-THEHP-tahn LEE-brahs ehs-tehr-LEE-nahs bree-TAH-nee-kahs)

Do you accept credit cards?

¿Aceptan tarjetas de crédito? (ah-THEHP-tahn tahr-KHEH-tahs theh KREH-thee-toh)

Can you change money for me?

¿Me puede cambiar dinero para mí? (meh PWEH-theh kahm-BYAHR thee-NEH-roh PAH-rah MEE)

Where can I get money changed?

¿Dónde puedo conseguir el dinero para cambiar? (THOHN-theh PWEH-thoh kohn-seh-GEER ehl thee-NEH-roh PAH-rah kahm-BYAHR)

May I get some Euros?

¿Puedo obtener algunos euros? (PWEH-thoh ohb-teh-NEHR ahl-GOO-nohs eh-oo-ROHS)

Can you change a traveler's check for me?

¿Puede cambiar un cheque de viajero para mí? (PWEH-theh kahm-BYAHR oon CHEH-keh theh byah-KHEH-roh PAH-rah MEE)

Where can I get a traveler's check changed?

¿Dónde puedo obtener un cheque de viajero cambiado? (THOHN-theh PWEH-thoh ohb-TEH-nehr oon CHEH-keh theh byah-KHEH-roh kahm-BYAH-thoh)

What is the exchange rate?

¿Cuál es el tipo de cambio? (KWAHL ehs ehl TEE-poh KAHM-byoh)

Where is an automatic teller machine (ATM)?

¿Dónde está un cajero automático (ATM)? (THOHN-theh ehs-TAH oon kah-KHEH-roh ow-toh-MAH-tee-koh)

Eating

A table for one person/two people, please.

Una mesa para una persona/dos personas, por favor. (OO-nah MEH-sah PAH-rah OO-nah pehr-SOH-nah/thohs pehr-SOH-nahs, pohr fah-BOHR)

Can I look at the menu, please?

¿Puedo mirar el menú, por favor? (PWEH-thoh mee-RAHR ehl meh-NOO, pohr fah-BOHR)

Can I look in the kitchen?

¿Puedo ver en la cocina? (PWEH-thoh behr ehn lah koh-SEE-nah)

Is there a house specialty?

¿Existe una especialidad de la casa? (ehk-SEES-teh OO-nah ehs-peh-thyah-lee-THAHD theh lah KAH-sah)

Is there a local specialty?

¿Existe una especialidad local? (ehk-SEES-teh OO-nah ehs-peh-thyah-lee-THAHD LOH-kahl)

I'm a vegetarian.

Soy vegetariano/na. (soy beh-kheh-tah-RYAH-noh/nah)

I don't eat pork.

No como carne de cerdo. (noh KOH-moh KAHR-neh theh THEHR-thoh)

I don't eat beef.

No como carne de vaca. (noh KOH-moh KAHR-neh theh BAH-kah)

I only eat kosher food.

Sólo como alimentos kosher. (SOH-loh KOH-moh ah-lee-MEHN-tohs KOH-shehr)

Can you make it "lite", please? (less oil/butter/lard)

¿Puedes hacerlo "lite", por favor? (PWEH-thehs ah-THEHR-loh "lite", pohr fah-BOHR)

fixed-price meal

comida de precio fijo (koh-MEE-thah theh PREH-thyoh FEE-khoh)

a la carte

a la carta (ah lah KAHR-tah)

breakfast

desayuno (theh-sah-YOO-noh)

lunch

almuerzo (ahl-MWEHR-thoh)

tea (meal)

té (TEH)

supper/dinner

cena (THEH-nah)

I want _____.

Quiero _____. (KYEH-roh....)

I want a dish containing _____.

Quiero un plato que contiene_____. (KYEH-roh oon PLAH-toh keh kohn-TYEH-neh...)

chicken

pollo (POH-yoh)

beef

carne de vaca (KAHR-neh theh BAH-kah)

fish

pescado (pehs-KAH-thoh)

ham

jamón (khah-MOHN)

sausage

embutido (ehm-boo-TEE-thoh)

cheese

queso (KEH-soh)

eggs

huevos (WEH-bohs)

salad

ensalada (ehn-sah-LAH-thah)

(fresh) vegetables

vegetales (frescos) (beh-kheh-TAH-lehs (FREHS-kohs))

(fresh) fruit

frutas (frescas) (FROO-tahs (FREHS-kahs))

bread

pan (pahn)

toast

tostada (tohs-TAH-thah)

noodles

fideos/tallarines (FEE-theos/tah-yah-REE-nehs)

rice

arroz (ah-RROHTH)

beans

fabas/judias (FAH-bahs/KHOO-thyahs) [Basque region is "alubias" (ah-LOO-byahs)]

May I have a glass of _____?

¿Puedo tener un vaso de_____? (PWEH-thoh TEH-nehr oon BAH-soh theh....?)

May I have a cup of _____?

¿Puedo tener una taza/copa de_____? (PWEH-thoh TEH-nehr OO-nah TAH-thah/KOH-pah theh......?)

May I have a bottle of _____?

¿Puedo tener una botella de_____? (PWEH-thoh TEH-nehr OO-nah boh-TEH-yah theh....?)

coffee

café (kah-FEH)

tea (drink)

té (TEH)

juice

zumo (THOO-moh)

(bubbly) water

Agua (burbujada) (AH-gwah (boor-boo-KHAH-thah))

water

agua (AH-gwah)

beer

cerveza (thehr-BEH-sah)

red/white wine

rojo/vino blanco (ROH-khoh/BEE-noh BLAHN-koh)

May I have some _____?

¿Puedo tener algun_____? (PWEH-thoh teh-NEHR AHL-goon....?)

salt

sal (sahl)

black pepper

pimienta negra (pee-MYEHN-tah NEH-grah)

butter

mantequilla (mahn-teh-KEE-yah)

Excuse me, waiter? (getting attention of server)

Perdone, camarero/ra? (pehr-THOH-neh, kah-mah-REH-roh/rah)

I'm finished.

Estoy acabado/da. (ehs-TOY ah-kah-BAH-thoh/thah)

It was delicious.

Estaba delicioso/sa. (ehs-TAH-bah theh-lee-THYOH-soh/sah)

Please clear the plates.

Por favor, clara la mesa. (pohr fah-BOHR, KLAH-rah lah MEH-sah)

The check, please.

La cuenta, por favor. (lah KWEHN-tah, pohr fah-BOHR)

Bars

Do you serve alcohol?

¿Sirven alcohol? (SEER-behn ahl-KOH-khohl?)

Is there table service?

¿Hay servicio de mesa? (eye sehr-BEE-thyoh theh MEH-sah?)

A beer/two beers, please.

Una cerveza/dos cervezas, por favor. (OO-nah thehr-BEH-thah/thohs thehr-BEH-thahs, pohr fah-BOHR)

A glass of red/white wine, please.

Un vaso de vino tinto/blanco, por favor. (oon BAH-soh theh BEE-noh TEEN-toh/BLAHN-koh, pohr fah-BOHR)

A pint, please.

Una pinta, por favor. (OO-nah PEEN-tah, pohr fah-BOHR)

A bottle, please.

Una botella, por favor. (OO-nah boh-TEH-yah, pohr fah-BOHR)

whiskey

whisky (WEES-kee)

vodka

vodka (BOHD-kah)

rum

ron (rohn)

water

agua (AH-gwah)

club soda

club soda (kloob SOH-thah)

tonic water

agua tónica (AH-gwah TOH-nee-kah)

orange juice

zumo de naranja (THOO-moh theh nah-RAHN-khah)

Coke (soda)

Coca-Cola (KOH-kah KOH-lah)

Do you have any bar snacks?

¿Tiene alguna merienda del bar? (TYEH-neh ahl-GOO-nah meh-RYEHN-thah thehl bahr?)

One more, please.

Una vez más, por favor. (OO-nah behth MAHS, pohr fah-BOHR)
Another round, please.
Otra ronda, por favor. (OH-trah ROHN-thah, pohr fah-BOHR)
When is closing time?
¿Cuando es la hora de cerrar? (KWAHN-thoh ehs lah OH-rah theh thehr-RAHR?)
Cheers!
¡Salud! (sah-LOOD) (literally this means "health" and may also be said after someone sneezes. Occasionally, one might say ¡Salud, pesetas, y amor! [sah-LOOD, pay-SAY-tuhz, ee uh-MOR] or "health, wealth, and love".)

Shopping

Do you have this in my size?
¿Tiene esto en mi talla? (TYEH-neh EHS-toh ehn mee TAH-yah?)
How much is this?
¿Cuánto es esto? (KWAHN-toh ehs EHS-toh?)
That's too expensive.
Eso es demasiado caro. (EH-soh ehs theh-mah-SYAH-thoh KAH-roh)
Would you take _____?
¿Tomaría _____? (toh-mah-RYAH....?)
expensive
caro/costoso (KAH-roh/kohs-TOH-soh)
cheap
barato (bah-RAH-toh)
I can't afford it.
No puedo pagarlo. (noh PWEH-thoh pah-GAHR-loh)
I don't want it.
No lo quiero. (noh loh KYEH-roh)
You're cheating me.
Usted me está engañando. (oos-TEHD meh ehs-TAH ehn-gah-NYAHN-thoh)
I'm not interested.
No me interesa. (noh meh een-teh-REH-sah)
OK, I'll take it.
OK, lo cogeré. (oh-kay, loh koh-KHEH-reh)
Can I have a bag?

¿Puedo tener una bolsa? (PWEH-thoh TEH-nehr OO-nah BOHL-sah?)

Do you ship (overseas)?

¿Hacen envíos (en el extranjero)? (AH-thehn ehn-BYOHS (ehn ehl eks-trahn-KHEH-roh)?)

I need...

necesito... (neh-theh-THEE-toh....)

...toothpaste.

...pasta de dientes (PAHS-tah theh THYEHN-tehs)

...a toothbrush.

...un cepillo de dientes. (oon theh-PEE-yoh theh THYEHN-tehs)

...tampons.

...tampón. (tahm-POHN)

...soap.

...jabón (khah-BOHN)

...shampoo.

...champú. (chahm-POO)

...pain reliever. (e.g., aspirin or ibuprofen)

...relevista de dolor (reh-leh-BEES-tah then DOH-lohr)

...cold medicine.

...medicinas para el resfriado (meh-thee-THEE-nahs PAH-rah ehl rehs-FRYAH-thoh)

...stomach medicine.

...medicina para el estómago. (meh-thee-THEE-nah PAH-rah ehl ehs-TOH-mah-goh)

...a razor.

...una navaja de afeitar (OO-nah nah-BAH-khah theh ah-FAY-tahr)

...an umbrella.

...una paragua. (OO-nah pah-RAH-gwah)

...sunblock lotion.

...loción de protección solar. (loh-THYOHN theh proh-tehk-THYOHN SOH-lahr)

...a postcard.

...una tarjeta postal. (OO-nah tahr-KHEH-tah POHS-tahl)

...postage stamps.

...sellos de correos. (SEH-yohs theh koh-RREH-ohs)

...batteries.

...baterías. (bah-teh-RYAHS)

...writing paper.

...papel para escribir. (pah-PEHL PAH-rah ehs-kree-BEER)

...a pen.

...una pluma. (OO-nah PLOO-mah)

...English-language books.

...libros en Inglés. (LEE-brohs ehn een-GLEHS)

...English-language magazines.

...revistas en idioma Inglés. (reh-BEES-tahs ehn ee-THYOH-mah een-GLEHS)

...an English-language newspaper.

...un periódico de idioma Inglés. (oon peh-RYOH-thee-koh theh ee-THYOH-mah een-GLEHS)

...an English-Castilian dictionary.

...un diccionario de inglés-castellano. (oon deek-thyoh-NAH-ryoh theh een-GLEHS-kahs-teh-YAH-noh)

Driving

Most of the signs in major cities in Spain are by pictures instead of actual lettered signs so refer to a European travel guide which will contain the rules for road or city signs.

I want to rent a car.

Quiero alquilar un coche. (KYEH-roh ahl-KEE-lahr oon KOH-cheh)

Can I get insurance?

¿Puedo obtener un seguro? (PWEH-thoh ohb-TEH-nehr oon seh-GOO-roh?)

stop (on a street sign)

stop (stohp)

one way

unica manera (oo-NEE-kah mah-NEH-rah)

yield

Ceda el paso (THEH-thah ehl PAH-soh)

no parking

No aparcamiento (noh ah-pahr-kah-MYEHN-toh)

speed limit

límite de velocidad (LEE-mee-teh theh beh-loh-THEE-thahd)

gas (petrol) station

estación de gasolina / gasolinera (ehs-tah-THYOHN theh gah-soh-LEE-nah/gah-soh-lee-NEH-rah)
petrol
gasolina. (gah-soh-LEE-nah)
diesel
diesel (THEE-thehl)

Authority

I haven't done anything wrong.
Yo no he hecho nada malo. (yoh noh eh EH-choh NAH-thah MAH-loh)
It was a misunderstanding.
Fue un malentendido. (fweh oon mah-lehn-tehn-THEE-thoh)
Where are you taking me?
¿Adónde me llevas? (ah-THOHN-theh meh YEH-bahs?)
Am I under arrest?
¿Estoy bajo arresto? (EHS-toy BAH-khoh ahr-REHS-toh?)
I am an American/Australian/British/Canadian citizen.
Yo soy un americano/australiano/inglése/ciudadano canadiense. (yoh soy oon ah-meh-ree-KAH-noh/ows-trah-LYAH-noh/een-GLEH-seh/thyoo-thah-THAH-noh kah-nah-THYEHN-seh)
I want to talk to the American/Australian/British/Canadian embassy/consulate.
Tengo que hablar con la embajada / el consulado estadounidense / australiano / británico / de canadá / canadiense . (TEHN-goh keh AH-blahr kohn ehl ehs-tah-THOW-nee-thehn-seh/ ows-trah-LYAH-noh/ bree-TAH-nee-koh/ ehm-bah-KHAH-thah theh kah-nah-THAH oh ehl kohn-soo-LAH-thoh)
I want to talk to a lawyer.
Quiero hablar con un abogado. (KYEH-roh AH-blahr kohn oon ah-boh-GAH-thoh)
Can I just pay a fine now?
¿Puedo pagar una multa ahora? (PWEH-thoh PAH-gahr OO-nah MOOL-tah ah-OH-rah?)

Made in the USA
San Bernardino, CA
26 April 2016

VACUUM MECHATRONICS
FIRST INTERNATIONAL
WORKSHOP

CONFERENCE PROCEEDINGS NO. **192**

AMERICAN VACUUM SOCIETY SERIES 7

SERIES EDITOR: **GERALD LUCOVSKY**
NORTH CAROLINA STATE UNIVERSITY

VACUUM MECHATRONICS
FIRST INTERNATIONAL
WORKSHOP

SANTA BARBARA, CA 1989

EDITORS: STEVEN E. BELINSKI, MAJID SHIRAZI,
SUSAN HACKWOOD, AND GERARDO BENI

University of California

AIP

American Institute of Physics   **New York**

L.C. Catalog Card No. 89-045905
ISBN 0-88318-394-3
DOE CONF-8902123

Printed in the United States of America.

CONTENTS

First International Vacuum Mechatronics Workshop

THURSDAY, FEBRUARY 2, 1989

WELCOME AND OPENING REMARKS
Dr. Robert Mehrabian
Dean of the College of Engineering, UCSB

SESSION 1—OVERVIEW OF VACUUM MECHATRONICS
Susan Hackwood, Center for Robotic Systems in Microelectronics, UCSB

SESSION 2—VACUUM ENVIRONMENT AND APPLICATIONS
CHAIR: THOMAS SEIDEL

Alex Ignatiev, Space Vacuum Epitaxy Center, University of Houston
Proposed Epitaxial Thin Film Growth in the Ultra-Vacuum of Space
Peter Borden, High Yield Technology
Particle Monitoring and Control in Vacuum Process Equipment
Hiroshi Saeki, T. Sekiguchi, Junji Ikeda, Matsushita Electric Ind. Co., Ltd.
Hajime Ishimaru, National Laboratory for High Energy Physics, Japan
The Electronic Dust Collector for Use in Vacuum Systems

SESSION 3—VACUUM MECHATRONICS DESIGN 1:
MATERIALS, ENERGY TRANSFER AND LUBRICATION
CHAIR: THOMAS SEIDEL

Tim O'Donnell, Jet Propulsion Laboratory
Materials Evaluation of an Electrically Noisy Vacuum Slip Ring Assembly
Brad Scott, Ball Aerospace Systems Group
An Overview of Lubrication and Associated Materials for Vacuum Service
Don Lewis, Dicronite Dry Lube and August Weilbach, Helvart Associates
The Usage of Lubricants in a Vacuum Environment
Ron Christy, TRW
Guidelines and Practical Applications for Lubrication in Vacuum

SESSION 4—VACUUM MECHATRONICS DESIGN 2:
MECHANISMS, ACTUATORS AND SENSORS
CHAIR: GERARDO BENI

Y. Tito Sasaki, Quantum Mechanics Corporation, Lyle Bergquist, Martin Marietta
Recent Developments in Leak Detector and Calibrator Designs
Junji Ikeda, T. Sekiguchi, Hiroshi Saeki, Matsushita Electric Ind. Co., Ltd.
Hajime Ishimaru, National Laboratory for High Energy Physics, Japan
The Durability of Ballscrews for Ultra-High Vacuum
S. Nio, T. Suzuki, H. Zenpo, K. Yokoyama, H. Wakizako, Yaskawa Electric Manufacturing Co., Steve Belinski, CRSM
Vacuum-Compatible Robot Design for Self-Contained Manufacturing

TOUR OF CRSM LABORATORY

KEYNOTE ADDRESS: *UHV Growth of Quantized Electronic Structures*
Dr. Arthur C. Gossard
Professor, Materials Department, Electrical and Computer Engineering Dept., UCSB
Member, NSF Center for Quantized Electronics Structures, UCSB

FRIDAY, FEBRUARY 3, 1989

SESSION 5—VACUUM MECHATRONICS DESIGN 3: CONTROL
CHAIR: GERARDO BENI

Brad Paden, Center for Robotic Systems in Microelectronics
Robot Motion Planning for Self-Contained Manufacturing Systems
Toshio Matsumoto, Yaskawa Electric Manufacturing Co., Ltd.
Magnetic Levitation for Vacuum-Compatible Wafer Transfer Systems

SESSION 6—VACUUM MECHATRONICS SYSTEM DESIGN
CHAIR: SUSAN HACKWOOD

Neil Reid, Space Sciences Laboratory, University of California, Berkeley
Space Payload Calibration Using Advanced Vacuum Robotics
Robert M. Warden, AEC—Able Engineering Co. Inc.
Design Criteria for Mechanisms Used in Space

SESSION 7—VACUUM MECHATRONICS APPLICATIONS
CHAIR: SUSAN HACKWOOD

Brian Hardegen, Brooks Automation
Concepts and Requirements for Semiconductor Multi-Process Integration in Vacuum
Thomas Seidel, SEMATECH
Self-Contained Systems for Microelectronics Processing

PREFACE

The First International Vacuum Mechatronics Workshop was held February 2–3, 1989 at the University of California, Santa Barbara. It was jointly sponsored by the National Science Foundation, the California Department of Commerce, and the American Vacuum Society.

The discipline of vacuum mechatronics is the design and development of vacuum-compatible, computer-controlled mechanisms for manipulating, sensing and testing in a vacuum environment. It encompasses the fields of vacuum science, automation in special environments, mechatronics (computer-controlled mechanisms) and robotics. The components of vacuum mechatronic systems include intelligent mechanisms, intelligent sensors, and intelligent measuring devices. The system integrating elements are the vacuum chamber and the system computer control. Vacuum mechatronics is relevant to research engineers in integrated circuit manufacturing, surface physics, food processing, biotechnology, materials handling, space sciences and manufacturing.

Vacuum mechatronics is gaining importance due to the increased use of vacuum in applications such as space studies, manufacturing, material processing, medicine, microelectronics, emission studies, lyophylisation, freeze drying and packaging. As the benefits of the vacuum environment (e.g., low pressure, long mean free path length, and cleanliness) become better defined and understood, the desire to implement more processes in vacuum will increase.

The space program has provided much of the forward momentum in vacuum mechatronics due to the numerous vacuum-related challenges which had to be worked out for space missions. These solutions have recently been applied and extended for use in chamber-based production environments. In this and other vacuum production applications, the sensing, transfer and/or positioning functions provided by the mechatronics equipment is critical to the overall process.

The newly developing field of vacuum mechatronics is also the driving force for the realization of an advanced era of totally enclosed clean manufacturing cells. High-technology manufacturing has increasingly demanding requirements for precision manipulation, *in situ* process monitoring and contamination-free environments. To remove the contamination problems associated with human workers, there is a tendency to move towards total automation for manufacturing. This will become a requirement in the near future, e.g., for microelectronics manufacturing. Automation in ultraclean manufacturing environments is evolving into the concept of self-contained and fully enclosed manufacturing. For example, at the CRSM we are developing a self-contained, automated robotic factory (SCARF™) as a flexible research facility for totally enclosed manufacturing of integrated circuits. The construction and successful operation of a SCARF will provide a novel, flexible, clean, vacuum manufacturing environment. In relation to this work, the CRSM has published a 360 page book entitled *Vacuum Mechatronics* which includes six chapters and 30 reprints of the latest papers on the subject.

The objective of the first Vacuum Mechatronics Workshop was to bring together scientists and engineers active in various fields of vacuum technology, mechatronics and related application areas for technical interchange. The common ground is a desire to make effective use of the vacuum environment (ground-based or space) by examining the obstacles which currently block flexible and reliable automation. The workshop was an information exchange for those who share this goal.

The total attendance of the workshop was about 75. Fifteen papers were presented, about half pertaining to space applications and half pertaining to the microelectronics field. As evidenced by the many questions and discussions during the sessions, the group was very interested in advancing the state-of-the-art in vacuum mechatronics. It was the first time that a group with a common interest in vacuum mechanisms was brought together from these various disciplines. As a result, much information was exchanged and many contacts made.

We would like to thank all of the speakers and attendees of the workshop. The speakers deserve special credit for their efforts in writing and submitting their manuscripts, which were not due until after the workshop. All but two of the talks are represented here, and even Dr. Alex Ignatiev, who could not attend the workshop, submitted a manuscript for publication. We would also like to thank the sponsors for their support of this new endeavor. The support from the National Science Foundation allowed us to keep the registration costs down; American Vacuum Society sponsorship allowed for the publishing of this proceedings through the American Institute of Physics; funding for the printing of the proceedings was provided by the California Competitive Technology Program, California Department of Commerce.

Credit is also due to the many people at the Center for Robotic Systems in Microelectronics who made the workshop a success. Directors Susan Hackwood and Gerardo Beni conceived the idea for the workshop and set the stage with an overview to open the sessions. Steve Belinski was the main organizer along with Karen Gundersen and Joan Bonetti. Other support staff included George Munson, Majid Shirazi, Bill Stout, Lois Bell, Mary Flores and Scott Smith.

Steve Belinski
Majid Shirazi
Susan Hackwood
Gerardo Beni

Center for Robotic Systems in Microelectronics
University of California, Santa Barbara

PROPOSED EPITAXIAL THIN FILM GROWTH IN THE ULTRA-VACUUM OF SPACE

A. Ignatiev, Space Vacuum Epitaxy Center
University of Houston, Houston, TX 77204-5507

ABSTRACT

A unique ultra-vacuum environment in space has been proposed for research and development in enhanced epitaxial thin film growth. This unique low earth orbit space environment is expected to yield vacuum levels of 10^{-14} torr or better, semi-infinite pumping speed and large ultra-vacuum volume (~ 100 m^3) without walls. These space ultra-vacuum properties promise major improvement in the quality, unique nature, and the throughput of epitaxially grown materials. Advanced thin film materials to be epitaxially grown in space include semiconductors, magnetic materials, and thin film high temperature superconductors.

INTRODUCTION

The attainment of reliable ultra-high vacuum through improvements of vacuum technology in the 1960's critically drove science in the areas of surface physics and chemistry, and technology in thin film materials epitaxial growth. Epitaxial growth of thin-film materials has presently been exercised through a number of techniques with the vacuum-based beam techniques showing the greatest promise for tailoring epitaxial thin-films. The beam techniques are molecular beam epitaxy (MBE)[1] and chemical beam epitaxy (CBE)[2]. Epitaxy is the growth of thin crystalline films in which the substrate determines the crystallinity and orientation of the grown layers. This growth is accomplished in an atom-by-atom, layer-by-layer manner. Molecular beam epitaxy is the growth of thin-film materials by the reaction of one or more thermal molecular beams with a crystalline surface under ultra-high vacuum conditions. Chemical beam epitaxy is the reaction of one or more gaseous beams with a crystalline surface under high vacuum conditions. Note that in both instances, high vacuum is of prominence in the growth of high quality, defect-free, single crystal films. These vacuum-based growth techniques have, however, since indicated the need for further improvement[3,4] of the vacuum environment for high quality semiconductor epitaxial thin film growth.

Fig. 1 Two epitaxial growth chambers with inter-connecting vacuum stations and analysis chambers located at the Space Vacuum Epitaxy Center.

MBE/CBE growth is currently undertaken in rather sophisticated and large ultra-high vacuum systems with base pressures in the 5 x 10^{-11} torr range and operating pressures as high as 1 x 10^{-8} torr under MBE growth conditions and 5 x 10^{-5} torr under CBE growth conditions. These systems generally incorporate multiple-growth chambers, analysis chambers, and interconnecting ultra-high vacuum tubes within which samples are transported from one chamber to the other [Fig.1]. Such complexities are required for the critical growth of epitaxial thin-films, however, they tend to adversely affect the ability to further improve vacuum conditions.

The vacuum-related problems in MBE/CBE technology are currently identified as follows:
1. High background doping and interface contamination; this is principally due to the non-ideal vacuum environment of the thin film during growth—usually 10^{-8} to 10^{-9} torr, and the purity of the sources of the materials that are being used for the growth process.
2. Small throughputs; this is principally the result of limited chamber size. Most ultra-high vacuum chambers are of the order of 0.5 cubic meter volume, and as a result, can only have a limited number of samples processed by the epitaxial growth technique. In addition, because of the complexity and sophistication of the equipment utilized for the growth process[Fig. 2], there is a significant amount of down time in most all of the machines that are currently in use.
3. Sample nonuniformity; because of the limited chamber size, the source-to-sample distance remains relatively small (of the order of 20 centimeters). Under these conditions, the source output is not spatially uniform, and as a result, substrates must be rotated during exposure to the source beams. Such rotation improves uniformity of the grown layers but may add particulate contaminants to the growth. Therefore, larger source-to-sample distances not requiring rotation would improve the quality and uniformity of the grown films.
4. Chamber wall contamination; in the current technology, a finite size chamber is used for the growth process ($\sim 0.5 m^3$). During growth, the chamber walls are also generally coated with the growing material due to overspray. Such coatings on the walls later plague future thin film growths since these coatings are continually desorbing into the vacuum chamber. This contaminates the vacuum environment, and as a result contaminates the grown layers. Therefore, a vacuum chamber used for the growth of one material cannot be readily used for the growth of another. This, consequently, restricts the use of a given chamber (representing a significant amount of capital cost—~$1 million), to a one-material status. Such a situation does not make MBE/CBE suitable for the empirical approach that has shown in the past to be so productive in a generation of new materials and devices.
5. Limited, finite pumping speeds; terrestrial vacuum chambers have finite and limited pumping capabilities. As a result, especially in chemical beam epitaxy, effective removal of processing gases is restricted with resultant impact on the quality of grown material and interface integrity in layered heterostructures.
6. Toxicity of gases used; within the chemical beam epitaxy technique, the gases that are used are generally toxic, and as a result, have to be removed from the vacuum chambers within which they are used. This generally involves rather elaborate and quite expensive, pumping, scrubbing, and cleaning techniques for the gases.

SPACE ULTRA-VACUUM

A possibility for alleviating the above noted limitations and problems of the epitaxial growth technologies lies in the use of the ultra-vacuum environment of low earth orbit space for epitaxial thin film growth. Space ultra-vacuum has the following proposed advantages:
1. An ultra-high vacuum of the order of 10^{-14} torr hydrogen with 10^{-18} torr or lower pressures for other gases.
2. Semi-infinite pumping speed.
3. Large vacuum volume without walls.
4. Processing capabilities as a result of solar bakeout, atomic energy, atomic hydrogen, micro-gravity, and 4K background radiation.

These space ultra-vacuum benefits require the flight of unique space flight hardware – the ultra-vacuum *Wake Shield Facility* (WSF)[5]. The space ultra-vacuum concept was first described nearly fifteen years ago[6,7] with, however, little identification of needs for ultra-vacuum. The current needs of beam epitaxial growth for enhanced vacuum conditions, enhanced pumping speeds, and reduction of wall contaminants have refocused interest in the utilization of the ultra-vacuum of space for thin-film epitaxial growth. The vacuum environment at the low earth orbit (300 kilometers) is between 10^{-7} and 10^{-8} torr and is mostly atomic oxygen. This is a relatively poor environment for epitaxial thin-film growth processes; however, one should note that there is a strong anisotropy in gas density with respect to vehicle motion for a vehicle in orbit. This has been pointed out clearly in the initial studies of space ultra-vacuum with the analysis being based on a kinetic theory of a drifting Maxwellian gas[8,9]. Within these calculations, it is sufficient to note that a vehicle in orbit has a velocity 8 to 10 times greater than the mean thermal velocity of the ambient gas atoms. As a result, its motion through the low-earth environment produces a region behind the vehicle into which the ambient molecules simply cannot diffuse thereby, creating an ultra-vacuum region. This vacuum "wake" behind a space vehicle is, therefore, the region within which ultra-vacuum experiments can be undertaken(Fig. 2).

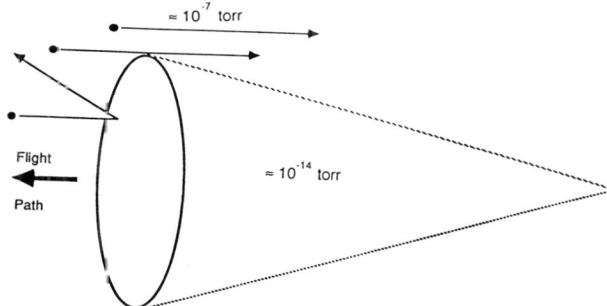

Fig. 2. A disc in low earth orbit space acting as a "wake shield". Atoms and molecules colliding with the shield are reflected, while those that miss the shield do not suffer a large number of collisions and hence have not imparted enough momentum transfer to allow them to diffuse behind the shield creating a "wake" of $\simeq 10^{-19}$ torr.

A proposal for an ultra-vacuum flight facility made early on in space vacuum studies[8,10] and recently refined, is that of a circular shield in orbit, behind which the ultra-vacuum experiments can be undertaken. Calculations indicate that behind such a shield, gas pressures (or more appropriately directional fluxes) would be on the order of 10^{-14} torr for hydrogen, 10^{-18} for helium, and lower for other species[9]. This basic concept for space ultra-vacuum, the wake shield, is shown in Fig. 3. The ultimate wake-shield facility is expected to be a free flyer with self-contained power, electronics, attitude control, and experimental package. The first version of this shield, however, will be shuttle-deployed as shown in Fig. 3.

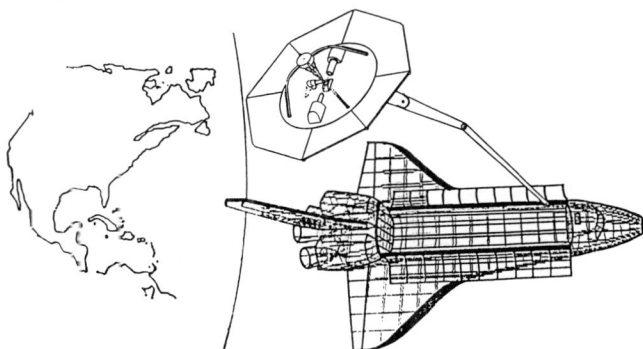

Fig. 3. The University of Houston Space Vacuum Epitaxy Center-designed Wake Shield Facility deployed in low earth orbit space by the shuttle on the shuttle arm (RMS). The apparatus behind the shield (in the wake region) is for epitaxial growth of thin films in the space ultra-vacuum.

This deployment will encompass stages of shield-operation:

1. Shield being oriented by the RMS (shuttle arm) such that the experiment package is facing the velocity vector for clean-up by the atomic oxygen present in that low-earth orbit. Atomic oxygen has been shown to be very reactive, especially with organics, forming volatile $CO-CO_2$ complexes[11]. It is expected, therefore, that the atomic oxygen would readily clean the working surface of the shield and the experiment package under these conditions.

2. The shield being turned toward the sun for solar bakeout. Preliminary calculations[12] indicate that the stagnation temperature for the shield is expected to be from 250 to 350°C. This is adequate to degas the working surface of the shield which is expected to be stainless steel. Vacuum-baked 304 stainless steel has an outgassing rate of ~8.7×10^{-15} torr l/sec[13] which equates to ~1.6×10^5 molecules/cm^2 sec. This flux is well within the minimum 5×10^{10} molecules/cm^2 sec allowed[9] for a pressure of 1×10^{-14} torr behind a 5 meter diameter wake shield.

3. The shield being turned with the experimental package opposite the direction of the velocity vector, attainment of ultra-vacuum within that experimental region, and the initiation of the experiment. Shuttle-based use of a wake shield would partially degrade the expected vacuum conditions to ~10^{-11} to 10^{-12} torr due to shuttle off-gassing, however, it is expected that these vacuum levels combined with semi-infinite pumping speeds will still significantly impact epitaxial thin-film growth.

THIN-FILM EPITAXIAL GROWTH IN SPACE ULTRA-VACUUM

Materials that are being considered for epitaxial growth within the space ultra-vacuum include semiconductors, metals, and superconductors. In the semiconductor area, III-V materials (mainly gallium arsenide based materials) have been projected to significantly impact semiconductor technology. This is principally due to the strong infrared response, the high electron mobility and the low power consumption of the materials. These characteristics result in possibilities for high speed/low power transistors, for opto-electronic devices (lasers and detectors) and for optical computing, The majority of these benefits, however, have not yet been realized.

Current quality measures of MBE and CBE grown materials are far from ideal, although some MBE grown *GaAs/AlGaAs* heterostructures are finding technology applications with their compromised characteristics[14]. The present records in compound semiconductor quality (defect densities and mobilities) are, however, being set by MBE growths where extreme efforts have been taken to maximize vacuum quality (to the point of baking vacuum chambers for up to 8 weeks[3,4]). The space ultra-vacuum based MBE experiments with exceptional vacuum levels and pumping speeds are, therefore, expected to identify new higher limits in compound semiconductor quality.

It must be added that the environment of low earth orbit space has not yet been completely and critically characterized, and as a result, special precautions may have to be exercized in epitaxial thin film growth in space. Low energy (100 eV to 20 KeV) charged particles (possibly present at LEO) may generate defects in growing films and thus degrade their performance, solar ultraviolet (generally shielded by the atmosphere) may affect film growth, though either in a detrimental or beneficial manner and micrometeorites (including space debris) present in low earth orbit could damage unprotected growing epitaxial films. Solutions are being addressed for these problems and, as a result, they are not expected to significantly hamper the possibilities of enhanced quality epitaxial thin film growth in space.

Finally, the Wake Shield Facility noted above is an ambitious, exciting and approved flight program. The design and construction of the Facility is currently underway in the Space Vacuum Epitaxy Center with a projected launch date of October 1991. The Facility will allow for both the initial mass spectrometric characterization of the ultra-vacuum environment behind the wake shield, and the controlled MBE growth of *GaAs* epitaxial thin films with future flights dedicated to other semiconductor and superconductor thin film growth systems. The Wake Shield Facility will be user-oriented flight hardware and is expected to yield information from the space research and development efforts which will both improve terrestrial vacuum-based epitaxial thin film growth technologies and more clearly delineate future space-based application of the epitaxial technologies.

SUMMARY

As has been noted. MBE/CBE is a powerful laboratory tool with the promise of growth of new and advanced materials and devices. The space ultra-vacuum environment is expected to allow exploitation of the full potential of the MBE/CBE technology both in the research arena and in future commercial areas. We expect the utilization of space ultra-vacuum for epitaxial growth to result in the fabrication of new and near-perfect materials and devices for use both on earth and in space. It will allow for the attainment of new knowledge to improve earth-based technologies and will allow for the discovery of new sciences.

ACKNOWLEDGEMENT

The author wishes to acknowledge extensive assistance and support from Dr. C. W. Chu on his topic and the critical discussions with all members of the Space Vacuum Epitaxy Center especially R. Sega, H. Shih, A. Bensaoula, and K. Jamison in the refining of the space epitaxial growth concept. Specific credit goes to R. Naumann of NASA Marshall Space Flight Center and T. Bonner and co-workers at Space Industries, Inc. Support is acknowledged from NASA through Grant NAGW-977.

REFERENCES

1.) A. Y. Cho and J. R. Arthur, Prog. Sol. State Chem. 10, 157 (1975).
2.) W. T. Tsang, Appl. Phys. Lett. 45, 1234 (1984).
3.) J. M. Harris, Appl. Phys. Letters, 49, (1986).
4.) L. Pfeiffer, K West, H. Stormer, and K. Baldwin, Bull. Am. Phys. Soc. 34, 549 (1989).
5.) A. Ignatiev and R. Sega, The Wake Shield Facility Flight Program, NASA Grant Augmentation, NAGW-977.
6.) H. F. Wuenscher, New Scientist 47, 54 (1970).
7.) L. T. Melfi, Proc. 27th Intl. Astronautical Congress. (Anaheim, Oct. 1976).
8.) L. Melfi, R. Outlaw, J. Hueser and F. Brock, J. Vac. Sci. Technol. 13, 698 (1976).
9.) R. J. Naumann, J. Vac. Sci. Technol. A7, 90 (1989).
10.) W. A. Oran and R. J. Naumann, Vacuum 28, 73 (1978).
11.) L. Leger, AIAA '83 Reoc 21 Aerospace Sciences Meeting, 83-0073, 1983.
12.) D. Perkinson, NASA-MSF, private communication, 1986.
13.) R. Barton and R. Gorier, Proc. 4th Intl. Vac. Cong., Inst. of Physics, London, 1986, p. 775.
14.) MESFET and HEMT MBE Grown *GaAs/AlGaAs* wafers are currently being sold by PICOGIGA, Les Ulis, France

PARTICLE MONITORING AND CONTROL IN VACUUM PROCESSING EQUIPMENT

Dr. Peter G. Borden and John Gregg
High Yield Technology, Mountain View, Ca. 94043

ABSTRACT

Particle contamination during vacuum processes has emerged as the largest single source of yield loss in VLSI manufacturing. While a number of tools have been available to help understand the sources and nature of this contamination, only recently has it been possible to monitor free particle levels within vacuum equipment in real-time. As a result, a better picture is available of how particle contamination can affect a variety of processes.

This paper reviews some of the work that has been done to monitor particles in vacuum loadlocks and in processes such as etching, sputtering and ion implantation. The aim has been to make free particles in vacuum equipment a measurable process parameter. Achieving this allows particles to be controlled using statistical process control.

It will be shown that free particle levels in load locks correlate to wafer surface counts, device yield and process conditions, but that these levels are considerably higher during production than when dummy wafers are run to qualify a system. It will also be shown how real-time free particle monitoring can be used to monitor and control cleaning cycles, how major episodic events can be detected, and how data can be gathered in a format suitable for statistical process control.

INTRODUCTION

In recent years, particle contamination during vacuum processes has become one of the chief sources of yield loss in VLSI manufacture. Wafers are extremely susceptible to contamination in these processes because they are directly exposed to environments that are often reactive, violent, or produce particulate by-products. Control of this contamination is often made difficult because the sources are process and process tool specific.

Nevertheless, significant strides have been made in reducing contamination from vacuum process equipment. This has been accomplished through an improved understanding of tool design and the use of measurement tools such as the surface defect scanner, which provides a measure of the particle contamination on wafers as a result of a complete pass through the process tool. More recently, tools have been available to monitor free particle levels in real-time. This provides the added benefits of localizing particle sources within the process tool, and, by knowing when particle sources are active, tying particle generation to phases of the process cycle.

Over the past two years, the authors of this paper have worked closely with a number of VLSI manufacturers to evaluate and develop applications for a real-time free particle monitoring technology for vacuum process equipment. The aim has been to make free particles a process variable that can be monitored in real-time. This opens the door for the use of standard techniques such as statistical process control (SPC) to rapidly detect and correct out-of-control conditions, thereby providing a significant improvement in process yield.

This work has involved use of a new real-time particle sensor that can monitor free particles independent of pressure. The sensor, which has been described elsewhere,[1,2] uses light scattering to detect particles as they pass through a laser beam. It is compact and self-contained, so that it can fit within load locks, process chambers and exhaust lines to detect particles near the wafers as they are generated.

This paper describes some of the most significant recent results of work with this sensor. Observations from a variety of process tools, including plasma etchers and ion implanters are presented. These show that it is indeed possible to obtain particle count levels during routine production that are high enough to apply SPC. It will be seen that out of control conditions often directly relate to wafer contamination and yield. However, process control conditions are often due to problems with process steps prior to that being monitored.

A REPRESENTATIVE EXAMPLE – THE END STATION OF A MEDIUM CURRENT ION IMPLANTER

Most process equipment is loadlocked. That is, the process chamber always remains under vacuum and wafers are brought down to vacuum and back to air through small loadlocks. A typical configuration is shown in figure 1, in this case for a medium current ion implanter. This is a top view of the implanter, showing the input cassette, input loadlock, and end station where the wafer sits exposed to an ion beam. The output loadlock and output cassette are below the input loadlock and cassette.

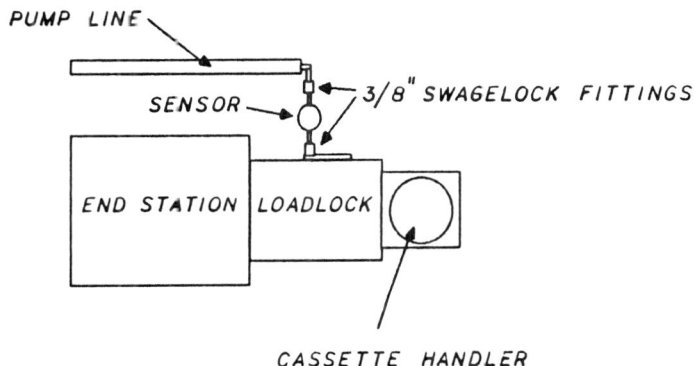

Fig. 1. Top view of the end station of a medium current ion implanter.

In this sort of equipment, a major source of particle contamination is stirring up of particulate during pumping and venting of the loadlock. Contamination in the end station is relatively small because the pressure is so low that the particles fall vertically, and the wafers mount vertically. The contamination can be monitored for every wafer that passes through by placing a particle monitor in the pump line for each loadlock. Free particles that are stirred up will be pulled through the pump line and seen with these monitors.

Because these stirred-up particles are a primary source of contamination, it is expected that particle counts in the exhaust line will correlate to counts on the wafer surface. Figure 2 shows evidence of this. A commonly used procedure to qualify loadlocks after maintenance is to run a sequence of two cassettes of dummy wafers followed by a monitor that is read with a surface defect scanner. The dummies gradually clean out the loadlock and the monitor is used to determine when the loadlock is sufficiently clean. In figure 2, the two particle counts for the two cassettes of dummies is compared to the surface counts for the monitor for three cycles on this sequence. Note how the two read relatively high counts for the first cycle. The counts are low for the second cycle, and change very little for the third. This suggests that the free particle monitor is trending with the surface scanner counts.

8

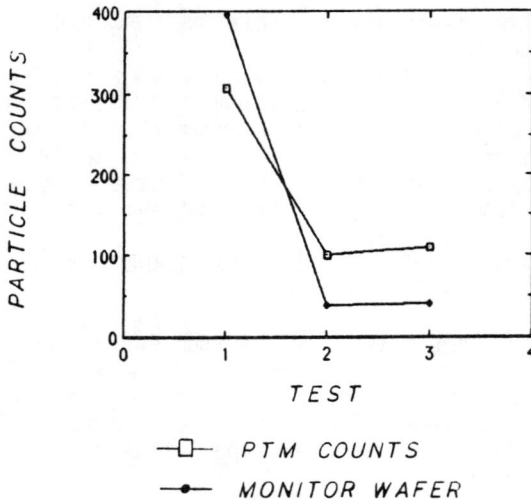

Fig. 2. Free particle counts for two cassettes and surface counts for a single monitor wafer over three sequential tests during an implanter particle requalification procedure

Output loadlock particle counts in 30 second intervals over a four hour period of production are seen in figure 3. The clean-up procedure described above was performed at 19 hours. Note how the counts drop consistent with the results shown in figure 2. In fact, particle counts are negligible for the third and fourth cassette. When production resumes, however, particle counts return to higher levels immediately. This suggests that particle levels observed with monitor wafers may not reflect the particle levels existing in production. This is plausible, because product wafers are more likely to generate particles than monitors. After all, monitor wafers are bare silicon wafers that have undergone relatively little handling, while product wafers usually have a number of coatings and have undergone a number of process and handling steps.

Also seen in figure 3 are particle counts during 14 lots of production. Note that some lots show considerably higher particle levels than others, and, at least for the lots just after 17 and 18 hours, one high counting lot is followed by a second. Assuming that the particle

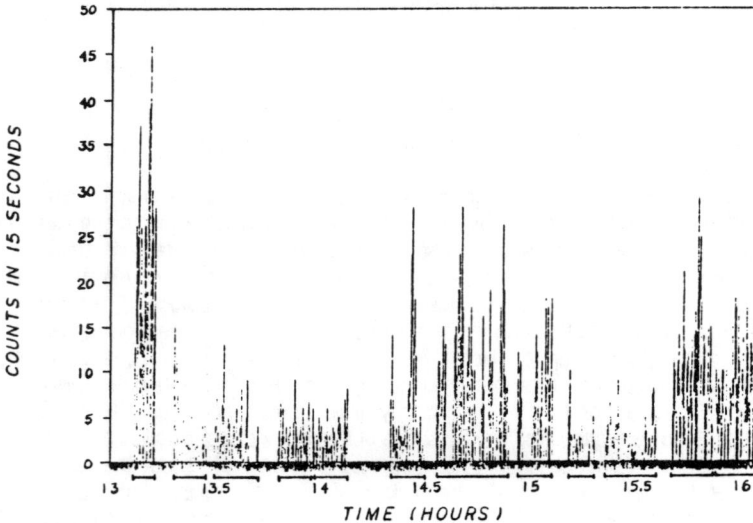

Fig 3. Particle counts in the pump line of the input loadlock of a medium current implanter during four hours of production.

counts seen with the monitor correlate to wafer surface contamination, and that this process is particle sensitive, these lots are at serious risk of reduced yield. The advantage of real-time particle monitoring is that processing can be halted after a high counting lot is seen, so that following lots are not put at risk.

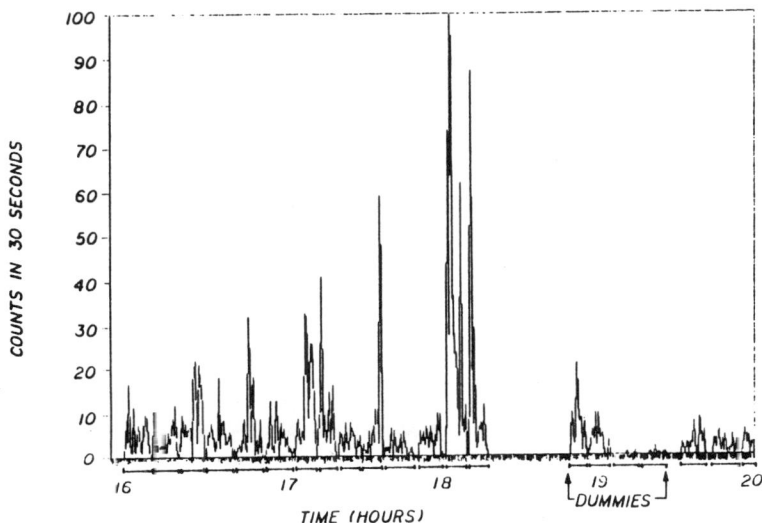

Fig. 4. Particle counts in the pump line of the output loadlock of a medium current implanter during three hours of production.

Input loadlock particle counts in 15 second intervals over a three hour period of production are seen in figure 4. Note that some sets of lots are seen to have significantly lower counts than others. Tracking of the production logs showed that these lots came from two different resist lines. This suggests that the particle problem is not arising from the implanter, but from the feeder process. It also suggests that monitoring the implanter gives information on the control of feeder processes.

In summary, these results show that:
- In loadlocks, where the primary contamination mode is particles stirred up during pumping and venting, levels of free particles during pumping and surface contamination correlate,
- Particle levels are higher when product is run through the loadlocks than when monitor wafers are run,
- Particle levels may be influenced by problems in earlier processes, and
- Real-time monitoring can flag potential yield hits when they occur, and allow the process to be stopped before subsequent lots are put at risk.

ANOTHER EXAMPLE: THE PUMP LINE OF A PLASMA ETCHER

A single wafer plasma etcher is another example of loadlocked system. Here, however, contamination in the process chamber can be a significant problem. These systems must be monitored in the exhaust line because the chamber is small and carefully designed to control the plasma uniformity. It is in fact possible to obtain meaningful results in the pump line because the etcher typically runs at pressures of 1-2 Torr. At these pressures, small

10

particles will remain suspended in the gas flow for a few seconds, long enough to be carried past the wafer into the exhaust line.

Another consideration in this application is etching of the optics by the reactive fluorine species that are typical by-products. While this necessitates careful sensor design, it is in fact possible to design sensors that will operate properly for several months in this environment.

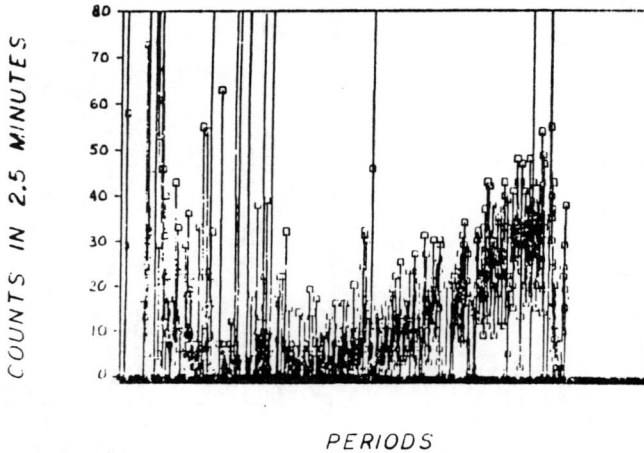

Fig. 5. Particle counts in the exhaust line of a single wafer oxide etcher during a period in which 372 wafers were etched.

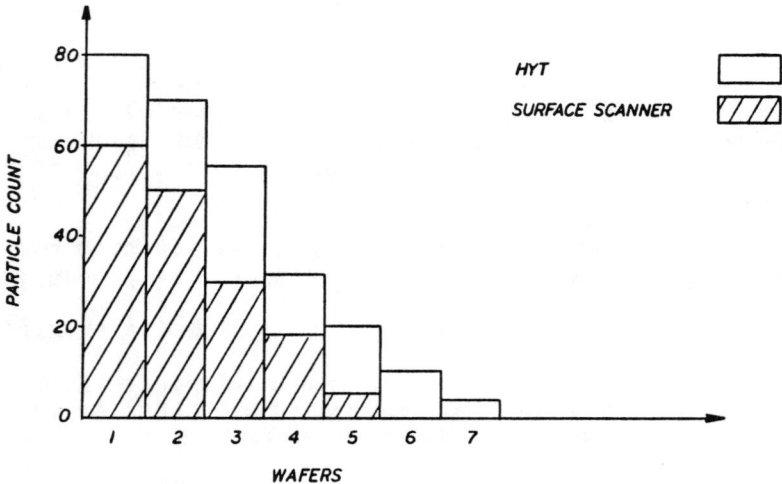

Fig. 6. Particle counts in the exhaust line of a single wafer oxide etcher and corresponding monitor wafer surface scan particle counts during a requalification after maintenance.

The aim here, as with the implanter loadlock, is to provide an immediate warning of when the process particle level may be out of control. Figure 5 shows particle counts in 2.5 minute intervals over a period in which 372 wafers were etched. This process generates a polymer, which is one of the primary particle sources. The very high counts that go off the vertical scale are due to an etchback process intended to remove the polymer from the chamber. The baseline level, however, is seen to rise over time. Near the peak, monitor wafers indicated that the particle level was above the control limit, and the etcher was brought down for cleaning. In this case, the free particle monitor was able to see the rise in the background particle level.

The free particle monitor is also useful to requalify a process chamber after maintenance. An example in a plasma etcher similar to that shown in figure 2 is seen in figure 6. In this case, the etcher was cleaned by running a series of monitor wafers through the chamber and passing the monitors through a surface scanner. The free particle monitor counts dropped along with the surface scan counts, showing that either monitor can be used to indicate when the chamber has become clean enough to resume processing.

SUMMARY

The aim of this work has been to make free particles in vacuum process equipment a measurable process parameter. This allows application of common techniques such as Statistical Process Control (SPC) to bring particle levels to consistently low levels, thereby increasing VLSI process yield. It has been shown that in many cases real-time count rates obtained in production applications are sufficient to enable use of SPC. While this is a meaningful first step, it is now necessary to couple this monitoring technology to process management systems. Completion of this challenging task will open the door to the realization of major benefits form in-situ, real-time particle monitoring.

ACKNOWLEDGEMENTS

The authors would like to thank Dr. Lawrence Larson of National Semiconductor and David Becker of Micron Technology for their help in providing data presented here.

REFERENCES

1. P. Borden and W. Knodle, "Process Control Through the Measurement of Particle Flux to Wafer Surfaces in Vacuum Process Equipment," Institute for Environmental Sciences 1988 Proceedings, page 429.

2. P. Borden, Y. Baron, and B. McGinley, "Monitoring Particles in Vacuum-Process Equipment," Microcontamination, October 1987.

ELECTROSTATIC DUST COLLECTOR FOR USE IN VACUUM SYSTEMS

H. Saeki, T. Sekiguchi, and J. Ikeda
Matsushita Electric Industrial Co.,Ltd.
Matsuba-cho 2-7, Kadoma-shi, Osaka-fu, 305, Japan.

H. Ishimaru
National Laboratory for High Energy Physics
Oho 1-1, Tsukuba-shi, Ibaraki-ken, 305, Japan.

ABSTRACT

An electrostatic dust collector was developed for use in vacuum systems. The particles was collected using an electrostatic force only or using an electron beam. A dust collecting method in which a thin film tape is rolled together to collect the particles was developed and used. The potential of the tape can be varied to a maximum of 10 kV. The current of the electron beam was 14 μA, and the vacuum pressure in the test chamber ranged from 10^{-6} -10^{-7} Torr. The dust collecting device was tested with several conducting and nonconducting particle materials about 60 μm in size on substrate materials of stainless steel, Al, Si wafers, and quartz. Particle removal was monitored using an optical microscope with a video camera or a photographic camera. The results show that the electrostatic dust collector removes all of the particles from the four substrates.

INTRODUCTION

An ultraclean environment is needed for the production of high-density integrated circuits. The yield of semiconductors is particularly influenced by particles. The performance of accelerators and of fusion machines is also influenced by particles.

Usually the method to protect vacuum chambers from the contamination of particles has been aimed at preventing particles from the external environment from entering. This method is powerless for particles produced inside vacuum chambers.

We propose that particles in vacuum chambers should be actively removed.

A new dust collector for use in vacuum chambers was developed and tested using an electron beam and an electrostatic force. The test showed that more than 90% of particles generated from pure metals (Fe, Al, Ni etc.) were collected using the electrostatic force only, and that all of the particles made from semiconductors or insulators were collected using both the electron beam and the electrostatic force.[1]

But there is a limit on the particle collecting volume of the test device, since the surface area of the dust collecting electrode was limited. Therefor, a more practical dust collecting method to roll a thin film tape together with collected dust was tested.

PRINCIPLE OF OPERATION

Figure 1 shows the principle of operation for the electrostatic dust collector using a thin film tape. A positive potential is applied to a thin film tape of the dust collecting electrode. The thin film tape is in direct contact with the electrode. The electrode is made from a conductor covered with a dielectric. The thin film tape is made from a dielectric.

If the particle has been generated from a conducting material, it can only be collected by an electrostatic force.

If the particle was generated from a semiconductor or an insulator, it can be collected using both an electron beam and an electrostatic force.

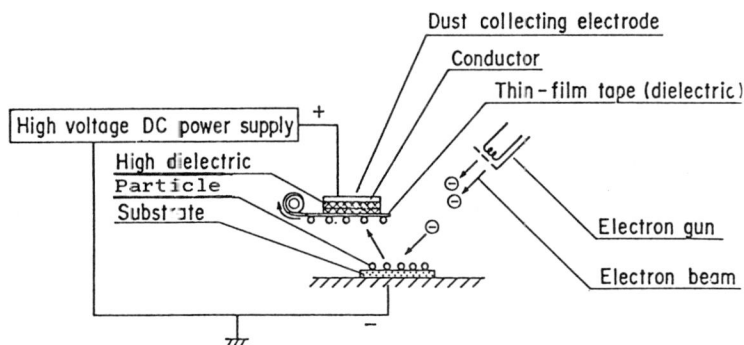

Figure 1. Principle of operation for the electrostatic dust collector.

EXPERIMENTAL APPARATUS

Figure 2 shows a schematic diagram of the experimental apparatus. The vacuum chamber is made of A1050-H24 aluminum alloy. Most of the internal components of the chamber are made of A2219-T87 aluminum alloy.

Particles for experiments were scattered on a substrate (20 x 20 mm size). A substrate holder was mounted on manipulator 1 (X axis stroke: ±10 mm, Y axis: ±10 mm, Z axis: 170 mm, and rotational angle of the θ axis: ±180). The potential of manipulator 1 was at ground.

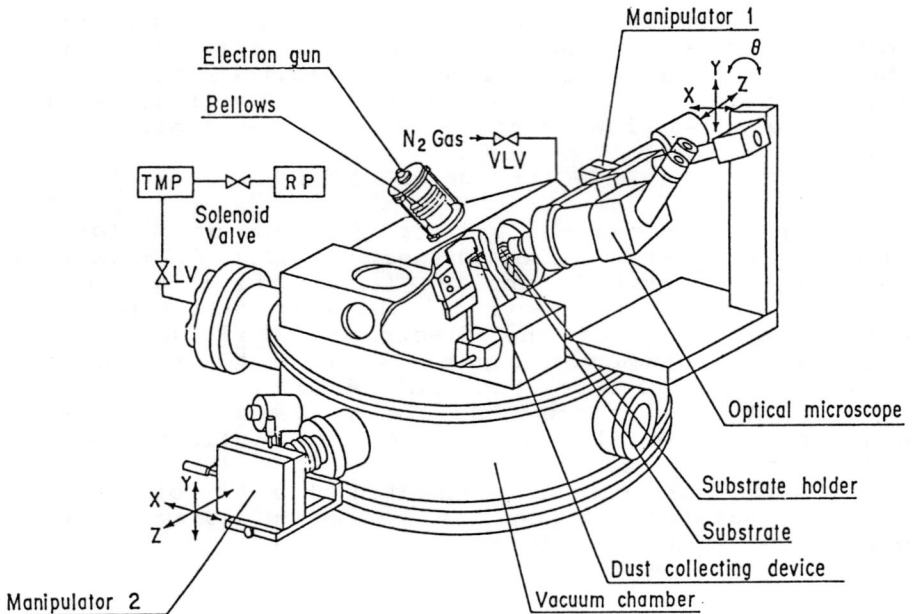

Figure 2. Schematic diagram of the experimental apparatus.

The dust collecting device was mounted on manipulator 2 (X axis stroke: ± 10 mm, Y axis: ± 10 mm, and Z axis: 70 mm).

A unipotential focus type electron gun is mounted on the chamber. The electron gun was moved 10 mm using bellows for collecting the path of the electron beam. The current of the electron beam was 14 μA, and the accelerating voltage was 1 kV. The diameter of the electron beam was about 10 mm at the substrate using a screen.

Four optical windows were mounted on the chamber. Particle removal was monitored through one of the windows using an optical microscope with a video camera or a photographic camera, where the maximum magnifying power was 40. The other three windows were used to introduce light for viewing.

Figure 3 shows the dust collecting device for the preliminary experiment. The tape is made of polyethlene, 3 mm wide and 0.1 mm thick. The electrode is made of copper covered with fiberglass epoxy. A high voltage (Max. 10 kV) was applied to the electrode from an external dc power supply. The thin film tape was rolled into a casette by a dc motor, driven from an external dc power supply. The tape speed was 3 mm/s.

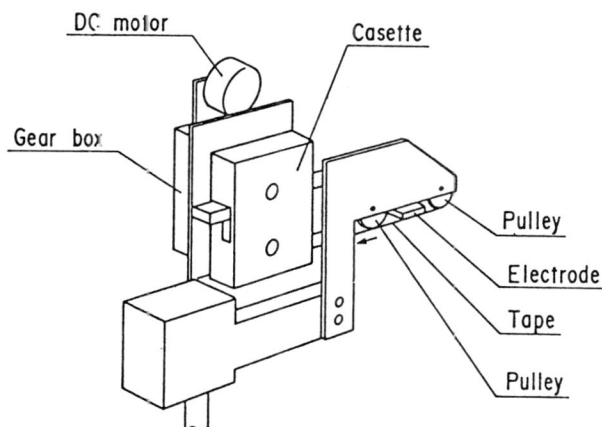

Figure 3. Schematic diagram of the dust collecting device.

The pumping system consisted of a 250 ℓ/s turbomolecular pump (TMP) and a rotary pump (RP). An L valve (LV) was operated slowly to prevent the experimental particles from scattering.

When nitrogen gas was introduced into the chamber, a variable leak valve (VLV) was used to prevent the particles from scattering.

EXPERIMENTS AND RESULTS

Experimental method

The experiments were carried out according to a flow chart as shown in Figure 4. Particles for the experiments were deposited on a substrate (made of stainless steel, Al, Si, or quartz glass). The particle size was about 60 μm. The substrate was set on the substrate holder and the chamber was pumped down slowly to the order of 10^{-6} -10^{-7} Torr. The experiment was then started.

In the case of conducting particles, a high voltage was initially applied to the tape (ie. to the electrode). The tape was then started. After the distance between the tape and the substrate was fixed, the dust collecting device was moved across the substrate.

In the case of semiconducting or insulating particles, at first, the electron beam was showered on the particles. After the electron beam was stopped, the experiment was carried out using the same process as in the case of conducting particles.

```
┌─────────────────────────────────────────┐
│ Particles are deposited on a substrate.  │
└─────────────────────────────────────────┘
                     │
┌─────────────────────────────────────────┐
│ The substrate is set on the substrate holder. │
└─────────────────────────────────────────┘
                     │
┌─────────────────────────────────────────┐
│ The chamber is pumped down. ($10^{-6}$-$10^{-7}$ Torr) │
└─────────────────────────────────────────┘
                     │
┌─────────────────────────────────────────┐
│ A high voltage is applied to the tape.   │
└─────────────────────────────────────────┘
                     │
       ┌──────────────────────────┐
       │ The tape starts running.  │
       └──────────────────────────┘
                     │
┌─────────────────────────────────────────┐
│ The distance is varied. (the tape and the substrate) │
└─────────────────────────────────────────┘
                     │
       ┌──────────────────────────┐
       │ The dust collecting device is moved │
       │ across the substrate.     │
       └──────────────────────────┘
                     │
                   ◇ ◇
         OK                  NO
┌──────────────────────────┐  ┌──────────────────────────────┐
│ The experiment is finished. │  │ The electron beam is showered on the │
└──────────────────────────┘  │                      particles │
                               └──────────────────────────────┘
```

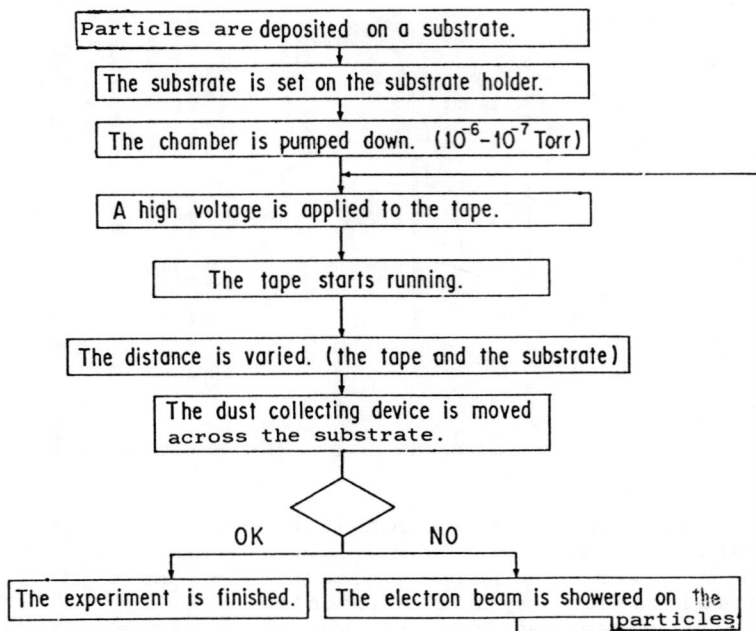

Figure 4. Experimental method

During experiments, the particle removal was observed using an optical microscope. After experiments, nitrogen gas was slowly introduced into the chamber.

Results

Table I shows the results. The experiments were carried out on particles of pure metals, semiconductors, and insulators. Substrates made of conductors, semiconductors, and insulators were also tested.

The collecting methods, the distance between the tape and the substrate, and the voltage applied to the electrode are also listed in Table I . The results were evaluated by visual inspection of how many particles were removed (good: more than 90% were removed, intermediate: from 10% to 90%, and bad: less than 10%).

It was found that all of the particles were collected using the thin film tape.

Table I.   Dust collection from stainless steel substrate, Aℓ substrate, silicon wafers, and quartz substrates.

Materials	Collecting method (a)	Distance between the tape and the substrate (mm)	Voltage applied (kV)	Evaluation (b)
Aℓ	1	3 – 5	± 3	G
Fe	1	3 – 5	± 3	G
Ti	1	3 – 5	± 3	G
Stainless steel	1	3 – 5	± 3	G
Aℓ-alloy	1	3 – 5	± 3	G
Si	2	3 – 5	+ 3	G
GaAs	2	2 – 4	+ 3	G
SiO	2	2 – 3	+ 3	G
Photo resist	2	2 – 6	+ 3	G
Ceramic (Zr series)	2	2 – 3	+ 3	G

(a) Collecting method

　　1: Using the electrostatic force only.

　　2: Using both the electron beam and the electrostatic force.

(b) Evaluatation

　　G: Good, I: Intermediate, B: Bad

DISCUSSION

It was found that many more particles were collected using the dust collecting device than using a small plate. But the distance between the tape and the substrate was shorter in comparison with the results using a small plate. Better results are expected when the thin film tape is made of high specific permittivity dielectric. The dust collecting device was originally made for use in atmosphere and was unsuitable for precise experiments. The dust collecting device now generates particles and uses lubrication on various parts. It is necessary to improve the dust collection device for practical use and for use in vacuum.

A semiconductive device containing particles may be damaged by an electron beam. It will be useful to charge particles by thermionic emission or photoelectric effect.

Further studies are necessary in order to apply this technique to small size particles.

SUMMARY

A dust collecting method in which a thin film tape is rolled together with collected particles was tested. All of the particles were collected on the tape using an electrostatic force and an electron beam. Dust collecting experiments for small size dust in the production of semiconductors will be carried out during the next research phase.

18

ACKNOWLEDGMENT

The authors would like to thank Dr. T. Momose and Dr. K. Kanazawa for their many helpful suggestions. This work was supported by Hakudo Co.,Ltd. and Musashino Engineering Co.,Ltd..

REFERENCE

1. H. Saeki, J. Ikeda, I. Kohzu, and H. Ishimaru, "New electrostatic dust collector for use in vacuum systems" was presented at the 35th National Symposium of the AVS, Atlanta, Georgia, 1988.

MATERIALS EVALUATION OF AN ELECTRICALLY NOISY VACUUM SLIP RING ASSEMBLY

Tim O'Donnell
Jet Propulsion Laboratory, Pasadena, California   91109

ABSTRACT

A vacuum slip-ring subassembly forms a primary part of the Jet Propulsion Laboratory Galileo spacecraft Spin Bearing Assembly (SBA). This SBA provides the nonimal 3 rpm spin rotation between a spun and despun portion of the spacecraft. Also the slip ring subassembly part of the SBA, provides the mission critical function of electrical power and signal transfer between the spun and despun spacecraft sections.

During vacuum testing of two flight-spare slip ring subassemblies, spurious, nonacceptable, electrical signals developed with one module. This article gives an overview of the materials evaluation involving various slip-ring components. A mechanism to explain the anomalous electrical signals is described. Finally, the solution to the electrical noise problem is presented.

INTRODUCTION

The Jet Propulsion Laboratory Galileo spacecraft is scheduled for late 1989 launch on the Space Shuttle for a mission to Jupiter. This spacecraft has spinning and nonspinning sections. In order to provide power and electrical signal communication between rotating portions of the spacecraft, a Spin Bearing Assembly (SBA) operating at approximately 3 rpm is used. The SBA contains four slip-ring modules that were designated "A", "B", "C", and "D".

The Galileo spacecraft slip-ring modules incorpcrated multiple solid, electrically conductive, signal and power brushes held in contact to a cylindric ring surface by metal flexures. For redundancy two brushes were used in each hard silver ring groove as part of the slip-ring cylinder. There were a total of 12 ring grooves therefore 24 total brushes (16 power brushes and 8 signal brushes) for each of the four slip ring modules. The use of sliding, dry lubricated, electrical contacts has considerable heritage from commercial and military space applications.[1]

After early engineering life test units were successfully tested for many millions of cycles, the Galileo Project procured flight units, spares, and additional units for life testing. Life testing was initiated on two slip-ring units designated "C1" and "C2" considered to be identical in design and construction to the four units installed in the spacecraft.

Within 2-5 days of operation in vacuum the C1 unit began
to exhibit out-of-spec electrical noise from all brush
pairs, whereas unit C2 was performing quietly, as
expected. Possible external causes for the noise were
investigated. Power supplies, recorders, cabling, output
signal detectors, etc. were all found to be operating
normally. Additionally, support test equipment and test
unit mechanical features such as drag torque, torque
ripple, ring circular runout and brush spring tension were
evaluated. However, none of these mechanical aspects were
responsible for the electrical noise.

When no immediate explaination for the noise was found,
a team of materials-related personnel was formed to
investigate the problem more extensively. Besides the
author the other lead team members were G. Lane, E.
Cuddihy, and Dr. G. Blue. A significant amount of time
and effort was expended in material evaluation of
slip-ring module components and fabrication processes
involving surface, bulk, inorganic, organic, and elemental
chemistries, molecular weight characterization, surface
morphologies and subsurface microstructures. Analytical
techniques used and results obtained are too numerous for
a single paper. This paper emphasizes visual, Scanning
Electron Microscopy (SEM), Energy Dispersive Spectroscopy
(EDS), and electrical resistance measurement techniques.
Other techniques used included X-ray Photo-electron
Spectroscopy (XPS), Fourier Transform Infrared
Spectroscopy (FTIR), Liquid Chromatography (LC), Mass
Spectrometry (MS), and Nuclear Magnetic Resonance (NMR)
imaging. The results obtained from using these latter
techniques are in general not reported on here.

DESIGN FEATURES AND MATERIALS

A close up of the Spin Bearing Assembly, slip ring
brush cylinder and slip ring brushes contacting the brush
cylinder is shown in Figure 1. Electrical contact brushes
are a sintered solid compaction of 85% silver, 12%
molydisulphide and 3% graphite. The cylindrical contact
surface is built up electroplated layers of copper, 0.030
inch fine or coin silver, with an external layer (0.001
inch) of 120 Vickers hardness silver. The slip-ring
barriers were an aluminum silicate (AST 400) filled epoxy
resin (DER 332). Brush springs were made of beryllium
copper and were originally coated with a dielectric epoxy
polyamide primer (Chemglaze 9922) and a white polyester
urethane Chemglaze A276 topcoat. After wiring harnesses
are soldered to the ends of the brushes a final Chemglaze
coating is applied to the terminal end of the brushes.
Temperature bakes of 66 degrees Centigrade were utilized
after 24 hours room temperature cure.

ELECTRICAL NOISE CHARACTERISTICS

The first electrical noise for each brush appeared in module C1 from two to five days after 3 rpm vacuum testing began on slip-ring modules C1 and C2. Signal brushes exhibited noise quicker than power brushes. The random, variable level, bursts of noise exhibited: 1) single spikes, 2) noise periods lasting several minutes and 3) significant periodicity within noise periods. Variable noise-free operation occurred between bursts and lasted several minutes to over a day. Noise events were still evident after hundreds of thousands of rotation cycles. Some individual ring channels or brush pairs cleared up after 300,000 cycles.

POSSIBLE NOISE GENERATION MECHANISMS

Prior to materials evaluation activities several noise generation hypotheses were developed through discussions with component manufacturers, other slip ring users and a literature survey. These hypotheses were used to help guide the materials evaluation efforts. The following is a summary of these hypotheses:

1. Inorganic environment degradation of the brushes or silver ring surface[1,2]
2. Low MoS_2 content in manufactured brushes[2]
3. Formation of frictional polymers as discovered by Hermance and Egan[3] of AT&T Bell Labs, 1967
4. Vapor phase contamination as was observed for a gold slip ring system[4]
5. Irregular as-manufactured silver ring surface[2]

VISUAL AND SEM/EDS EXAMINATION

Initially the C1 module brush assembly was viewed under a binocular microscope (10 - 30X magnification) with particular attention to the sliding surfaces. These surfaces appeared to be mottled with light areas and dark, discrete splotches (Figure 2). This was expected as the brushes are a sintered, heterogenous product of silver, molydisulfide, and graphite. Unless otherwise stated all discussion of Module C1 observations pertains to a slip-ring subassembly after 5 days 3 rpm vacuum testing (when testing of this unit was stopped due to noise).

Due to the seriousness of the concern, the destructive mechanical removal (clipping off) of several brushes was allowed in order to facilitate SEM evaluation. The initial SEM evaluation of brush surfaces did not reveal anything more enlightening than visual inspection. However, it should be pointed out that initially there was no appreciation of what exactly the sliding surface of a properly working slip-ring brush should look like.

EDS analysis of a C1 power brush surface detected silver, carbon, oxygen, molybdenum, and sulfur. Elemental mapping of the brush surface revealed that silver was distributed continuously over the whole surface, with discrete regions containing MoS_2. Surprisingly, carbon was found to be continuous over the whole surface, with no discrete domains of pure carbon being found. Along with carbon, oxygen was continuous over the whole surface. This observation was not consistent with a particular brush degradation hypotheses where oxidation of molybdenum to MoO_3 was anticipated.

A Module C2 power brush was examined by SEM. The appearance of the sliding surface of the C2 power brush sharply contrasted with the appearance of the sliding surface of the C1 power brushes (Figures 3 and 4). Visual evidence now pointed to an abnormal, dark surface material residing in discrete locations on the Module C1 brush sliding surface. This evidence was very apparent when imaging in the backscattered SEM mode (Figure 5). For the noise free C2 brush, SEM examination readily revealed the three material phases of the brush, silver, MoS_2, and carbon (graphite). The SEM backscatter mode very clearly displayed the contiguous silver (near white), Mo/S_2 (light grey), and graphite (black) (Figure 5).

EDS chemical analysis of the C2 brush surface revealed that each of the visually observed material phases were confined exclusively to its own domain. For example, elemental carbon readings were only found at the discrete sites of the graphite (black) phase. Also, no oxygen was found on the C2 brush sliding surface.

In order to obtain more chemical information about the abnormal, discrete splotches of dark material on Module C1 brushes, XPS analysis (also known as ESCA) was conducted. The key chemical information provided was that the carbon and oxygen on the surface were best associated with an organic compound. Though there was difficulty in obtaining a usable XPS signal due to surface charging, the chemical information provided strong support for the brush contamination hypotheses.

Mechanically removed sections of Module C1 ring surfaces were examined by optical microscopy, SEM, XPS, and surface profilometer. These efforts were instrumental in showing that the double wear track pattern observed over two diametrically opposed 45 degree arc ring surface areas were due to noncontact with the brush in the center. These double wear ring surfaces were slightly concave with up to 0.0005 inch depression measured in the center of track width. In addition, a surface roughness in the range of 5 - 10 microns RMS was measured.

High magnification SEM examination of Module C1 ring surfaces revealed the existence of a nodular surface. Nodule peak to valley distances ranged from 5 - 20 microns typically. The surface morphology observed was consistent with an unpolished electroplated hard silver layer. Nodules that had been in contact with the sliding brush were partially worn, and it appeared that wear products had accumulated in the valleys between adjacent nodules as well as up on the ring surface in larger accumulated areas. These observations are exhibited in Figure 6.

A significant breakthrough came from XPS analysis of a module C1 ring on the surface outside of the brush wearing path. XPS clearly and decisively detected an organic contaminant. Carbon, which was not expected on this surface, was found, and it was identified to be all organic carbon, none of it graphitic. The nominal composition of the this organic carbon was 67 atomic % aliphatic hydrocarbon, 25 atomic % ether and/or alcohol carbon, and 8 atomic % ester carbon. Locations of carbon - oxygen elements on the C1 ring are exhibited in EDS displays shown in Figure 7. Also, a strong carbon signal was apparent on the coated brush spring (Figure 7).

Other material evaluation and visual observations included: 1) Finding ring surfaces exhibiting various degrees and patterns of orange-brown stains; however no correlation of these stains (silver sulfidation/ oxidation) to electrical noise events could be found, 2) From 5 to 50 % of each C1 module brush wear surface was covered by the dark contaminant (Figure 8), 3) On some of the module C1 brush sides and coated brush spring surfaces a pale yellow, semi-transparent, pasty material was observed (Figure 1 and 9). This material was not found on Module C2 brush/spring surfaces.

Faced with brush surfaces that had been organically contaminated, the decision was made to ultrasonically clean a C1 power brush in tetrachloroethylene. After one minute cleaning the surface was reevaluated in the SEM/EDS. The regions of dark contamination, when now obseved at high magnification, revealed: 1) a dry mud-cracking appearance, 2) pieces of the contaminate had been removed revealing another brush surface underneath, 3) the contaminant was constructed of very finely divided particulates dispersed in a continuous matrix, i.e. 1 - 10 micron debris particles mostly silver embedded in a carbon rich organic matrix, 4) the contaminant on the brush surface was from 1 - 10 microns thick, 5) ultrasonic cleaning of contaminated brushes was relatively ineffective, and 6) nylon brush cleaning with ethanol proved the most successful, i.e. about 95 % of visible contaminate was removed from each brush wear surface. Figures 10 - 12 exhibit the above mentioned observations.

Calculations of organic contaminant thickness existing on the Module C1 surface prior to wear operation were made separately based on analytical chemistry mass quantity results and SEM observations. Calculated thickness ranged from approximately 300 angstroms to approximately 900 angstroms.

Organic contamination cleaned from Module C1 ring surfaces was characterized by various analytical chemistry techniques mentioned above. The material solvently removed from the ring surface was found to consist of several components covering a molecular weight range from nominally 200 to over 1000, and to contain the following chemical groups, esters, aliphatic hydrocarbons, and organic acid salts. These results were in agreement with XPS findings, but included a new component, organic acid salts. In comparison, analysis of material solvently removed from the quietly operating Module C2 contained only di-octyl phthalate (DOP). C2 surfaces did not contain any high molecular weight components as C1 did.

ELECTRICAL RESISTANCE OF CONTAMINANT

Multiple measurements of contact resistance were made between various points on Module C1 brush / spring surfaces using a four point probe technique. Table 1 gives a summary of measurement results. The brush wear contaminant exhibited electrical resistances 5 to 1200 times higher than other brush wear surfaces.

SPECULATED NOISE GENERATION MODEL

Key features of this authors speculation on a physical model to descibe the occurrence and characteristic traits of the observed electrical noise include:

1. A high molecular weight, organic, precursor contaminant (from a thermally decomposed polyester urethane) was present on ring and brush surfaces prior to wear operation. Highly suspected sources for this precursor contaminant are discussed below.

2. The quantity of precursor contaminant brought into contact with the brush wear face during initial operation was partially controlled by silver plating topology and contour.

3. Precursor contaminant binds up generated debris (silver, molydisulfide, and graphite) into a paste-like composite;

4. This composite paste predominately accumulates under brushes due to their relative softness and topology, and in between hard silver plating nodules (low contact stress sites).

5. Composite contaminant is basically a dielectric causing high resistance.

6. Some accumulated brush contaminant randomly transfers to ring surface through mechanical shear and stick/slip.

7. Brush contact with built up ring surface contaminant debris a) knocks the ring contaminant off, i.e. single event, b) gradually wears it away, i.e. periodic short or long lived noise, and c) causes exposure of accumulated debris contaminant in nodule valleys to high brush shear forces and due to silver nodule wear could randomly result in pull out/drag of high resistance contaminant debris.

POSSIBLE CONTAMINATION SOURCES

After considerable review the following potential external or internal sources of contamination were identified. The possible external sources could be:
1. Freon TES cleaning solvent
2. Vinyl gloves used in handling and fabrication
3. Cross-contamination from fab or test enviroments

The possible internal contamination sources could be:
1. The Chemglaze materials used as an electrical insulation coating on brush springs
2. Epoxy materials used in the slip ring assembly
3. KG-80 oil used as a lubricant in the SBA

One highly suspected source was the insulation coating on the brush springs. Soldering operations could have exposed this material to unacceptably high temperatures. The thermal decomposition byproduct for the coating used has many similar characteristics to the precursor contaminant discussed in this paper.

When all analytical results were cross-correlated with possible contamination source materials, in order of priority, the following sources were considered most probable:
1. Chemglaze A276 (brush spring insulation coating)
2. Freon TES
3. Epoxy adhesive

MITIGATION OF ELECTRICAL NOISE

The following actions resulted in noise free operation of a flight test slip ring unit and sufficient confidence in construction quality to resolve all concerns:
1. Replaced commercial Freon TES solvent with a JPL blend of liquid chromatographic grade Freon TF and absolute ethanol (ratio: 96.2 wt. % TF and 18% ethanol).
2. Liquid chromatograph tests were performed on solvent used to clean ring surfaces. A go-no go cleanliness criteria was established.
3. JPL provided solvent extracted fabric gloves for handling/fabrication activities.

4. An additional 24 hour, 65 degree centigrade bake in nitrogen was performed on the slip ring assembly.

5. The polyester urethane primer and topcoat used on the brush spring was replaced with a single coat of polyurethane, Solithane 111/113. This coating was applied after all heating operations.

SUMMARY

A series of materials evaluation activities were performed on components of an electrically noisy slip-ring assembly and a noise-free slip ring assembly. Likely causes and sources of contamination were determined. The discovered mechanism of noise generation was unlike any of those in the open literature. Based on materials evaluation results a set of slip-ring rework elements were instituted. Implementation of rework elements resulted in noise-free slip ring operation.

ACKNOWLEDGEMENTS

Credit for solving this tough problem must be given to the tireless work of Ed Cuddihy, Gerry Lane and Gary Blue. These individuals and myself had the pleasure of working with Ron Ruiz (SEM), Ken Evans (electrical resistance measurements and SEM), Ray Haack, Marc Anderson (chemical analysis and cleaning), Lois Taylor (consultant), and Carl Marchetto, Bob Shrake and Bob Summers (Spin Bearing Assembly project personnel).

REFERENCES

1. E. W. Roberts, European Space Agency Contract Report No. ESA 4099/79/NL/PP, October 1981
2. Private communication with manufacturers
3. R. Holm, Electrical Contacts Theory and Application, Springer-Verlag New York Inc., 1967
4. E. W Glossbrenner and A.M. Jenney, An Investigation of the Effect of the Environment in a Closed System in the Performance of Sliding Contacts, 7th International Conference on Electrical Contacts, 1974

TABLE 1

GLL SLIP RING FAILURE ANALYSIS
ELECTRICAL RESISTANCE MEASUREMENT OF BRUSH CONTAMINANT

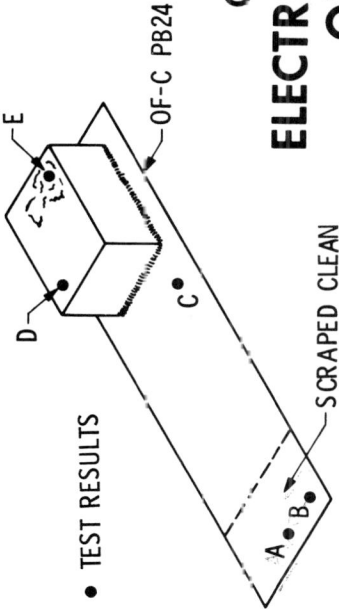

• TEST RESULTS

OF-C PB24

SCRAPED CLEAN

ELECTRICAL PATH	J-PROBE RESISTANCE, OHMS		POINT PROBE, Ω
	INITIAL CONTACT	AFTER BURNISHING	
A - B	0.12 ± 0.05	–	
A - C	1.0	0.125 ± 0.005	
A - D (11 READINGS)	100 HIGH 450 LOW 3.5	32 HIGH 260 LOW 0.64	1 HI 3.7 LO 0.18
A - E (11 READINGS)	2900 HIGH 15,000 LOW 50	137 HIGH 290 LOW 6	1288 HI 5000 LO 1.8
ACROSS CONTAMINANT CHIP	> 1000		

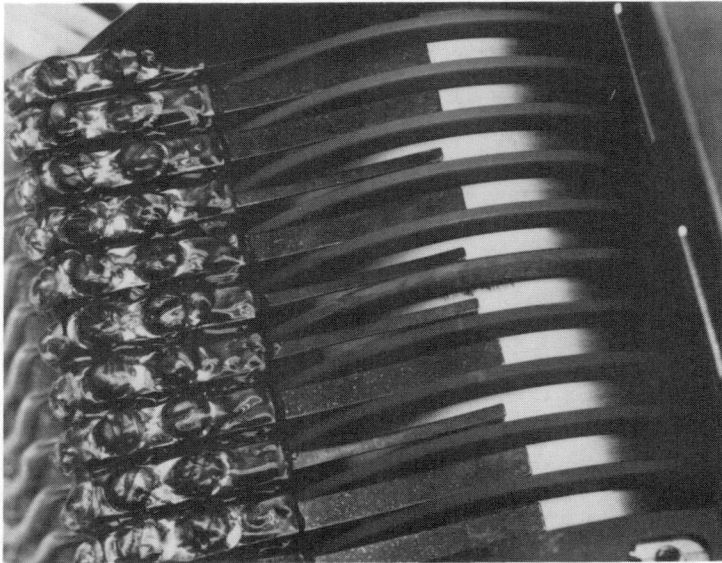

Figure 1 - Spin Bearing Assembly (top),slip-ring cylinder
(center) and brushes on cylinder (bottom)

Figure 2 - Close up of several brush blocks (wear face)
and the spring arm attached. Larger brush is
power brush (contact surface is 0.10 x 0.125
inch); smaller brush is the signal contact

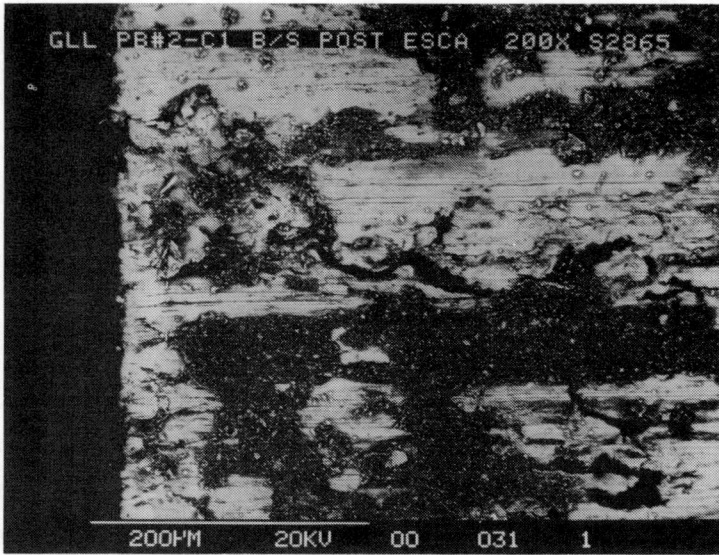

Figure 3 - Contaminated wear face of Module C1 brush

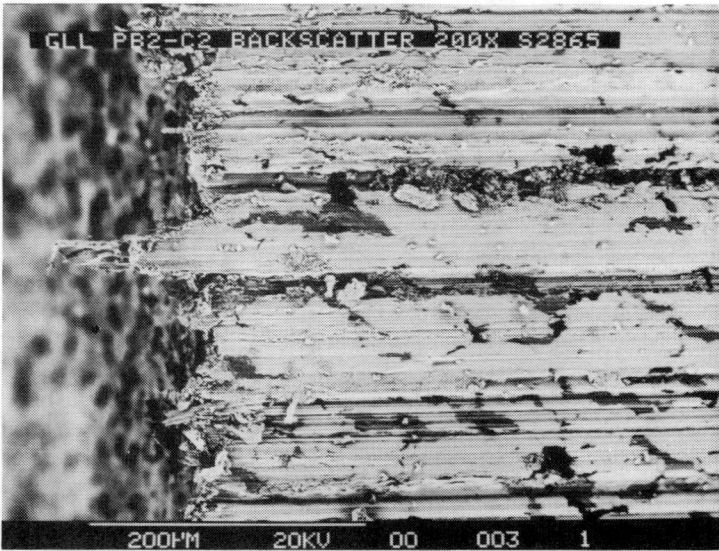

Figure 4 - Noncontaminated wear face of Module C2 brush

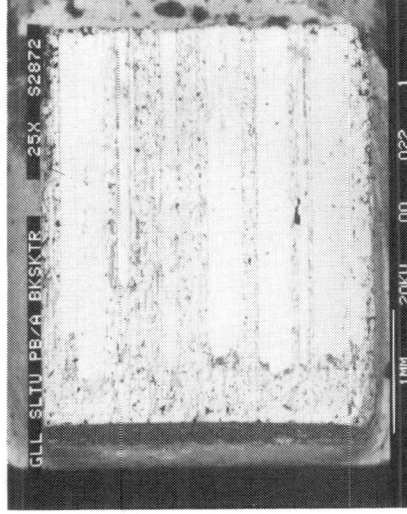

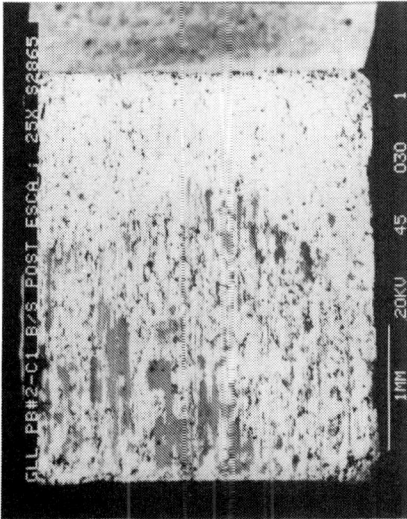

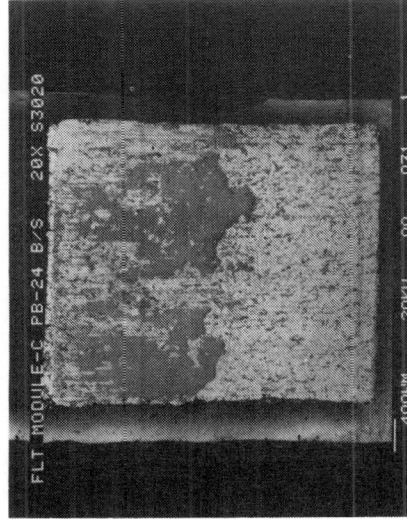

Figure 5 – SEM backscatter images of conataminated brush wear faces (left) and noncontaminated brushes (right).

32

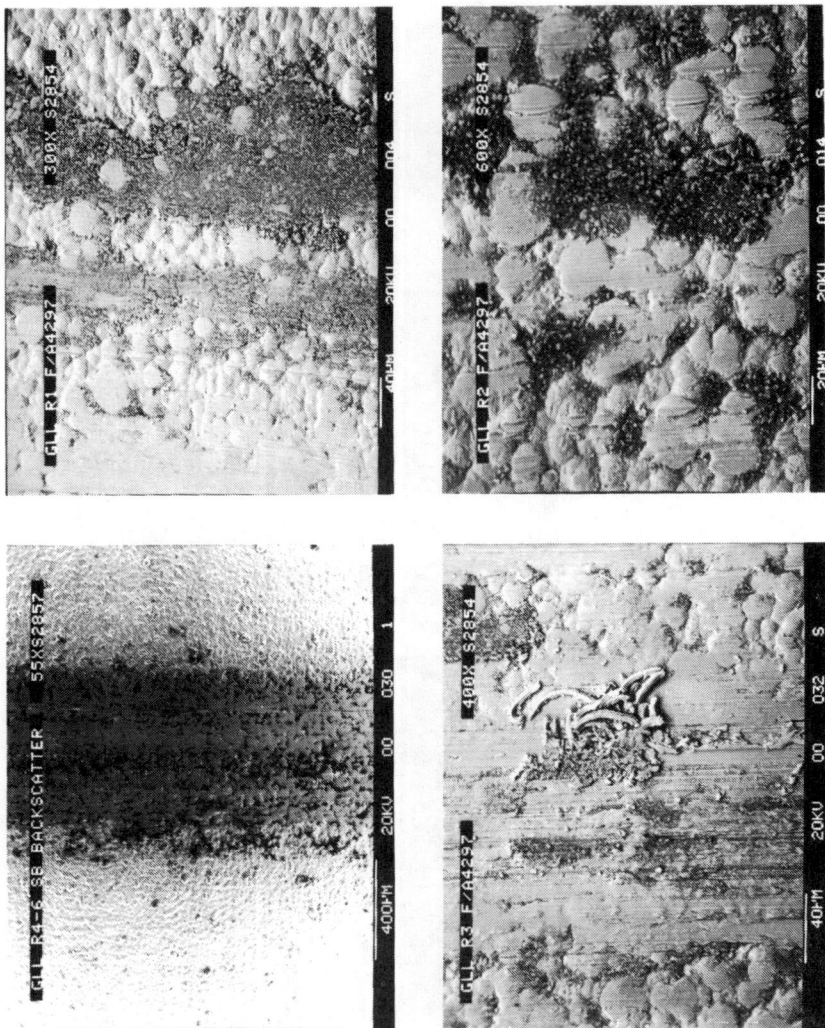

Figure 6 - SEM images of hard silver wear track showing debris build up in contact area (vertical dark zone in upper left photo) and nodular feature of unworn surface.

33

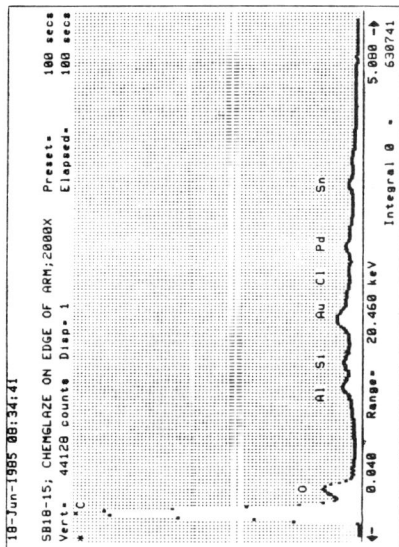

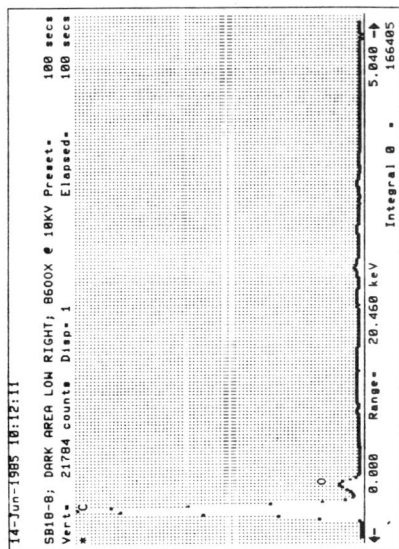

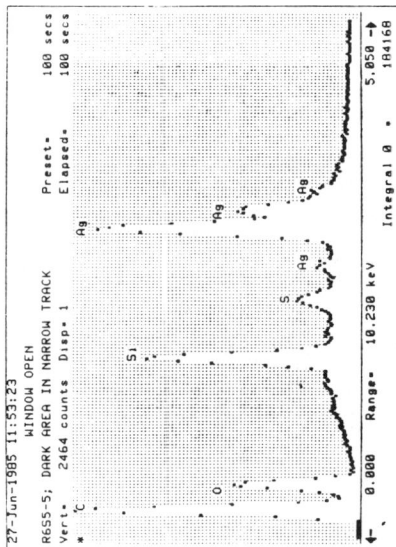

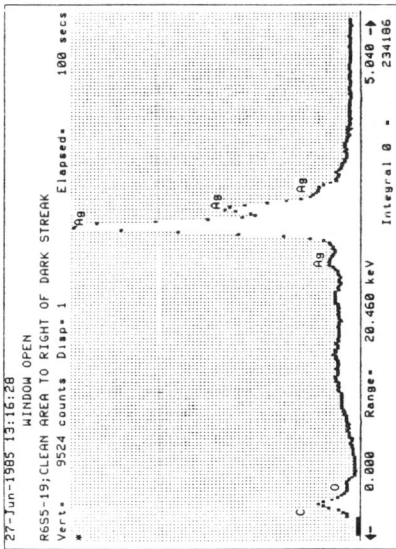

Figure 7 – EDS displays of brush arm urethane encapsulant (photo A), contaminant on ring wear surface (photos B and C) and ring surface outside of wear track (photo D)

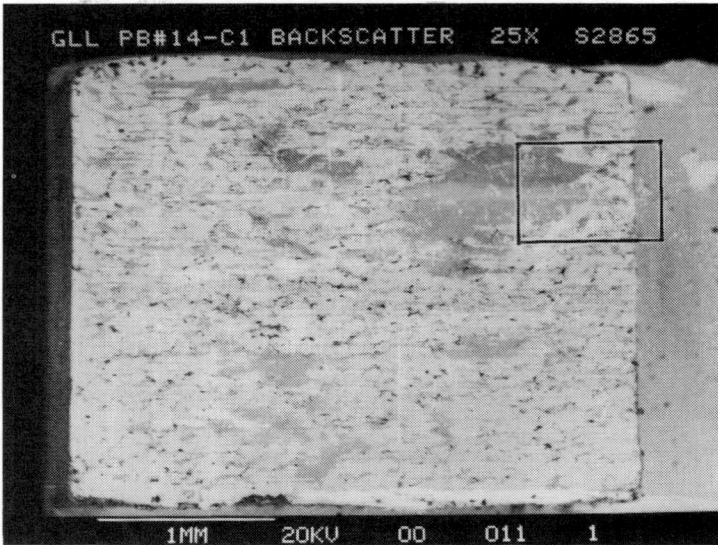

OVERALL BACKSCATTER SEM PHOTO OF MODULE
C-1 POWER BRUSH 14 WEAR SURFACE. DARKER
GRAY PATTERNS ARE REGION OF BRUSH
CONTAMINATION

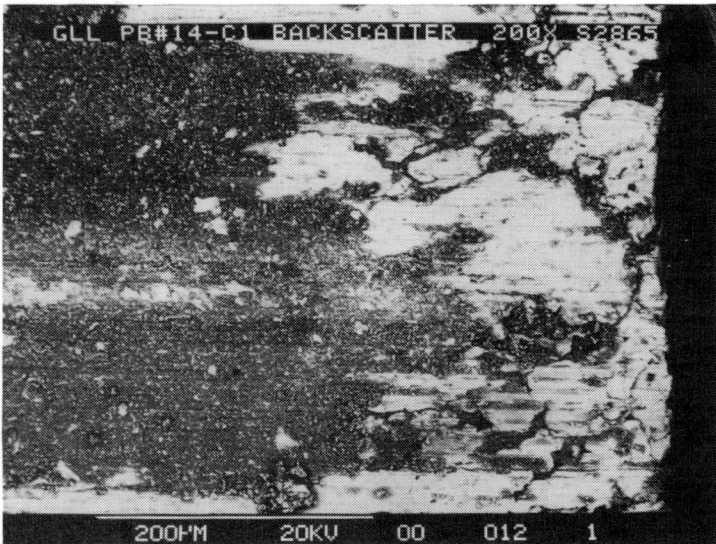

CLOSE UP OF AREA IN BOX (FIGURE ABOVE)

Figure 8

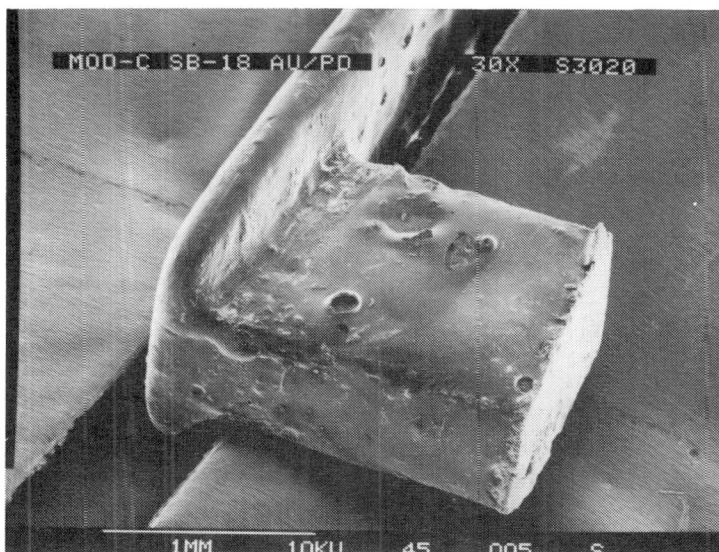

Figure 9 - Contaminant found on side of brushes

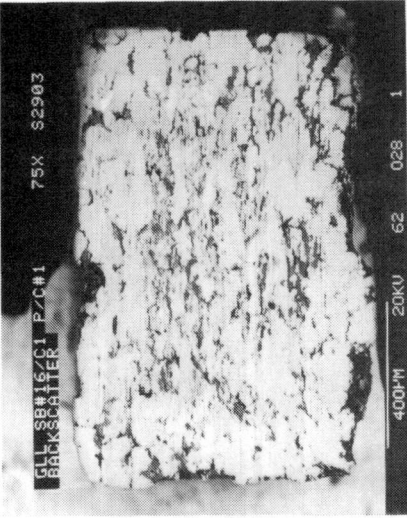

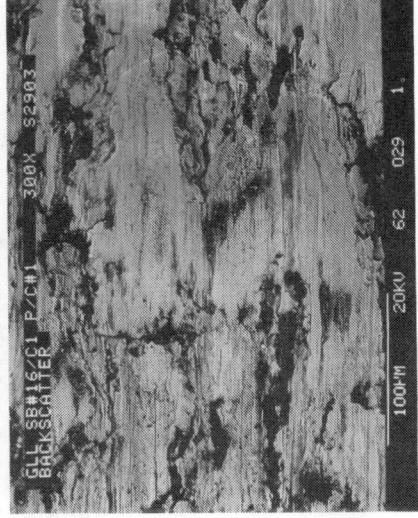

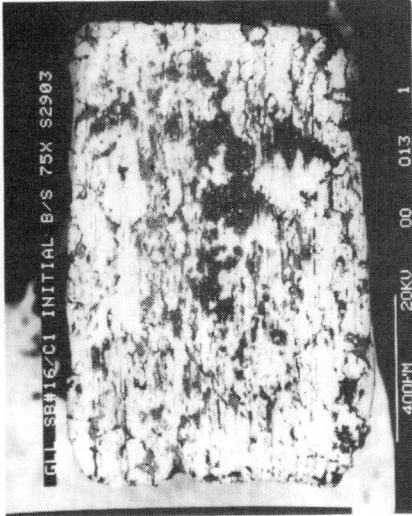

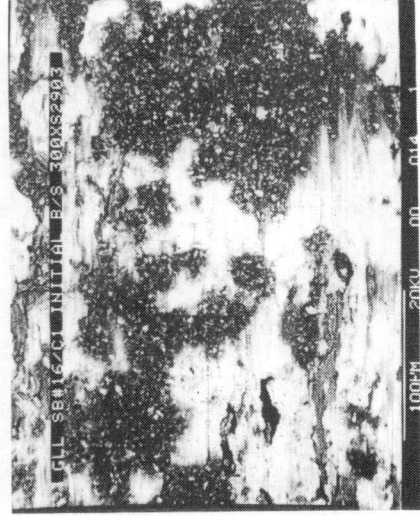

Figure 10 – Brush wear face before (left side photos) and after ultrasonic cleaning (right side photos)

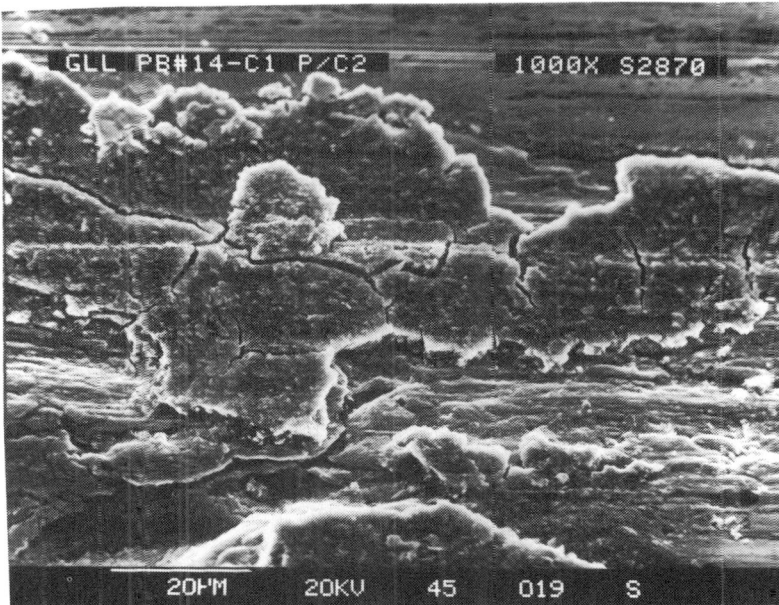

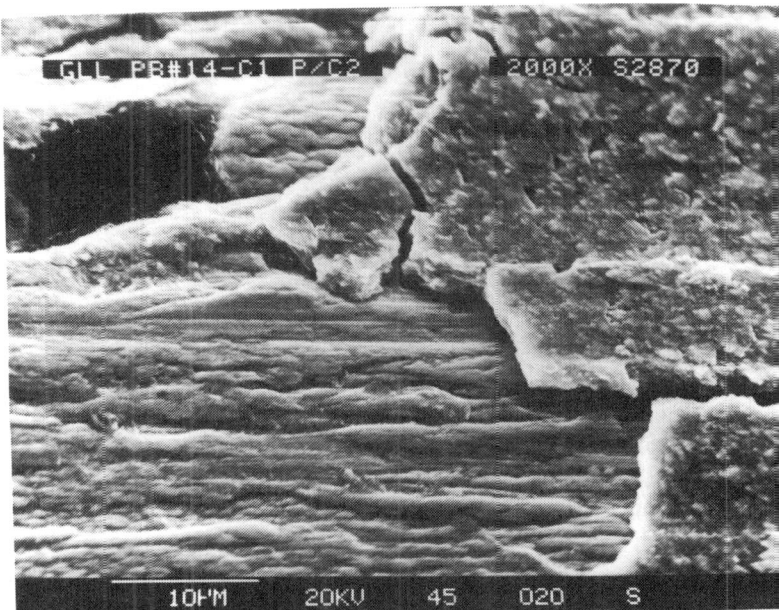

Figure 11 - Close up brush face contaminant showing
"mudcrack" pattern

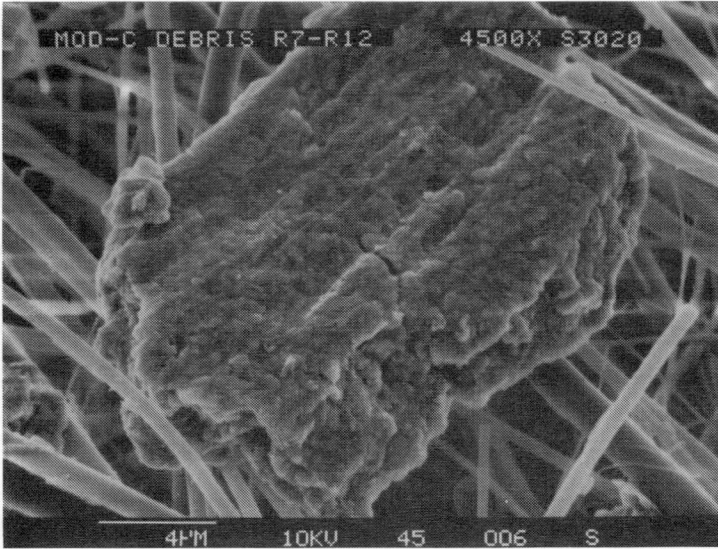

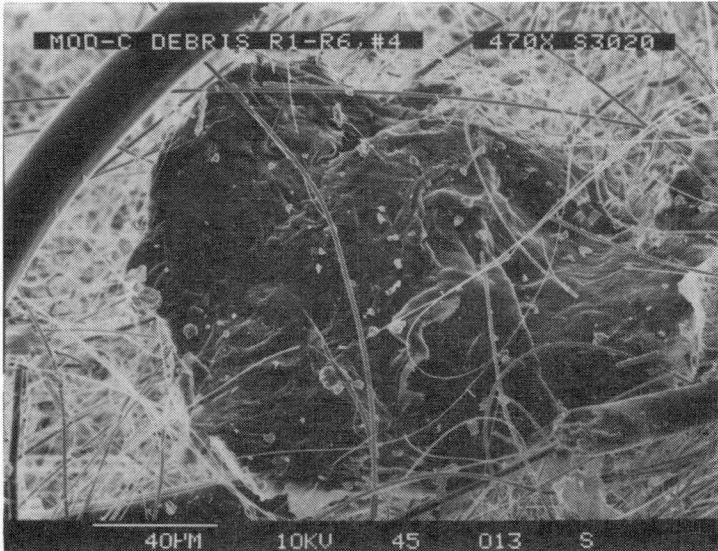

Figure 12 - Piece of wear face contaminant collected after ultrasonic cleaning

AN OVERVIEW OF LUBRICATION AND ASSOCIATED MATERIALS FOR VACUUM SERVICE

B. A. Scott

Ball Aerospace Systems Group, Boulder, CO 80306

ABSTRACT

For mechanisms to function reliably with extended life in vacuum environments, special consideration must be given to the selection of lubricants and materials. Generally, for the lubrication of mechanisms in a vacuum environment there are two types of acceptable lubricants: fluid lubricants which include oils and greases; and dry lubricants which include soft metals, polymers such as PTFE, and dichalcogenides such as MoS_2.

Advances have introduced new methods of lubricant application such as sputtering and state-of-the-art techniques to modify wear surfaces, as exemplified by ion implantation. Even the lubrication of electrical contacts must be addressed to assure a successful mechanism life. Other materials associated with a lubricated component must also be carefully chosen. Aspects such as chemical compatibility with the lubricant and the possibility of contamination by outgassing of a selected material are additional concerns.

INTRODUCTION

Since the late 1950's and 1960's the aerospace industry has been faced with the task of lubricating mechanisms for use in vacuum. Initially, well known techniques of lubrication were applied with only moderate success to spacecraft. New lubricants were soon developed to solve the challenges of space lubrication. As more stringent demands have evolved for space mission parameters such as increased temperature, speed, load, life, and mechanism complexity, correspondingly, the vacuum lubrication technology has evolved to satisfy the requirements. These lubrication techniques can also be applied to the more terrestrial fields of vacuum service including semiconductor manufacturing, chemical analysis instrumentation, vacuum robotics, and vacuum chamber accessories such as pumps and feed-throughs.

Lubrication in general serves several purposes. Primarily lubrication reduces friction and wear. Along with a reduction in friction comes the additional benefit of lower power requirements for a mechanism to function. Another beneficial aspect of lubrication is that it provides a media for increased thermal conduction to reduce temperature gradients, which, with decreased wear will increase the life of a mechanism. Other benefits are the improved uniformity of motion and mechanism positioning.

The inherent nature of vacuum service poses many challenges for choosing a suitable lubricant. Water, air and other "uncontrolled contaminants" are absent and so clean, degassed materials at a friction interface may fuse or cold-weld causing catastrophic failure. While a ball bearing, for example, may operate for months or years in an air atmosphere due to the presence of these "contaminants", in a vacuum the bearing could cold-weld within minutes to hours of operation. Because of the cleaner atmosphere that a vacuum provides, proper lubricant selection is especially important.

Oils and greases evaporate. Low environmental pressure and elevated temperature increase the rate exponentially. The loss of a lubricant by evaporation can be severe enough that a mechanism can become starved of its lubricant and possibly fail. As a lubricant evaporates it may condense on other surfaces such as optics, creating a potentially mission threatening contamination. And while a lubricant has an increased evaporation rate in vacuum, other materials in a mechanism may also outgas to a great extent. These materials can contaminate the lubricant and, in the case of cyanoacrylate adhesives, react with and destroy the lubricant.

An ideal lubricant has three major properties. It would be chemically and thermally stable. A zero shear strength would provide zero friction as long as there isn't any contact between the two surfaces in relative motion. And lastly, it would have an infinite compressive strength and so able to carry high loads. Unfortunately there isn't an ideal lubricant. A good definition of a lubricant is a controlled contaminant with known properties under known environments and known stresses which is applied to, or incorporated in, solid substrates.[1] To select a suitable lubricant several parameters need to be determined at the design phase of a mechanism. These are presented in Table I. Without the specification of these parameters the suitability and subsequent mechanism life is unknown.

Table I
Design Parameters for Lubricant Selection

- Speed, load and duty cycle
- Storage and operating life requirements
- Electrical loads and performance
- Temperature range
- Radiation exposure
- Vacuum or atmospheric pressure
- Contamination susceptibility and potential

Two major types of lubricants are usually considered for vacuum service: fluid lubricants such as oils and greases, and dry lubricants such as molybdenum disulfide. Ion implantation methods also can be considered a method of lubrication since this technique can beneficially change the surface characteristics of a substrate. Other methods of addressing mechanism motion, such as magnetic bearing supports, definitely have their applications but are beyond the scope of this discussion.

FLUID LUBRICANTS

Oils and greases provide lubrication by: a) separating surfaces, b) having low shear strengths and c) allowing particulates to escape the contact zone. Two different lubrication regimes are possible: boundary (thin film) or fluid (thick film) lubrication. These are illustrated for a ball bearing in Figure 1.[2]

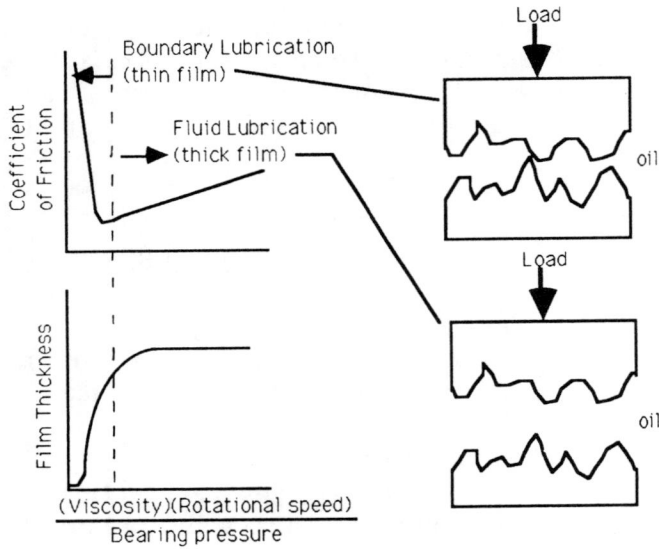

Figure 1 - Boundary and Fluid Lubrication

Full fluid, thick film lubrication completely separates surfaces preventing surface asperities from contacting. Breaking of asperities constitutes wear and leads to possible failure of a mechanism. But full fluid film lubrication only occurs at higher speeds, higher viscosities and lower bearing loads.

When viscosity, speed and load parameters are such that boundary, or thin film lubrication occurs, the surface asperities protrude through the oil or grease film and make contact. As a result friction increases as does the wear of the mechanism. It is when these conditions of low speed or high load exist that particular consideration of lubricant selection is necessary.

Fluid lubricants have been widely used in vacuum service applications. They do, however, have limitations. The comparative qualities of fluid lubricants are presented in Table II.

Table II - Fluid lubricants: advantages and disadvantages

Advantages	Disadvantages
High reliability	Possible outgassing contamination
Well understood	Viscosity a function of
Replenishable	temperature
Carry high loads	Vapor pressure a function of
Lower friction	temperature
Good heat transfer media	Susceptible to failure by
	contamination

A myriad of fluid lubricants are available in today's market. Base fluids suitable for vacuum service can be categorized into five general classes.[3]

Petroleum lubricants are produced by refining crude oil stocks. Some yield base lubricants with low vapor pressures suitable for vacuum service. This class generally has excellent lubricating properties, but has limited temperature ranges.

Synthetic esters have been extensively used in the aircraft industry for decades. When they were initially produced many people felt that this class would constitute the perfect lubricant for all applications. While synthetic esters are not a panacea, they definitely have excellent properties for some applications. They are useful because of their low viscosity and low volatility over a wide temperature range (i.e. -65 °F to 250 °F).

Polyalphaolefins (PAO's) are a more recent class of synthetic base oils. Having a high viscosity index, PAO's are used over a broad temperature range. They are of a more uniform molecular weight and have excellent shear stability.

Silicones are a unique class of lubricants with very attractive properties, such as applicability over a broad temperature range and provision of good lubricity for solid polymers. Typically they are not good for boundary lubrication regimes. Since silicones have a low surface energy and spread rapidly, the migration can cause a severe contamination threat. Silicones are notorious for causing problems with electrical contacts. Still, for many applications such as lubricating plastics and in marine applications, silicones are excellent lubricants and moisture barriers.

Fluorinated polyethers are a specific class of base oils. Chemically inert and with a broad useful temperature range, these oils can be used in many applications. Frequently they are chosen for manned aerospace missions since they are nonflammable. Limiting factors of fluorinated polyethers are that they are expensive and will show increased friction torque at higher speeds.

Vapor pressure of an oil is a significant property when considering vacuum service applications. Typical values of vapor pressures for the five classes of base oils are presented in Table III.

Table III

Vapor pressures for vacuum service oils

Base oil class	Vapor pressure at 296 K (mm Hg)
Petroleum	10^{-8}
Synthetic esters	10^{-10}
Polyalphaolefins	10^{-10}
Silicones	10^{-8} to 10^{-9}
Fluorinated polyethers	10^{-10} to 10^{-12}

The evaporation rate of a given oil must be considered when selecting a lubricant for vacuum service. The Langmuir equation gives the rate of evaporation as:[4]

$$G = \frac{P}{17.14}\left(\frac{M}{T}\right)^{1/2} \qquad (1)$$

where G is the rate of vaporization $(g/[cm^2 s])$, P is vapor pressure of the base oil (mm Hg), M is molecular weight (g/mol), and T is temperature $(^{\circ}K)$. Using the Langmuir equation along with the known values of M, T and desired lifetime of a lubricated component, the quantity of oil needed can be calculated.

A convenient rule of thumb can be developed from this equation. Assuming that the molecular weight of an oil is 1000 g/mol, and that the T is room temperature, then the numerical value for the rate of vaporization (in $g/[cm^2 s]$) is approximately one tenth the value of the vapor pressure (in mm Hg). This estimate, of course, should be used cautiously.

Greases are simply oils that have been thickened to make them non-flowing. An exception to this are high viscosity oil residues, the heavier fractions of a natural petroleum distillate. The function of a grease is to provide a close proximity reservoir of oil, which bleeds into the contact region, while being thick enough to maintain the position of the grease nearby but out of the friction interface zone.

Examples of grease thickeners are quartz powders, modified Teflon, clays, and soaps. A soap thickener is formed by a chemical reaction within the base oil. A metal hydroxide and, for example, stearic acid, react in the base oil to produce a metal stearate (a soap) with the base oil. A useful addition to a grease is molybdenum disulfide. The MoS_2 added will increase the load carrying capacity of the grease, especially for sliding applications such as gear lubrication.

To improve the properties of a base oil, lubricant additives are usually incorporated. Lubricant properties can be improved by addition of one or more oxidation inhibitors, extreme pressure additives, antiwear additives, friction modifiers, corrosion inhibitors, or viscosity index improvers to the base oil. Most important are extreme pressure additives such as lead compounds and antiwear agents such as sulfur, phosphorous and zinc compounds.

Careful preparation of surfaces prior to applying fluid lubricants is necessary. Thorough cleaning of the parts by solvent washing and elevated temperature baking is recommended. When applying an oil, vacuum impregnation of all hardware to be lubricated is desirable to fill available voids. Lubricant reservoirs, highly porous materials impregnated with oil, can be installed near lubricated mechanisms to replenish oil that is lost by evaporation. Phenolic retainers in ball bearings can be used as a lubricant reservoir. Shields, seals, barrier film, and labyrinths can all be used to maintain and confine an applied fluid lubricant.

DRY LUBRICANTS

Solid film lubricants are materials that provide separation of, and reduced friction to, two surfaces under essentially dry conditions.[5] While sometimes regarded as unconventional lubrication, dry lubricants solve many particularly troublesome problems. Early on, dry lubrication was more of an art than a science, but as experience has grown, so too has scientific understanding. The benefits and drawbacks to using dry lubricants are presented in Table IV.

Table IV - Dry lubricants: advantages and disadvantages

Advantages	Disadvantages
Low vapor pressure	Limited life
No viscous friction	Lower load carrying ability for long term sliding use
Usable over a wide temperature range	Not easily replenishable
High radiation resistance	Catastrophic failure mode
Won't collect dust and grit	Requires design adjustment
Excellent storage stability	Requires particulate debris management

Graphite and molybdenum disulfide (MoS_2) are commonly used examples of dry lubricants. Both have a planar, hexagonal structure and will form in a lamellar fashion. Figure 2 illustrates how these lubricant platelets separate two surfaces in relative motion and provide a low shear strength, high load carrying film within the contact region. An analogous situation is playing cards in a deck. Each card will slide easily against another, even under high loads, and so the deck functions as a load carrying friction modifier. Dichalcogenides are the general class of dry lubricants that along with graphite exhibit this hexagonal/lamellar structure. Tungsten disulfide and MoS_2 are the two most widely used dichalcogenides.

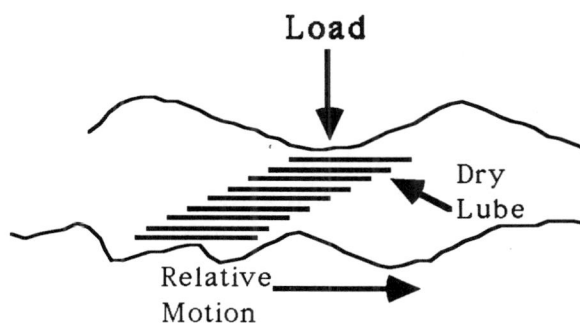

Figure 2

Powdered graphite isn't recommended for use in hard
vacuums . Graphite depends on residual moisture to aid in
sliding of its hexagonal platelets. In vacuum environments, at
most only isolated molecules of water are available, and so the
graphite is unable to produce adequate lubricity. Corrosion
problems are also associated with graphite, particularly with
steels. However, graphite does have its applications. A percent
or two of graphite will aid in ground performance at ambient
atmosphere of molybdenum disulfide and tungsten disulfide
films.

Polymers also can serve as dry lubricants. This class is
dominated by fluorocarbon compounds such as
polytetrafluoroethylene (PTFE) and fluorinated ethylene-
propylene for vacuum use. These polymers don't have a
structure like graphite and dichalcogenides, but have wax-like,
amorphous structures with low shear strength which provide
lubrication. Since these fluorocarbon polymers are chemically
inert they are suitable for liquid oxygen and harsh chemical
exposure.

One exceptionally good application of polymers as a
lubricant is as a base material for ball bearing retainers. Glass
reinforced PTFE retainers lubricate a bearing's balls during
operation with the PTFE component while the glass fiber ends
plow through any build up of PTFE on the balls, and so
maintaining a thin PTFE film.

Soft metals, such as lead, indium and gold, can be applied
as a thin films to a harder substrate and since they have low
shear strengths, this yields a low coefficient of friction. Gold is

especially useful for electrical contacts such as in sliprings and
encoders. It will flow some, but still provides electrical
conductivity and lubricity. Lead is frequently used in the
European aerospace industry. As a very thin film, lead provides
lubrication and since it is soft, it will transfer to contacting
surfaces, lubricating them as well. In the United States lead
isn't widely used because it readily converts to lead oxide, an
abrasive, if operated in air.

Techniques for applying dry film lubricants are more
varied and significant than for fluid lubricants. Dry film
lubricant behavior will depend on the type of application
process used. Pretreatment of the substrate is also an
important consideration. Thorough cleanliness along with
mechanical roughening or chemical treatments will increase
adhesion of a lubricant film to a substrate and so extend the
wear-life.

The simplest application method is to mechanically apply
a powdered dry lubricant by rubbing or burnishing it onto a
solid substrate, "cobwebbing" the lubricant across the peaks of
substrate surface asperities. Film thickness will range from 20
to 80 x10^{-6} in. In general, this type of lubricant film will have a
lower wear-life because of low adhesion to the metal compared
to those applied by other methods. It is good for low speed and
high load usages, for instance, as a lubricant for fasteners and
inserts.

An improvement on burnishing is to mechanically apply
the lubricant by high velocity impingement. Small spheres are
electrostatically coated with powdered lubricant, and sprayed
against a substrate causing the lubricant to transfer to the
substrate. This process produces a much more tenacious, thin
film of lubricant to bond to the substrate surface. Impinged
coatings are self-limiting in thickness and range from 8 to 20
X10^{-6} in. Very low operating torques in bearings can be
achieved with lubricants applied in this manner.

Resin bonded lubricants are the most widely used dry
lubricant films. Organic based resins such as polyimides,
phenolics, and epoxies are used to bond the lubricating pigment
to substrates. Pigments may be one or more of graphite,
molybdenum disulfide, tungsten disulfide or
polytetrafluoroethylene. Thicker than unbonded dry films, they
range from 2 to 4 X10^{-4} in. thick. While performance will

depend on the type of binder used, resin bonded lubricants can provide long wear-life, good solvent resistance and good abrasion resistance.

Inorganically bonded lubricants are also available. Using binders of silicates, phosphates or ceramics allows the lubricant film to be used at much higher temperatures, up to 1500 °F. Usually these are thicker films than organically bonded lubricants, being on the order of 2 to 50 $X10^{-4}$ in. thick.

Another application method is sputtering of lubricant films. Inert gas is ionized, accelerated and sputters the lubricant material from a target. The sputtered material is then deposited on the part being coated. Very thin films (up to 10 $X10^{-6}$ in.) of pure lubricant can be applied.

Ion implantation, since it modifies surface characteristics such as hardness and coefficient of friction, can be considered a dry lubricant. The process involves accelerating energetic ion species so that the ions strike the surface, for instance, of a ball bearing raceway.[7,8] The energies of ions are on the order of 50-500 keV and penetrate the surface 100-10,000 Å. Penetration produces alterations in the crystal structure of the substrate which, depending upon the ion species used, will change chemical, mechanical or tribological properties of the surface. One criticism of this method is that since the depth of penetration of the ions is relatively small, any wear will go completely through this thin surface. However, many critical applications arise that warrant the investigation and use of ion implantation.

GENERAL MATERIALS CONSIDERATIONS

In conjunction with lubricant selection for vacuum service, careful attention should be given to choosing hardware materials to ensure a fully satisfactory device. Table V summarizes general guidelines towards choosing acceptable materials for vacuum use. These guidelines are based mostly on outgassing properties of the materials. Other considerations are also involved. For instance, cyanoacrylates will outgas and when they come into contact with many lubricants they cause the lubricant to polymerize. Nylons are avoided since they

absorb water while in an ambient atmosphere, later releasing
the absorbed water when in vacuum.

These guidelines are only general suggestions based on
reasonable temperatures, chemical and radiation environments,
and time requirements. Many of the materials listed as
undesirable may be used if pre-cleaned by baking or solvent
extraction. Some materials listed as acceptable aren't
recommended for extreme temperatures. Most importantly,
each material should be examined based on the particular
environmental parameters anticipated.

Table V - Material Guidelines for Vacuum Service

Materials to avoid	Materials to use with caution
Vinyls (contain plasticizers)	Silicones
Polyethylene	Epoxies
Natural rubber	Urethanes
Synthetic rubbers	Nylons
Hot melt glues	Natural fibers
Cyanoacrylates	Most paints, adhesives
Unalloyed tin, zinc, cadmium, mercury	
Fluorinated rubbers	
Polyolefins	Most oils, greases
Leathers	Phenolics
	Waxes
	Graphite

Acceptable materials
Polyimides
PTFE, FEP, CTFE
Mylar
Diallylphthallate
Acrylics
Polycarbonates
Aluminum anodize
Most metals
Molybdenum disulfide
Tungsten disulfide

CONCLUSION

No single lubricant will satisfy all vacuum applications.
Yet, with the myriad of lubricants available, a very satisfactory
lubricant can be found for particular applications. This requires
specific testing or thorough knowledge of a candidate lubricant.

Materials associated with the lubricated component also must be carefully chosen. While there are few absolutes, usually excellent materials can be found to fulfill a particular use.

REFERENCES

1. G.H. Ahlborn, 'Introduction to Bearing and Lubrication Technology," Ball Aerospace Systems Division seminar (September 1984).
2. E.E. Bisson, "Advanced Bearing Technology," NASA SP38, (1964), p. 7.
3. C.G. Beecher, Inside Bearings (MPB Corporation), 3, 1,(1987).
4. E.E. Bisson, op. cit., p. 262-263.
5. Midwest Research Institute, Lubrication Handbook for the Space Industry (NAS8-27662), p. AI-1-AI-10.
6. European Space Tribology Laboratory Technical Bulletin, 2 (1984).
7. P. Sioshansi, Thin Solid Films, 118, (1984), p. 61-71.
8. R.A. Kant & B.D. Sartwell, J. Vac. Sci. Technol. A, 3, 6, (1985), p. 2675-2676.

THE USAGE OF LUBRICANTS IN A VACUUM ENVIRONMENT

Don R. Lewis
Dicronite Dry Lube, Covina CA 91723

August O. Weilbach
Helvart Associates, La Habra CA 90631

ABSTRACT

Lubrication systems which show substantially improved performance in a vacuum environment are the result of continuing development efforts. The availability of a variety of surface coatings and a better selection of high-tech ceramic and plastic materials with excellent wear and low friction qualities have permitted significant advances in the state of the art. The proper use of some wet lubricants, exhibiting very low vapor pressure, still can provide a viable vacuum lubrication system alternative.

Hybrid bearings, consisting of metal races and ceramic balls, may provide the answer to extended life and extreme temperature problems. Bearing friction can further be reduced through the deposit of certain solid lubricants. Some of the material and lubricant combinations will permit the use of plain sleeve bearings.

Combinations of a solid lubricant and a minimum amount of a wet lubricant have been chosen for a substantial number of spaceborne instrument actuators, rolling element and friction bearings.

A continuing effort to essentially eliminate particulate and vapor contamination is essential for low friction mechanisms operating in a vacuum environment dedicated to the production of micro-circuitry. Examples of such efforts are described.

The significance of surface hardness, surface finish and other characteristics of a selection of rolling snd sliding element materials is discussed.

INTRODUCTION

The search for and the testing of lubricants and materials useable within a vacuum environment is not new. However, to translate these materials into useful and reliable mechanisms presents many challenges. Low friction characteristics, essentially no contaminant generation and a life span of a decade or more in space are but a few of the requirements facing the engineer, designer and manufacturer of such mechanisms. This paper emphasizes material and surface treatment combinations that will meet these requirements.

Several solid lubricants, sometimes in combination with certain wet lubricants, are operational in numerous space probes including the Shuttle and will be used in the future Space Station. In a refined form, boundary lubrication will be of prime value in "Mechatronics" used in modular but self-contained ultra-clean processing equipment. Here, under artificial and mostly ultra-high vacuum conditions, Robotic Motion Systems will assist in performing the final production steps for today's extremely sophisticated and very contamination sensitive microelectronic devices.

Borden and Gregg[1] in their paper stated, "Particle contamination during vacuum processes has emerged as the largest single source of yield loss in VLSI manufacturing." This has to be taken as a serious statement and thus the materials and especially the lubricants for use in chip manufacturing vacuum chambers (Mechatronics) have to be most carefully selected.

Facetiously one could state that the best combination would be zero friction materials and no lubricant at all. With this in mind we should consider linear motors with a magnetic suspension (levitation) combination. Whenever possible we should use motion limited flex or torsion joints. When feasible, vacuum levels permitting, we should consider the use of low friction composite sliding element bearings. By necessity we must evaluate what rolling element bearings of both the rotating and linear type can do. At the present time rolling element bearings are the most promising and efficient approach.

BEARING COMPONENT MATERIALS

Today's choice of high-tech ceramics often offer several advantages over most metals used for bearing applications operating in a vacuum environment. Table I provides some comparative physical property values such as hardness and thermal coefficient of expansion. Other equally important properties such as wearability and coefficient of friction will be mentioned in the forthcoming discussions.

Table II will act as a rough guideline for which materials, metals, ceramics, coatings and/or plastics are suitable for Mechatronic components and assemblies. A few tested and promising lubricants are listed as choices for further evaluation.

The considerable difference in surface characteristics of ceramic materials is shown in the following photo-micrographs . Alumina exhibiting a structure of bonded crystals is shown in Fig. 1. It is a relatively inexpensive ceramic and is available in several grades. The sample shown forms an excellent substrate for the application of low friction solid lubricant layers such as modified tungsten disulfide and HELVALUB both of which are applied without a binder.

In contrast zirconia shown at the same magnification in Fig. 2 looks like a molten media with relatively few burst-bubble pores. Recent versions of this ceramic are essentially bubble free. The surface will not provide a reliable substrate bond for solid lubricants. The material however has by itself a low coefficient of friction and superior wearability. In contact with an suitable boundary on the opposite bearing surface it will form an excellent vacuum bearing material combination.

PROPERTY CHART		CERAMICS			METALS		
		Alumina	Silicon Nitride	Zirconia	M1	440C	17-4 PH
Mechanical Density	gm/cm^3	3.3	2.8	5.6	7.5	7.7	7.8
Hardness	HRA	87	94	80	56	58	60
Compressive Strength	Kg/cm^2	28'000		20'000		4200	
Young's Modulus	$10^6 kg/cm^2$	3.5	2.6	1.9	1.1	1.2	0.9
Poisson's Ratio		.25	.25	.22			
Tensile Strength	kg/cm^2	800	1000	1200	1800 (600)	5200 (2200)	4000 (1600)
Fluxural Strength	kg/cm^2	3000	9500	10'000			
Thermal Thermal Expansivity	$10^{-6} in./in ^\circ F$	7.7	3.3	11	6.5	5.6	6.0
Thermal Conductivity	$\dfrac{cal.cm}{cm^2/sec/^\circ C}$	.06	.02	.004	.08	.12	.10
Maximum Useful Temperature	$^\circ C$	1600	875	1500	450	500	500
Thermal Shock Resistance		good	good	good	fair	fair	fair

Properties of Selected Ceramics and Metals

Table I

```
                 TABLE II.    MATERIAL SELECTION

METALS:                                     Coat with
     Steel      52100              Dicronite or 2-141
     Steel      M 50               Dicronite
     SS Steel  440 C               Dicronite
     Steel      17-4 PH            Dicronite or 2-141
     Beryllium Copper              Dicronite
     Aluminum (Hard anodized)      Dicronite or 2-141

PLATING or SURFACE TREATMENT:
     High density Chrome           Dicronite
     Electroless Nickel            Dicronite
     Hard Anodize (Aluminum)       Dicronite or 2-141
     Ceramic Plasma Coat           Dicronite or 2-141

CERAMICS
     Alumina                       Dicronite or 2-141
     Silicon Nitride                     N/A
     Zirconia                            N/A

PLASTICS
     Polymers and its composites DUROID, TEFLON
     Polyimides  VESPEL,  MELDIN (9000)


WET-LUBRICANTS
     Braycote 601 (CASTROL); KRYTOX (duPONT)
      Do not use Silicones

SOLID-LUBRICANTS
     Tungsten disulfide (modified)
     Molybdenum disulfide (VAC-KOTE)
     Boron Nitride (formulated)
     Fluorides (experimental)

Note:  The above listed materials, surface treatments
and   lubricants   are   strictly   meant   as   guidelines
without endorsing  anyones product.  Other   materials
and coatings, tried and untried, are available.

     REGISTERED TRADENAMES:
          DICRONITE           Lubrication Sciences, Inc.
          VESPEL & TEFLON     Du Pont
          MELDIN 9000         Dixon Co.
          DUROID 5813         Rogers Co.
          BRAYCO 601          Castrol
          VAC-KOTE            Ball Aerospace
          KRYTOX              Du Pont
```

56

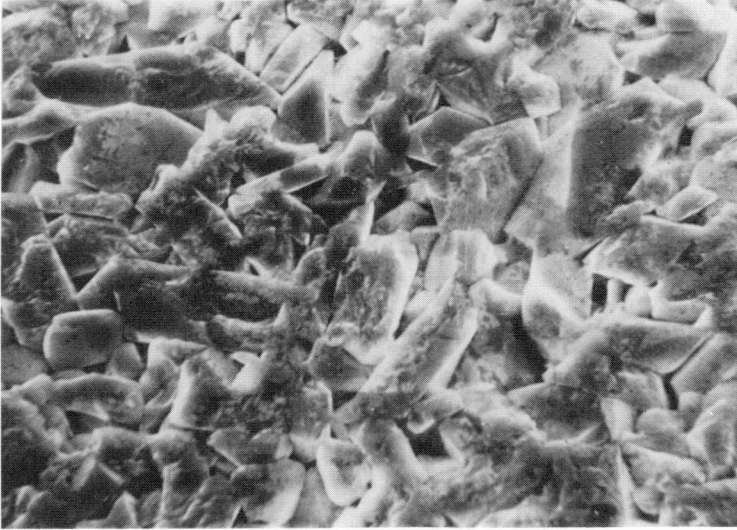

Figure 1 Alumina 96%
          Surface Finish of 8-15 rms
          Magnification 1000X

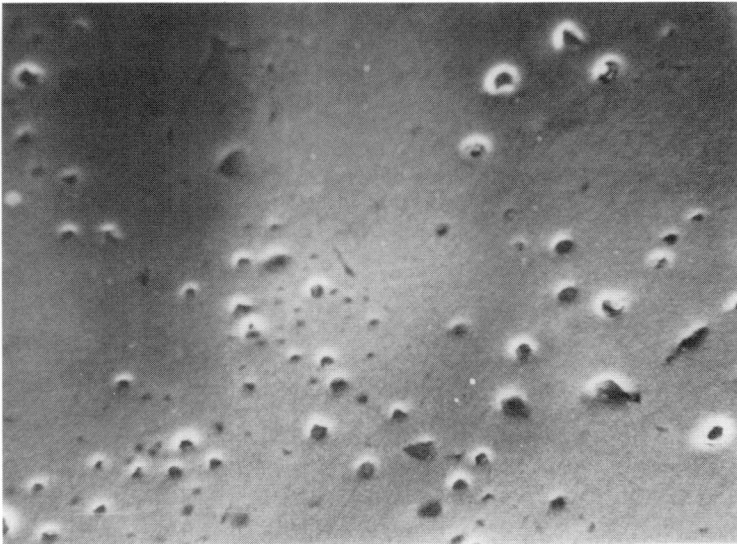

Figure 2 Magnesia Stabilized Zirconia
          Surface Finish of 4-8 rms,
          Magnification 1000X

NON-METALLIC BALL SEPARATORS

Despite the fact that some of the high-tech ceramics such as silicon nitride or zirconia allow the running of a full compliment of balls without a ball separator, we think it to be prudent to include it in most cases. If high temperature is not an important criteria, the use of polymers or polyimide materials is recommended. VESPEL, a polyinide, has passed many tests and is available on special order from several bearing manufacturers. So is MELDIN 9000, a porous polyimide made by the Dixon company. The finished part can be impregnated with a solid or wet lubricant and thus provide a limited lubricant "reservoir." Vespel will accept a coat of DICRONITE which will act as an excellent transfer lubricant to the ball surfaces which in turn will help lubricant transfer to the race-tracks. DUROID 5813, a polymer produced by the Rogers Co., has a very low coefficient of friction and, being a composite material containing molybdenum disulfide, will also provide permanent transfer lubrication.

PHENOLIC and its composites have been a long time stand-by for space instrument bearing retainers. The material will allow a certain amount of solid or wet lubricant impregnation. Shedding of relatively large particles can occur and outgassing in high vacuum cannot be prevented. For the reasons stated, it is a material not to be recommended for vacuum mechatronics used for the production of microelectronics. Its weight and possible shrinkage loss, due to elimination of small amounts of absorbed water, must, for critical applications, also be taken into consideration.

SOLID LUBRICANTS

The paper repeatedly mentions DICRONITE and HELVALUB as solid lubricants.
DICRONITE is a modified tungsten disulfide coating containing no auxiliary binder. The coating is deposited as a thin layer without the need of a baking or curing operation. It is applied under specification DoD L-85645.
HELVALUB is the name for a series of lubricants specifically mixed for high-temperature and/or vacuum applications. HELVALUB 2-142 is a boron nitride based lubricant[6] with rare earth oxide additives. These additives perform several functions including acting as binders that can penetrate the microstructure of most metals and anchor itself to some of the ceramic materials.

Other solid lubricants, mostly molybdenum disulfide based formulations, are readily available and have performed well in space and commercial applications. The relatively heavy build up and the need for elevated temperature curing make them usually unsuitable for the coating of ball bearing components. In contrast a modified tungsten disulfide coat such as DICRONITE will bond itself to the substrate with a maximum coating thickness of less than .000020" (0.5 microns).

Experience has shown that for sliding bearings a "hybrid" lubricant approach (Fig. 5) exhibits superior performance.

At this time the reasons for this improvement are not fully understood. It seems that differences in the laminar structure and differences in size and hardness of the laminates contribute to the phenomena. Pre-burnishing of each coat will essentially eliminate particle shedding from the lubricant layer and thus greatly minimize contamination. Molybdenum disulfide, tungsten disulfide and sintered TEFLON coatings will "even" out the asperities of the substrate materials and thus simulate the behavior of wet lubrication. See Fig. 3.

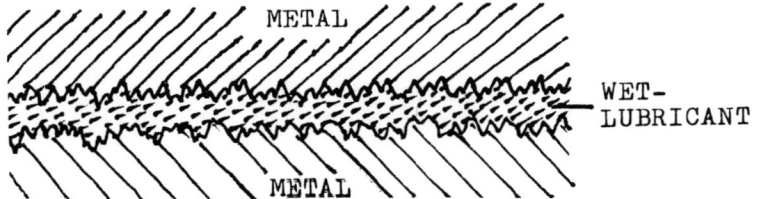

Figure 3   Conventional Wet Lubrication

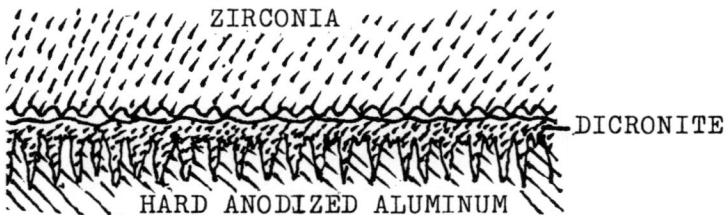

Figure 4   Boundary Lubrication

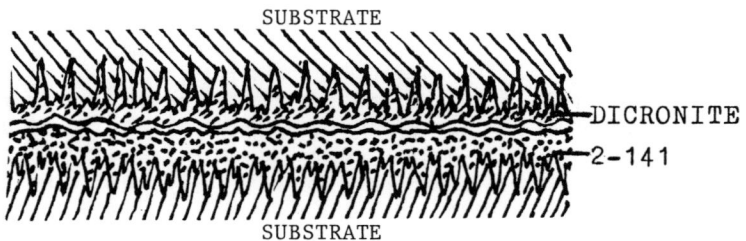

Figure 5   Hybrid Boundary Lubrication

WET LUBRICANTS

Since the beginning of space instrumentation the use of wet lubricants with low vapor pressure has been common. These lubricants have often performed well over many years of operational life. For example, the motors on PIONEER 10 and 11 made by Schaeffer Magnetics, Inc. of Chatsworth CA (Figure 6) have functioned for over 17 years and are now beyond our solar system. Both of these motors used conventional metal ball bearings lubricated with Krytox grease.

Figure 6 PIONEER 10 and 11 Spaceprobe Motor

Du Pont describes Krytox as fluorinated oil (perfluoroalkylpolyethers) with a thickener (tetra- fluoroethylene telomer). After 17 years in a space vacuum the oil has probably evaporated leaving a boundary layer consisting of the oil residue plus the thickener, which is similar to Teflon. This boundary layer is sufficient to permit the motors to operate.

Wet lubricants are suitable for use in some space applications, however, they are generally unsuitable for use in vacuum equipment for microelectronic processing where their relatively high vapor pressure may cause contamination problems.

BOUNDARY LUBRICATION

For a moment let us look at surface coatings, surface treatments and the control of boundary layers that will provide the desired results.

During the testing of bearing prototypes we found that some of the material combinations used in these models showed characteristics suitable for use in a vacuum environment. Fig. 7 shows a bearing demonstration sample.

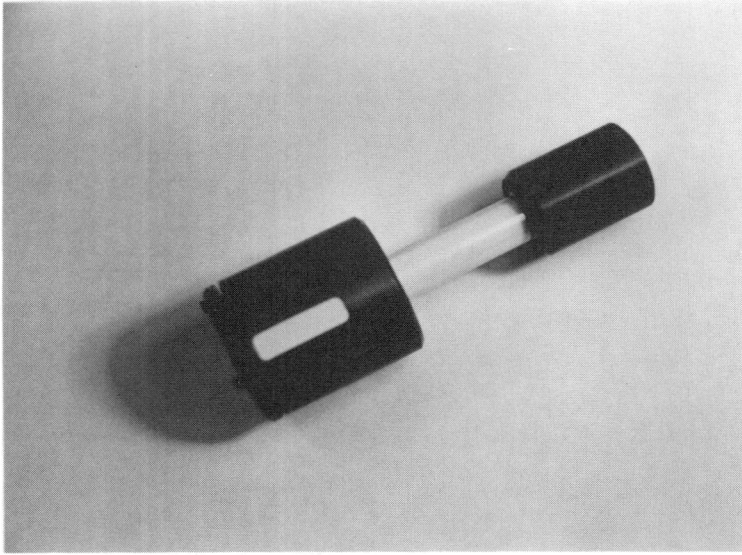

Figure 7   Bearing Demonstrator with a Zirconia Shaft and Hard Anodized Aluminum Sleeve Bearing

The shaft is made of zirconia. The sleeve is made of aluminum with a specially processed hard anodized surface coated with DICRONITE. This surface functions as a boundary layer. The coating has been heavily burnished and has a residual thickness of less than .00001" (0.00025 mm.). See Fig. 8.

Boundary lubrication is discussed by Fuller[2] and by Hamrock and Dowson[3]. They describe two lubrication regimes, fluid film (Fig. 3) and boundary lubrication (Fig. 4 and 5). In the fluid film regime the moving surfaces are separated by a film of liquid sufficient to prevent the opposing solids from coming into contact.

Boundary lubrication is present when very thin films adhering to the surfaces reduce the friction between the moving parts. In this case the moving parts are not separated by a fluid. Contact between the mechanical parts is governed by the physical and

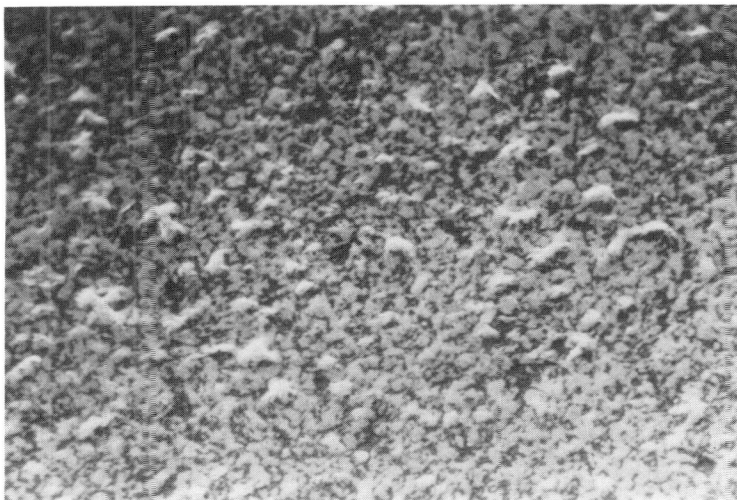

Figure 8   Aluminumum, Hard Anodized with DICRONITE Coating
            Magnification 1000X

chemical properties of a thin surface film of near molecular
proportions.

     Substances which produce good boundary layers have a strong
affinity   for   the surface of the structural   material.   In
conventional wet lubricants   fatty acids produce good boundary
layers on metals that they can react with to produce metallic soaps.
Solid lubricants may react with the material structure or may simply
interpose themselves as a layer in which shearing can take place
more easily than when the two surfaces contact each other directly.
This   can   be   accomplished when the solid lubricant   fills
irregularities in the contacting surfaces as shown in Figs. 4 and 5.

FRICTION

     A low coefficient of friction is essential in most mechanical
devices except for brakes and couplings. We have the problem of
reducing bearing friction (and its related contaminant producing
problems) to a minimum. Low friction and high wear resistance have
to be in concert with each other. In most cases friction under
vacuum conditions will increase a considerable amount. Graphite is
completely unuseable as a lubricant in vacuum.   Hardness and
wearability are only roughly related and are dependent on a
materials surface characteristics and material structure.   An
uncoated aluminum sleeve and bearing combination will cold weld in
no time but if the contact surfaces are hard anodized, friction is
low and wearability is high. The addition of a very thin layer of a
solid lubricant will substantially improve these conditions.
Additional steps, such as burnishing, are necessary to make it into

a viable bearing combination.

In sequence, and assuming a ficticious coefficient of friction of 10, the improvement will be as follows:

Aluminum to Aluminum	uncoated	10
Aluminum to Aluminum	with a molybdenum disulfide coating	5
Aluminum to Aluminum	hard anodized	1
Aluminum to Aluminum	hard anodized with DICRONITE coating	0.06

The friction characteristics of wet lubricants, despite their enormous selection, is a well researched and documented technology.

This is not so when it relates to available data for solid lubricants. It is often difficult to obtain up to date, reliable friction coefficient values. Information from different sources varies considerably.[4]

" Boundary " lubrication from solid lubricants is for all practical purposes not easily replenishable and thus has to be treated in a different way. The same applies if we are talking in terms of rolling or sliding friction. Solid lubricant transfer from impregnated separators, as discussed under NON-METALLIC BALL SEPARATORS, could be part of a solution to achieve replenishment. A review of the paragraph on the nature of "boundary lubrication" may help to shed light onto this important subject.

APPLICATIONS

As we have seen a generous selection of solid lubricants is available. The choice is dictated by the conditions of permissible contamination. For space applications, despite the extended life requirements, the selection is large. Where particle and vapor contaminants would be harmful, the choice is limited and low friction and non-galling characteristics of the bearing element materials and the choice of coatings will be of prime importance.

Figure 9 shows an example of a fully ceramic ball bearing. The rolling elements performed under conditions of +250 C temperature, an axial load of 50 kg. and with HELVALUB 2-141 lubricant. By changing the retainer to a specially treated refractory material the bearing was eventually operated at +800 C at a speed of 2000 rpm.[6] A similar version will shortly be tested at +400 C and at speeds up to 30,000 rpm.

GEAR-TRAINS to be operated under vacuum conditions have to be given special attention. No design will provide truly rolling friction and is at best a combination of sliding and rolling motion. In the absence of wet lubrication and again considering the need for eliminating particle contamination it is best to stay with a carefully generated simple spur-gear configuration used by alternating from metal to plastic materials such as polyimides. Lubrication can be provided by coating the metal with DICRONITE

Figure 9   Disassembled Ceramic Ball Bearing

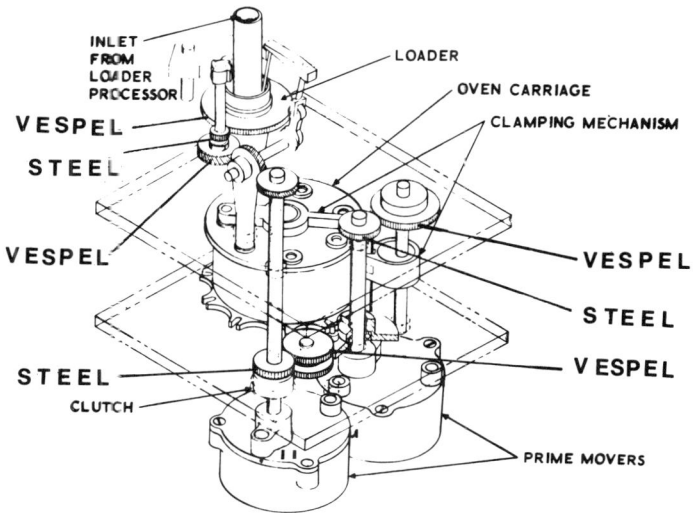

Figure 10   Pyrolysis Oven Loading Mechanism for the
Gas Chromatograph Mass Spectrometer (GCMS)
Instrument for the Viking Mars Lander

or suitable VAC-KOTE and a subsequent burnishing and/or run-in procedure that will provide an enduring boundary layer. This hybrid combination was successfully applied[5] in a mechanism running within the GCMS instrument as part of the payload on both of the Mars Landing VIKING probes. If loads and speed are within a relatively low range, just about all gear forms can be considered.

BALL-SCREWS and LINEAR BUSHINGS are two other mechanical devices frequently used in robotic devices. In this case the ball screw and the ball nut and the ball bushing would be made from zirconia, whereas the balls would be of silicon nitride. Such devices allow high precision positioning and in all likelihood could be operated without lubrication. Both items are presently in design stage and will be submitted for cost estimates. Feasability is assured.

PERFORMANCE MODELS

From the preceding discussion on THE USAGE OF LUBRICANTS IN A VACUUM ENVIRONMENT it is evident that no single solution will answer all the problems. From the best evaluation of which way to go it is prudent to build a basic but flexible working model of the final concept that will allow excercising the bearing materials and lubricant selection.

One starts out under ambient pressure conditions. If failure occurs at that stage further testing in a vacuum is futile.

It is best to start out with a "worst-case" combination of simply a shaft and bushing, consisting of the selected material and lubricant combination. Loads per surface area have to be known and controlled in order to translate the results into rolling element bearing conditions.

After the test it is best to scrutinize the surfaces under a good microscope for wear, lubricant retention and or lubricant transfer. Watch for debris generation. For that purpose it will be best to wash the parts in a volatile, non-toxic solvent such as alcohol. Analyse the debris, if any, for its origin and relative quantity. The survival of a sleeve bearing arrangement will indicate that rolling elements have lower torque requirements by possibly several orders of magnitude.

Such test can be conducted at vacuum levels of 10^{-6} to 10^{-7} torr without jeopardizing the results.

The next and important step is to build and test a prototype that can be subjected to all the rigors of testing within a high vacuum environment.

CONCLUSIONS

With the availability of high tech ceramics, advanced solid lubricant coatings and the selective application of several available surface coatings, one can think positively about using "clean" sliding or rotating "Mechatronics" in vacuum. Substantial progress has been made in this technology and solutions to some of the residual problems are in sight. Non-contact motion systems such as magnetic levitation holds much promise if further improvement is to be achieved. For the present the low friction systems described in this paper will fill the requirements for use in vacuum.

Solving contamination and lubrication problems will extend beyond the production of microelectronics into exciting diciplines such as biotechnology. In doing so it will further enhance improvements to ultra-clean manufacturing and processing equipment for use in a future SELF-CONTAINED AUTOMATIC FACTORY SYSTEM.

REFERENCES

1. Borden, P. and Gregg, J. International Workshop on Vacuum Mechatronics, University of Calif., Santa Barbara. Abstract of paper titled ' Particle Monitoring and Control in Vacuum Process Equipment' February 1989

2. Fuller, D. Theory and Practice of Lubrication for Engineers, Pub. John Wiley and Sons, Inc. pp 310-311 (1984).

3. Hamrock, B. J. and Dowson, D. Ball Bearing Lubrication Pub. John Wiley and Sons, Inc. pp 118-119 (1981)

4. Ludema, K. CRC Handbook of Lubrication Vol. II Pub. CRC Press, Inc. p 48 (1987)

5. Chase, P. and Weilbach, A. O. Viking GC/MS Mechanisms Design and Performance, Proceedings 10th Aerospace Mechanism Symposium , JPL (1976).

6. Weilbach, A.O. Helvart Associates High Temperature and Dry-Lubrication Concepts DARPA Contract N00014-82-C-0248 (1982). NTIS AD 121 386 and AD 122 542

GUIDELINES AND PRACTICAL APPLICATIONS
FOR LUBRICATION IN VACUUM

R. I. Christy
TRW, Redondo Beach, California

ABSTRACT

The many applications for lubrication in vacuum comprise a wide range of requirements. These requirements include temperature, cleanliness, load, speed, position accuracy, and life. In order to select the optimum lubricant, the selection process must be based upon the application requirements.

There is also a wide range of approaches to select from for lubrication in vacuum. These include fluid lubricants with containment and replenishment systems, fluids applied over dry lubricants, and a range of dry lubricant coatings and composites.

An attempt will be made to show the lubricant selection process based upon application requirements. Many specific examples will be given, including some bad choices that should be avoided. The intent will be to provide some useful information for solving today's needs for lubrication.

INTRODUCTION

The first step is to look at some logic behind the choices of lubricants for vacuum. The basic requirements for any lubricant system in vacuum are performance and life. The need is to select a system that meets all performance requirements and does this for the required life. To optimize the choice, it should meet (but not necessarily exceed) the performance, with minimum cost and maximum simplicity.

The logic above is straightforward, until an actual application is considered. For most applications, both performance and life are difficult to determine. Given a defined set of performance and life requirements, a further problem is the tribological uniqueness of each application. Because of the large number of variables that affect each tribological system, there is little correlation between different applications, This makes selection of a lubricant system more difficult for any new application. For this reason, testing is usually necessary for verification, unless there is past history on an identical system. For most new applications, identical systems with performance history cannot be found, so testing is necessary. The lubricant system selection is usually based upon the most closely related past history available. It is then necessary to use careful control to assure that both the lubricants, and methods of application on the tests can be repeated exactly on the application.

SOME DEFINITIONS

For each application, performance must be defined for a set of operating requirements over the life of the unit. These terms are defined below:

Performance   —A set of limits on torque or force.
                                A set of limits on position accuracy (wear).
                                Maintain the above sets of limits over the specified operating requirements.

Operating Requirements   — Loads vs. Time.
                                 Speeds or Motion vs. Time
                                 Temperature vs. Time.
                                 Outgassing or cleanliness requirements.
                                 Environment — (air, vacuum, gas).
                                 Storage conditions.
Life — The total time and "miles over the road" required.

THE FLUID LUBRICATION APPROACH

The two systems now used for lubrication in a vacuum, are the fluid, and dry lubricant systems. The fluid systems (oils and greases) will first be discussed. For long life unattended operation in vacuum, such as on spacecraft mechanisms, the fluid lubricants have been very successful. It is necessary to assure that an adequate oil film is maintained at the critical wear interfaces for the required life. Containment and replenishment systems are usually needed. Oil escapes by both surface and vapor transfer. To control surface transfer, all escape paths from the unit can be coated with low surface energy barrier coatings. The escape paths include all bolted flanges with interface paths going from inside to outside. To control vapor transfer, labyrinth seals are effective. Typical labyrinth gaps are 0.010 inches over a 0.5 inch length. Another escape path is from the lubricated part to any dry surface within the unit. For this reason, it is best to oil coat all internal surfaces during assembly. Using well designed labyrinth seals and surface migration barriers, it is possible to use oils with higher vapor pressure successfully.

For long life designs, methods of replenishment help assure oil is maintained where needed. On ball bearings, use of an oil impregnated porous retainer can store and supply oil exactly where needed. Commercial materials, such as Nitrite Acrylic Copolymer foam, cotton phenolic, porous polyinide and sintered nylon have been used successfully. Oil reservoirs may also be used to maintain the oil vapor pressure.

The oil selection should be based upon long term stability. Many fluids have been used successfully. The refined natural hydrocarbons that have been used for many years are now being replaced by synthetic hydrocarbons. In general, the oil viscosity should be maximized for each application. Some typical oils are shown in Table I. Extreme pressure additives are needed for slower speed boundary lubrication applications. The silicon oils and fluorinated ether oils are not suitable for long life boundary lubrication use. They break down to a jelly or sand consistency. One of the most important considerations is extreme care in cleaning and applications of the lubricant. Careful control is necessary to assure that the unit has 100% of the selected oil and 0% of anything else. This aspect is seldom given enough attention. Related to this is the selection of materials within the unit in contact with the oil. Some plastics or paint coatings will contaminate the oil.

The oil systems have the advantages and disadvantages shown below. Grease systems may also be used, but oil systems with containment and replenishment are usually preferred.

FLUID LUBRICANT ADVANTAGES

- Excellent for long life unattended operation.
- Smooth predictable operation (friction variation is low).
- Good data base of past performance (heritage).

68

Table I. Candidate Lubricants

Lubricant	Lubricant Class	Viscosity	Pour Point	Vapor Pressure or Evaporation	Additive Accept	Boundary Stability	Comments — Assessment
1. Krytox 143AB	Perfluoroalkylpolyether	85 CS at 100°F	-45°F	5% loss 400°F 6.5 hrs. 0.3 torr at 300°F	None	Poor	O.K. only for EHD — cannot use for long life boundary lube.
2. Bray NPT-4	Synthetic ester	19.8 CS at 100°F	<-80°F	94% loss 125°C 24 hrs.	Good	Good	High vapor pressure — low viscosity but works on many applications
3. Technolube XPA28C (+Sb)	Polyalpha-olifin	420 CS at 100°F	<-40°F	4% loss 125°C 24 hrs.	Good	Good	Excellent candidate for a new oil based on dither tests
4. Apiezon C + Pb	Natural Hydrocarbon	94 CS at 100°F	+15°F	78% loss 125°C 24 hrs. 7×10⁻⁹ torr at 25°C	Good	Good	"Standard" of the industry — limited temperature range
5. Pennzoil XT + Sb	Polyalpha-olifin	Not Avail.	Not Avail.	Very low – value not available	Good	Good	Best new oil based on properties and short wear tests.
6. Apiezon C + Sb	Natural Hydrocarbon	94 CS at 100°F	+15°F	78% loss 125°C 24 hrs. 7×10⁻⁹ torr at 25°C	Good	Good	"Standard" base oil and new additive best on dither test
7. NPE-UC-20	Synthetic ester	162 CS at 100°F	-40°F	3% loss 125°C 24 hrs.	Good	Good	Like NPT-4 but high viscosity
8. Bray NPT-9	Synthetic ester	55 CS at 100°F	-50°F	3.4% loss 400°F 6½ hrs.	Good	Good	Like NPT-4 but high viscosity
9. Technolube XPA28D (Pb)	Polyalpha-olifin	420 CS at 100°F	<-40°F	4% loss 125°C 24 hrs.	Good	Good	New base oil good on TRW dither tests and "standard" additive.
10. Bray 815Z	Perfluoroalkylpolyether	135 CS at 100°F	<-60°F	.03% loss 125°C 24 hrs. <1×10⁻⁹ torr at 100°F	None	Poor	OK for EHD or short term boundary only
11. Bray NPT-4 + Sb	Synthetic ester	19.8 CS at 100°F	<-80°F	94% loss 125°C 24 hrs.	Good	Good	Good base oil on units new add. best on dither test
12. Bray NPT-4 + TCP	Synthetic ester	19.8 CS at 100°F	<-80°F	94% loss 125°C 24 hrs.	Good	Good	

FLUID LUBRICANT DISADVANTAGES

- Limited temperature range.
- Contaminant and replenishment adds cost and complexity.
- Contamination from surface or vapor migration.
- Difficult for long term storage.
- Viscosity adds to torque at higher speeds.
- Accelerated testing is very difficult or not possible.

THE DRY LUBRICATION APPROACH

Many methods of dry lubrication have been used successfully in vacuum. These include a wide range of coatings, thick insert liners of dry lubricant composites, and fabrication of parts made of ceramic or composite materials that lubricate. There are two basic approaches. One is the use of a sacrificial material that transfers a dry lubricant coating to the critical wear surfaces. The other is a coating or composite designed to meet all requirements without lubricant transfer. For very short life low load applications, MoS_2 or Teflon can be burnished directly on to wear surfaces. This is inexpensive but is not repeatable, and often the burnished coating forms platelets that cover less than half of the area coated. More recently, the burnished coatings have been replaced by sputtered coatings that are well controlled.

Other thin film coatings include ion vapor deposition of soft metals, such as lead, gold or silver. These are excellent for many ball bearings or gear applications. A more recent approach is the use of extremely hard wear resistant coatings applied by reactive sputtering or reactive ion vapor deposition. These may be used with a soft overcoat such as MoS_2 or Pb, or they can be used with fluid lubricants, to reduce wear. For thicker coatings on less precise applications, there are many commercial bonded solid coatings. These consist of a lubricant pigment or pigments, a binder, and in some cases, a reinforcing filler. These are less expensive and can be sprayed, dipped, or painted. Care is needed to assure surfaces are clean and that adhesion is good.

Ceramic materials may be used, but they usually require lubricant coatings. This is more recent, and coating adhesion to ceramics has been difficult. For some limited applications, either balls, or both balls and races have been made of Si_3N_4 ceramic, but only on smaller size parts.

Many ball bearings have been operated in vacuum using retainers made from composite materials designed to transfer thin dry lubricated films by a sacrificial process. From some higher speed applications, this approach has been successful. At low speeds, transfer takes place in lumps that cause torque increases or jam the bearings. It is difficult to obtain optimum transfer. It is usually beneficial to first apply a thin dry lubricant coating to the balls and races to establish a better initial condition. The trend today is in the direction of hard coatings, overcoated with softer, low friction coatings. These can be applied by a variety of physical vapor deposition (P.V.D.) processes such as sputtering or ion plating. In a few cases, ion implantation is beneficial, but these are usually very specialized, and for light loads, and where the higher cost is justified. With rapid development of the new P.V.D. processes, along with all the applied research on cutting tool coatings, we now have many new candidate dry lubricants to evaluate. These include the nitrides, carbides and oxides of the refractory metals, along with various combinations of these. Both graded or layered coatings are also now being explored. As with the fluid lubricants, there are advantages and disadvantages to the dry lubricants as shown below.

DRY LUBRICANT ADVANTAGES

- Wide temperature range
- Very low outgassing
- Good for long term storage
- Accelerated testing is valid
- Provides corrosion protection
- No viscosity effects

DRY LUBRICANT DISADVANTAGES

- Limited history for long cycle life applications
- Some systems are difficult or expensive to re-apply
- Transfer systems can result in erratic torque at low speeds

SLIDING ELECTRICAL CONTACTS

For both slip rings and motor brushes in vacuum, oils may be used at low speeds. The ring and brush materials must be compatible for vacuum. Gold alloy brushes on hard gold rings work well oil lubricated. Special silver graphite motor brushes with Barium Fluoride work well oil lubricated on copper commutators. Again, contaminant and replenishment systems are needed, and temperature can be a problem. A better solution is the use of dry composite materials. For slip rings, silver-graphite-MoS_2 composite brushes on coin silver rings are excellent in high vacuum, but have a high wear in air. A copper-copper sulphide-graphite motor brush is excellent in air or vacuum on copper commutators. These dry systems allow higher speeds and temperatures.

CONCLUSIONS

In a short space, the present status of lubrication in vacuum has been outlined. There are many possible choices for each application. In general, the trend is away from the fluid systems in favor of the dry lubricants.

RECENT DEVELOPMENT IN LEAK DETECTOR AND CALIBRATOR DESIGNS

Y. Tito Sasaki
Quantum Mechanics Corp., Sonoma, Ca. 95476-1885

ABSTRACT

A reliable ultrasensitive helium leak detector capable of
measuring leaks as small as 1E-15 std cc He/s has been developed
and tested. Adjunctly to the leak detector, a leak calibrator
that can quickly calibrate a wide range of leaks from E-4 to at
least E-12 std cc He/s and beyond was developed. and tested. Leak
measurements by these devices can be made traceable to National
Institute of Standards and Technology (NIST).

INTRODUCTION

A need for ultrasensitive helium leak detectors has long been
recognized. Small volumes such as infrared sensor dewars require
leak-tightness better than 1E-12 std cc He/s for long shelf life.
The useful life of a 1 cc-dewar, if we disregard its built-
in getter pump, would be only a few days if there is a 1E-12 std
cc He/s leak. In order to guarantee a 10 year-shelf life, it must
be proven that the dewar is leak- and permeation-tight to 1E-
15 std cc He/s. (See Table I). "Std cc" in this paper refers to
a cubic centimeter of gas at 0°C and under 760 torr.

Table I. Pressure Inside a Dewar After Exposure
to Atmosphere (STP-Air).

Vessel Volume	Leak Rate (scc He/s)	Pressure Inside a Dewar After 1 Day	Time to Reach 1E-4 Torr
1 cc	1E-10	2.43E-3 Torr	59 min.
	1E-12	2.43E-5 Torr	4 Days 3 Hrs.
	1E-15	2.43E-8 Torr	11 Yrs 3 Mos.

Also, very large volumes, such as a vacuum chamber measuring
several cubic meters, may also require an ultrasensitive leak
detector because the partial pressure of the tracer gas leaking
into such a volume will be very low. For example, in order to
measure a 1E-8 leak in a 10 cubic meter chamber, a detector must
have a sensitivity to measure a 1E-12 leak in a 1-liter volume.
Two major obstacles for successful development of an ultrasensitive leak detector have been the interference of the
background noise and the lack of means to calibrate superfine
leaks. The background noise is created by stray and residual
helium, photons and excited neutrals, and other uncontrolled
behaviors of electronics. Typically the background noise limits

the usable sensitivity of conventional leak detectors to the E-11 std cc He/s range.

As for calibration, the finest primary leak standards certified by Sandia are in the E-10 range, and commercially available NIST certification is only up to 2E-7 std cc He/s. Both Sandia and NIST use the "accumulate and dump" method of calibration, which is time-consuming and not best suited for superfine leaks.

Radical solutions to all these problems were advanced in the early 80's by Lyle Bergquist of Martin Marietta Space Systems.

BERGQUIST'S SOLUTIONS

For the ultrasensitive leak detector, Bergquist proposed the following approach:

1. Accumulate the leaked helium and measure the rate of rise of the helium ion current signal rather than measuring the leak as it is pumped. This will effectively increase the sensitivity of the system and make it easy to separate noise from the signal. Then, compare the rate of rise of the ion current signal of the unknown leak against that of a reference leak to establish the leak rate of the test object.

2. Use a preferential pump to pump active gases while helium is being accumulated. This will keep the total pressure low during helium accumulation, and the sensitivity and linearity of the quadrupole mass analyzer (QMA) will not be impaired.

3. Use specially processed stainless steel components with a very low outgas rate. This will also reduce the total pressure.

4. Use only all-metal valves. This will prevent unwanted helium migration into the accumulation region.

5. Use a high-quality QMA with a 90° off-axis multiplier which reduces noise from photons and neutrals.

For the calibrator, Bergquist's solution was:

1. Obtain a certified mix of $He-4/N_2$ which is predominantly nitrogen and of which the proportion of helium-4 is precisely known.

2. Admit the gas mix under measured pressure and temperature into a precisely calibrated small volume. Now a known quantity of helium molecules is captured in the volume.

3. Release the captured gas mix to a chamber equipped with a QMA and a nitrogen pump. The nitrogen constituent of the gas mix will be pumped out immediately, decreasing the total pressure. The helium quantity, on the other hand, will remain intact.

4. Read the increase in the ion current registered by the QMA, and correlate it to the moles of helium that was admitted to the chamber. Now the QMA is calibrated in terms of helium sensitivity

73

under the specific configuration of the chamber. Open the exhaust valve and pump out the helium.

5. Close the exhaust valve and admit leak from an uncalibrated reference leak attached to the same chamber. An accurate temperature sensor should be attached to the orifice of the reference leak. Measure the rate of rise of the ion current signal using the calibrated QMA and an accurate timepiece. Also, record the temperature of the leak orifice.

6. Convert the observed rate of rise in amp/s to mole/s or std cc/s. The reference leak is now calibrated.

7. Repeat the above operations under different temperatures (of the reference leak orifice) to establish the temperature coefficient of the reference leak.

All the primary measurements used in the above operations, namely, helium mix, pressure, temperature, volume, and time, can be made traceable to NIST. Therefore, the resultant calibration of leak could be considered traceable to NIST.

Bergquist calculated the overall precision of measurement to be better than ± 0.5% under best conditions. Our proof-of-concept tests showed that it is quite possible.

Bergquist built an experimental leak detector and a calibrator of his designs, and later obtained patents on them. Quantum Mechanics Corp., under an agreement with Martin Marietta Corporation, then assumed the responsibility for developmental work, and completed a prototype of ULTRA-15 leak detector in 1987. This unit has logged over 3,700 hours of operation by this time, providing useful data on the objects that were leak tested as well as for the future versions of the ULTRA-15.

DETECTOR DESIGN AND OPERATION

The basic design of the ultrasensitive leak detector is as illustrated in Fig. 1.

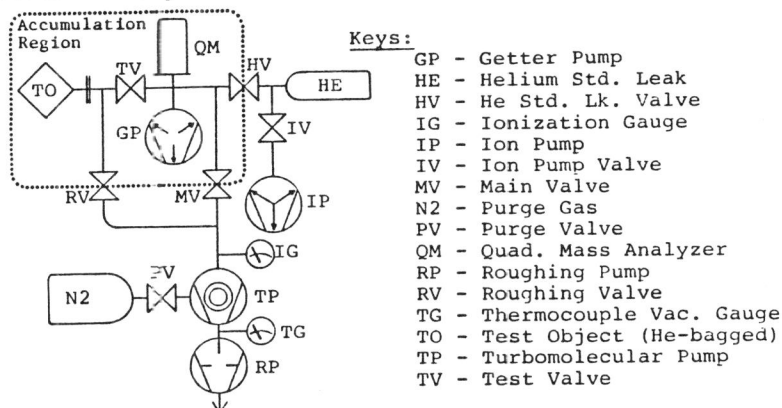

Keys:
GP - Getter Pump
HE - Helium Std. Leak
HV - He Std. Lk. Valve
IG - Ionization Gauge
IP - Ion Pump
IV - Ion Pump Valve
MV - Main Valve
N2 - Purge Gas
PV - Purge Valve
QM - Quad. Mass Analyzer
RP - Roughing Pump
RV - Roughing Valve
TG - Thermocouple Vac. Gauge
TO - Test Object (He-bagged)
TP - Turbomolecular Pump
TV - Test Valve

Fig.1. Schematic of Ultrasensitive Leak Detector

Operation can be either a flow-through mode for measuring large leaks of the E-6 to E-11 std cc He/s range, or an accumulation mode for finer leaks of the E-10 to E-15 range. (Fig. 2)

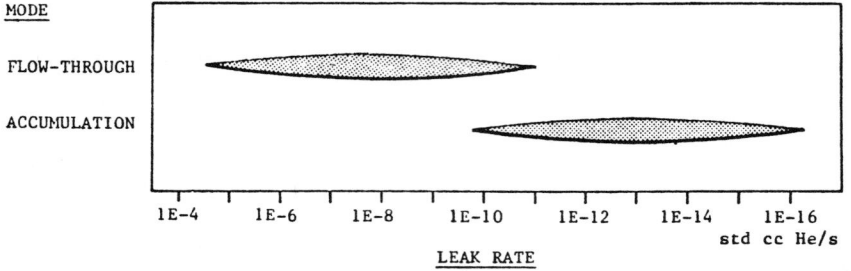

MODE

FLOW-THROUGH

ACCUMULATION

```
        1E-4    1E-6    1E-8    1E-10   1E-12   1E-14   1E-16
                                                        std cc He/s
                            LEAK RATE
```

Fig.2. Effective Range of Leak Detection, by Mode

In the flow-through mode, the main valve is kept open and the helium-bagged test object is continuously pumped. The ion current reading by the QMA is then compared with that for the standard leak, and the leak rate of the test object is calculated. This operation is the same as that of conventional helium leak detectors.

In the accumulation mode, the main valve is closed, and the rate of rise of the helium signal is measured. Three measurements are taken for each test: the background helium measurement, the test object leak measurement, and the leak standard measurement. Typically, each measurement is taken over a duration of 1 to 3 minutes. The background rate-of-rise is usually non-existent or less than 1E-14 std cc He/s-equivalent. If it is of a measurable quantity, it is subtracted from the test object leak rate-of-rise to arrive at the net leak figure. Subtraction of the background figure is not critical for leaks greater than, say, 1E-12 std cc He/s because the margin of error due to the background is negligible. For this reason, the background figure is not subtracted from the standard leak figure. (Fig. 3.)

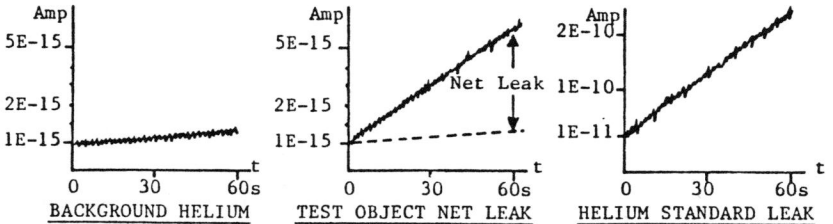

```
Amp |                    Amp |                  Amp |
5E-15|                   5E-15|          2E-10|
     |                        |                   |
     |                        |          Net Leak |
2E-15|                   2E-15|          1E-10|
1E-15|~~~~~~~~~~~         1E-15|                   1E-11|
     |_____t            |_____t           |_____t
     0   30   60s             0   30   60s            0   30   60s
   BACKGROUND HELIUM       TEST OBJECT NET LEAK    HELIUM STANDARD LEAK
```

Fig.3. Typical Measurements in a Leak Test.
        (Helium Accumulation Mode)

With the ULTRA-15, the entire leak test, except for installation of the test piece and helium bagging, is done fully automatically by a computer. A program developed by Quantum Mechanics performs all necessary control of valves and instruments, data analysis, operational decision making such as when to start and stop the rate-of-rise measurement, net leak calibration, and data presentation. Alternatively, the detector can be operated in a "manual" keystroke-per-command mode.

Fig.4. ULTRA-15 Leak Detector

The key to success in maintaining a high sensitivity during helium accumulation is to keep the background total pressure low. This is accomplished by the following design:

1. Use of a chemical getter which pumps active gases such as H_2, H_2O, N_2, CO_2, and O_2, while leaving He intact.

2. Use of Quantum-Passivated stainless steel components with an outgas rate of ca. 2E-13 torr-L/s/cm for construction of the accumulation region.

3. Use of all-metal valves in the system.

4. Careful design of the accumulation region to minimize its total surface area and volume. (Volume minimization is necessary for increasing helium partial pressure and sensitivity.)

With these features, the total pressure in the accumulation region can stay under 1E-9 torr throughout helium accumulation.

The background helium is kept minimal by use of all-metal valves. Elastomer-sealed valves cause helium permeation, absorption and desorption, but there is practically no such danger with metal-seal valves. They effectively isolate the accumulation region from the rest of the system which may trap and release helium.

Electronic noise limits the sensitivity of a detector when the detector is used in the flow-through mode. However, the background noise of purely electronic nature tends to stay constant regardless of small changes in pressure. Therefore, if we switch the operation to the accumulation mode, the helium signal is easily detected even when it is indistinguishable from the noise in the flow-through mode. (Fig. 5)

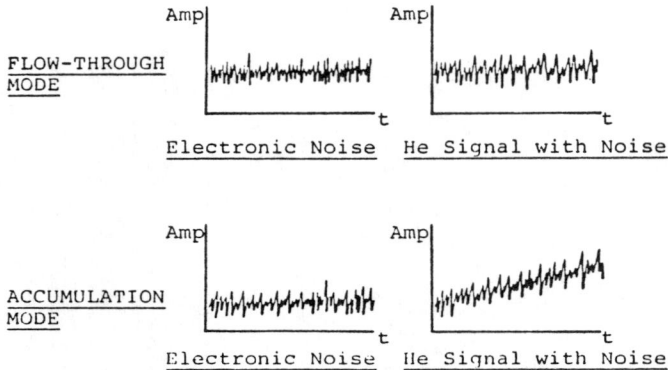

Fig.5. Helium Leak Signals in Flow-Through Mode and Accumulation Mode, vs. Electronic Background Noise.

LEAK TEST EXAMPLES

Three examples of typical fine leak test results are discussed here. The equipment and the methods used for these tests are as follows:

Leak Detector:	Quantum Mechanics ULTRA-15, with Balzers QMG112A/QMA120 modified by Quantum Mechanics.
Reference Leak:	3.8E-10 std cc /s @ 24°C ± 6.3%/°C, calibrated against Sandia Std. Leak.
Test Object Lk. Prep.:	Helium Bagging @ 15 psia.
Leak Test Method:	Helium Accumulation, Rate of Rise Comparison.
Mass Scan Range:	3.5 - 4.5 amu
Scan Speed:	1 sec/amu

The test results are summarized below in Table II.

Table II. Examples of Fine Leak Test Results.

Rate-of-Rise and Leak Rate	Unit	Test #1 Dewar	Test #2 Valve	Test #3 T-250
1. Background	A/s	1.1E-17	6.9E-16	1.05E-17
2. Test Object Leak	A/s	4.1E-17	2.8E-15	1.11E-17
3. Net Rate of Rise (2)-(1)	A/s	3.0E-17	2.1E-15	6E-19
4. Reference Leak	A/s	2.3E-12	2.8E-12	2.9E-12
5. Reference Leak @ Test Temperature	cc/s	2.6E-10 @19°C	3.6E-10 @23°C	2.8E-10 @20°C
6. Conversion Factor (5)/(4)	cc/A	113	129	95
7. Test Object Leak (3)x(6)	scc He/s	3.4E-15	2.7E-13	5.7E-17

Test 1, Dewar

This was one of the ten infrared sensor dewars tested at one time. Seven of the ten showed leak rates in the mid E-15 std cc He/s; two had no detectable leaks; and one had a mid E-14 leak. We suspect that the mid E-15 figures probably represent permeation rather than leak.

For the test object leak and the reference leak, measurement of the rate-of-rise was started about ten seconds after the accumulation region was valved off, when a steady rate of rise of the ion current was observed. The measurement was terminated when a trend was well established, typically 90 to 180 seconds after the start. The background count, on the other hand, could be started immediately after the valve was closed off. This is because the background had been stabilized after a long period of pumping. The actual beginning and ending readings of the background current were 3.0E-15A and 4.0E-15A, and the elapsed time was 92 seconds.

Test 2, Valve

A nominal 1/2" all-metal valve was leak tested from the bonnet bellow side. The detected leak could be through the valve seat or the bonnet seal or both.

Beside this test, two additional tests were conducted on the same valve. The results were 2.6E-13 and 3.0-13, as against this test of 2.7E-13 std cc He/s.

The relatively high background readings as well as a somewhat large variance in the net leak figures may have been caused by the adsorbed helium on the bellow surface. The pump-down time between the tests was approximately 5 minutes.

Test 3, T-250

T-250 is a 250 cc tritium vessel constructed from Quantum-Passivated 304 stainless steel. The design of the vessel is very simple and all welds had been liquid penetrant tested and radiographed; no leaks were expected except, possibly, from the 2.75" Conflat connection between the vessel and the leak detector.

As expected the measurable leak was extremely small, taxing even the ultrasensitive leak detector to its maximum potential. The background reading was 4.0E-15A at the start of measurement, and it reached 5.0E-15A after 95 seconds. With helium bagging, the same rise took 90 seconds. Thus, the net rate of rise was 6E-19A/s. Comparing this to the reference leak, we calculated the leak rate to be 5.7E-17 std cc He/s.

This figure, however, has a relatively low confidence factor because the fluctuations in the noise current were great. Normally this magnitude of leak is presented as an "unmeasurable leak," but the figure is presented here as an illustration of the ultrasensitive leak detector's potential.

CALIBRATOR DESIGN AND OPERATION

Fine leak measurements by the ultrasensitive leak detector as discussed earlier rely on the assumption that the helium sensitivity of the QMA is constant over several decades of helium partial pressure. The only solid checkpoint is the range close to the calibrated reference leak: in our case, around 3E-10 std cc He/s.

By monitoring the linearity of the ion current rise of a presumably stable fine leak or permeation, one could get some assurance for the sensitivity uniformity. In the case of ULTRA-15, the uniformity can be checked for up to three decades because the rate of rise can be measured reliably for durations ranging from several seconds to several hundred seconds.

In order for the ultrasensitive leak detector to measure an E-15 std cc He/s leak with good confidence, it is therefore highly desirable to have a calibrated reference leak in the order of E-12 std cc He/s. Here again, Bergquist has come up with a simple solution as outlined earlier.

A proof-of-concept unit of Bergquist's calibrator was constructed by utilizing the ULTRA-15 leak detector and incorporating a few additional components. (Fig. 6)

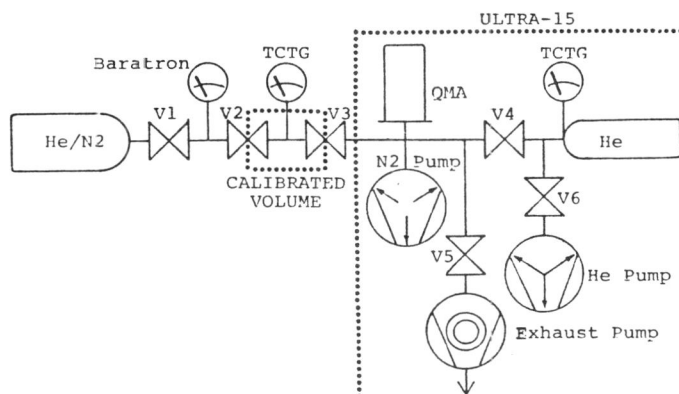

Fig.6. Leak Calibrator Schematic.

The main additional components are as follows:

1. Calibrated Helium-4/Nitrogen mix of 5139±4 ppb, certified by the Bureau of Mines.
2. Calibrated Volume: Quantum Mechanics Aliquot Volume, 0.33±0.005 cc. (QM Aliquot Volume is a calibrated volume between two valves, made for measured dispensing of tritium gas.)
3. Pressure Transducer gauge: Baratron 310-CHS-1, 0-1 torr.
4. Thermocouple Temperature Gauge attached to the calibrated volume.
5. All metal valves.

The principle of operation was discussed earlier. The specific steps are as follows: (see Fig. 6)

1. Open valves V2, V3, and V5, and pump down to E-10 torr range.
2. Close V3, and admit a small amount of Helium/Nitrogen mix through V1. Then, close V1.
3. After pressure and temperature are stabilized, record both measurements, and close V2. Calculate the quantity of helium (in moles or std cc) captured in the calibrated volume.
4. Close V5, open V3, and measure the increase in the helium ion current by QMA.
5. Open V5 and pump out the system. Verify that ion current reading has dropped to the same level as that before the He/N introduction.
6. Open V4, close V6, and close V5, and start measuring the rate of rise of ion current caused by the "unknown" leak entering the system. Complete the measurement, and correlate it to the value obtained through Step 4. Record the helium leak orifice temperature.

The entire calibration steps described above can be completed in less than one hour.

CALIBRATION EXAMPLES

Three calibration tests were conducted using a "3.8E-10 scc He/s @ 24°C ±6.3%/°C" reference leak as an "unknown leak to be calibrated." The results are summarized below.

Table III. Calibration Test Results.

	Unit	Test #1	Test #2	Test #3
1. Helium Mix Pressure @ Temperature	Torr @ °C	0.490 @23.0	0.555 @20.5	0.606 @21.0
2. Computed Helium Quantity	scc He	1.01E-9	1.15E-9	1.25E-9
3. Ion Current Reading	A	3.81E-10	4.31E-10	4.60E-10
4. Conversion Factor (2)/(3)	scc/A	2.65	2.67	2.72
5. "Unknown Leak" Rate of Rise	A/s	1.41E-10	1.16E-10	1.64E-10
6. Calibrated Leak Rate (5)x(4)	scc He/s	3.74E-10	3.10E-10	4.46E-10
7. Reference ("unknown") Leak Rate adjusted to Orifice Temp.	scc He/s @ °C	3.8E-10 @24.0°C	3.08E-10 @21.0°C	4.49E-10 @26.9°C
8. Deviation (6)/(7)	%	-1.6%	+0.6%	-0.6%

As seen, the test results showed remarkable consistency and accuracy in calibration. We consider that the deviations are well within the reading errors of time and temperature and of the temperature adjustment factor of the reference leak.

Finer leaks down to the E-12 std cc He/S range can be similarly calibrated by increasing the electron multiplier gain, by increasing the accumulation time, by decreasing the calibrated volume size, or by their combination.

As for calibrating grosser leaks, up to the E-4 std cc He/s range leaks can be calibrated by using a higher-pressure transducer, a larger calibrated volume, and a Faraday cup.

Thus, the calibration method discussed herein is usable for a wide range of helium leaks from E-4 to E-12 std cc He/s, is very accurate, and required no more than one hour per calibration.

CONFIDENCE FACTOR

The maximum error in each step of measurement can be held to a small value as follows:

Gas Mix	0.078%
Calibrated Volume	0.1%
Pressure Measurement	0.085%
Temperature Measurement	0.3%
QMA Stability/Linearity	0.1%
Time Measurement	0.05%

If the calibrator system is carefully constructed and properly operated, an overall confidence factor of 99.5% can be achieved.

CONCLUSIONS

A series of tests have proven that Bergquist's designs of the ultrasensitive leak detector and the calibrator are sound.

The ULTRA-15 leak detector is fully operational and reliable with a practical sensitivity of 1E-15 std cc He/s.

The calibrator needs to be made traceable to NIST in order to have universal acceptability. All measurements except QMA stability and linearity can readily be made traceable to NIST. The stability and linearity can also be made indirectly traceable to NIST by using the same calibrator system if the size of the expansion volume (i.e., accumulation volume) is calibrated by NIST-traceable means.

The ultrasensitive leak detector and the calibrator discussed herein open up a new frontier of superfine leak measurements.

THE DURABILITY OF BALLSCREWS FOR ULTRAHIGH VACUUM

J. Ikeda, T. Sekiguchi, and H. Saeki
Matsushita Electric Industrial Co.,Ltd.
Matsuba-cho 2-7, Kadoma-shi, Osaka-fu, 571, Japan.

H. Ishimaru
National Laboratory for High Energy Physics.
Oho 1-1, Tsukuba-shi, Ibaraki-ken, 305, Japan.

ABSTRACT

Recently an ultrahigh vacuum environment has been necessary to reduce impurities in the production of high-density integrated circuits. Generally, driving apparatuses used in ultrahigh vacuum environments are required. Ballscrews for ultrahigh vacuum are also required for those apparatuses. But the durability of ballscrews has not been confirmed.

A test of the durability of ballscrews has been carried out on two sets of screws and nuts made of stainless steel. Electrochemical buffing was performed on the surfaces of the screws and nuts. One screw/nut pair was then coated with TiC and Ag, while the other pair was left uncoated. The stainless steel balls were coated with Ag. Each ballscrew was directly connected to an ultrahigh vacuum-compatible stepping motor. The test was carried out in an ultrahigh vacuum environment on the order of $10^{-10}-10^{-11}$ Torr. The ballscrew coated with TiC and Ag was moved 21000 times with a reciprocating motion. However, the uncoated ballscrew moved only 1310 times before failure.

INTRODUCTION

With the recent technological advances in semiconductors, higher reliability in thin-film processing equipment and surface analysis systems is required for the production of high-density integrated circuits. Therefore, ultrahigh vacuum fabrication environments are necessary to improve the quality of the films and to eliminate impurities.

A precision table for ultrahigh vacuum made of aluminum alloys was developed for thin-film processing equipment and surface analysis systems.[1] In the course of the development of the table, it was necessary to confirm its durability.

Especially, it is important to know the durability of the ballscrews in the table, since a heavy load is applied on the ballscrews.

This paper reports on the durability of ballscrews for ultrahigh vacuum.

APPARATUSES

This section describes two types of ballscrews, and a newly developed experimental apparatus for ballscrews.

Figure 1 shows the newly developed experimental apparatus for ballscrews. The durability for two types of ballscrews was compared. These ballscrews are the same structure as a constant pressure type using springs, except for the surface treatment. The ballscrew consists of a screw and two nuts. The lead of the ballscrew is 3 mm. The screws and nuts of the ballscrews are made of stainless steel 304 with electrochemical buffing (roughness of about 0.1 μm). One screw/nut pair was further coated with TiC (thickness of about 1.5 μm), and Ag (thickness of about 0.3 μm). Another pair was not coated. Both ballscrews used stainless steel 440C balls coated with Ag (thickness of about 0.3 μm).

The driving sources for the ballscrews are built-in stepping motors. The motors consist of a rotor made of a samarium-cobalt magnet and silicon steel, a stator made of silicon steel, and a stainless steel sheath cable using MgO for insulation, 0.5 mm in outer diameter.

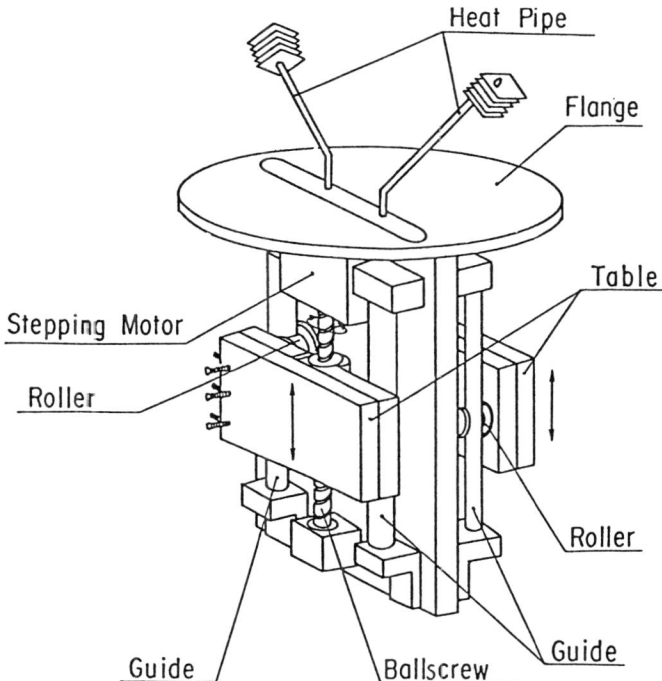

Figure 1. Experimental apparatus for ballscrews.

Each of the ballscrews is directly connected to the rotor of the stepping motor. The nuts of the ballscrews are connected to tables which allow linear movements parallel to the axis of the corresponding screw.

The linear sliding guides for the tables consist of cylindrical guides made of stainless steel 304, and rollers made of A2219 aluminum alloy. The rollers are coated with TiC (thickness of about 1.5 μm). The rollers move on the guides. All the rotational bearings are made of stainless steel 440C, and the balls are coated with Ag (thickness of about 0.3 μm). The main material for the apparatus is A2219-T87 or T852 aluminum alloy machined in an oxygen and argon atmosphere.[2] The surface roughness is less than 1 μm. The weight of the table is about 2 kg.

Two heat pipes were used to prevent localized heating of the stepping motors.

All the fasteners (bolts, nuts, and washers) are made of stainless steel and were treated with acids and degassed before assembly at 300 °C, 10^{-8} Torr for about 24 h.

Figure 2 schematically shows an experimental ultrahigh vacuum system made of aluminum alloys for testing the ballscrews. The chamber has an inside diameter of 250 mm, a length of 420 mm, and a volume of 25 l. The walls of the chamber were made of A1050-H24 aluminum machined in an oxygen and argon atmosphere.[2] The flanges were made of A2219-T87 aluminum alloy machined in an oxygen and argon atmosphere.[2]

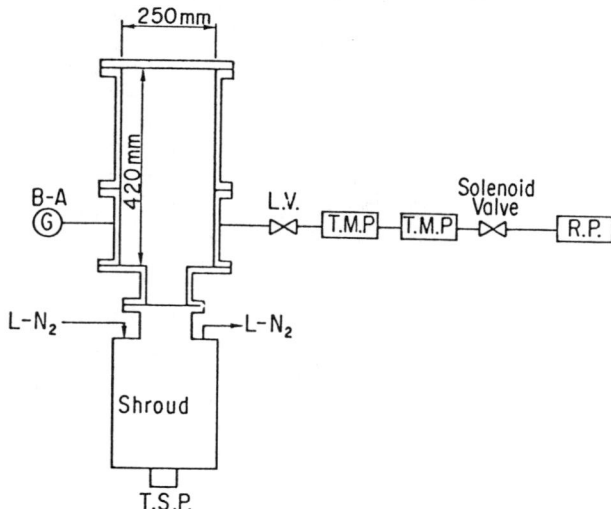

Figure 2. Experimental ultrahigh vacuum system for testing the ballscrews.

A Bayard–Alpert gauge (954–7902, ANELVA Co.,Ltd.) for a
vacuum gauge was used.
    The pumping system consisted of a 250 l/s
turbomolecular pump (TMP) with magnetic floating
bearings, turbobacked (50 l/s), and a titanium
sublimation pump (TSP) with a liquid–nitrogen shroud.
The TMPs and the vacuum chamber were connected through
an L valve (LV) made of aluminum alloys. Aluminum
gaskets (A1050–H18) were used for the seals between
flanges.

EXPERIMENTS AND RESULTS

    Figure 3 shows the pumpdown curve of the chamber,
with the ballscrews stationary throughout.
    At first, the system was pumped down from 1 atm by
the turbomolecular pumps, and then baked at 140 °C for
about 27 h. The vacuum gauge was degassed at the end of
the baking process. After that, liquid nitrogen was
introduced into the shroud, and the TSP was also fired.
As the result, the ultimate pressure was 9 x 10^{-11} Torr.

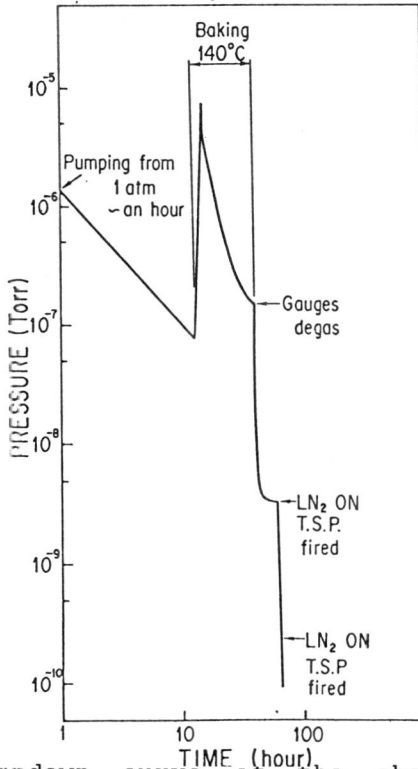

Figure 3. Pumpdown curve of the chamber, with the
ballscrews stationary.

86

    After that, the two tables made a reciprocating
motion of 45 mm, at a speed of 2.25 mm/s (60 sec/1
stroke). Thermocouples showed the temperature of the
motors to be 60 °C. The experiment was carried out in an
ultrahigh vacuum environment of the order of 10^{-10} Torr.
    The ballscrew coated with TiC and Ag moved 21000
times without failure. The uncoated ballscrew failed
after 1310 times.

DISCUSSION

    It can be expected that the film of TiC prevents
the material of the balls from adhering to the material
of the screw or the nuts, and that the ballscrew with
all of the track coated with Ag will have an extended
life due to the increase in volume of lubricant metal.
    The experiment was conducted only once. Further
trials are necessary to establish quantitative results.

SUMMARY

    An experimental apparatus for the testing of
ballscrews was developed. It was found that the
ballscrew consisting of balls coated with Ag and screws
and nuts coated with TiC and Ag on mirror surfaces has
extended life.

ACKNOWLEDGMENTS

    The authors would like to thank Dr. T. Momose for
his many helpful suggestions. This work was supported
by Hakudo Co.,Ltd., Musashino Engineering Co.,Ltd.,
Koyo Co.,Ltd., and Toho-Kaken Co.,Ltd.

REFERENCES

1. H. Saeki, J. Ikeda, and H. Ishimaru, J. Vac. Sci.
Technol. A6, 2883 (1988).
2. H. Ishimaru, "Ultimate pressure of the order of 10^{-13}
Torr in an aluminum alloy vacuum chamber" was presented
at the 35th National Symposium of the AVS, Atlanta,
Georgia, 1988.

VACUUM-COMPATIBLE ROBOT FOR SELF-CONTAINED MANUFACTURING

Satoru Nio, Takeo Suzuki, Hideharu Zenpo, Kazuhiko Yokoyama
and Hitoshi Wakizako
Kitakyushu-city, JAPAN
Yaskawa Electric Manufacturing Co. Ltd.

Steve Belinski
Center for Robotic Systems in Microelectronics
University of California, Santa Barbara, CA 93106

ABSTRACT

Recently, vacuum mechatronics technology has been increasingly
desired for high quality automation in the field of high-technology
manufacturing processes such as microelectronics, space applications, surface treatment of new materials and medicine. In response
to those demands, YASKAWA has been actively researching vacuum-
compatible mechatronics since 1985. As a result of that research
and development, YASKAWA has successfully manufactured a number of
key products for vacuum mechatronics, including various types of
pulse motors (axial gap, radial gap and linear), horizontally
articulated and frog leg type robots, and magnetically levitated
wafer transport systems.

Recently, through joint work with the CRSM, a new cylindrical-
type vacuum-compatible robot, especially designed for wafer handling
in the CRSM self-contained automated robotic factory (SCARF), has
been developed.

Three goals of the SCARF robot are : minimization of
particulate generation in order to maintain clean vacuum, smooth
motion for precise handling, and high reliability for maintenance-
free operation. YASKAWA's approach to elementary technologies for
such requirements in vacuum-compatible actuators and robots is
described below.

VACUUM-COMPATIBLE MOTORS

For vacuum-compatible actuators, direct-drive methods are
desirable for minimizing dust-particles caused by gear contact-
friction. Pulse motors are suitable as direct-drive actuators
because of their relative ease of structual gas-sealing in addition
to their low speed / high torque / high thrust characteristics.
YASKAWA's vacuum-compatible pulse motors (hybrid type) are listed
in Table 1. Generally these motors are wholly located in a vacuum
chamber and optionally they can be mounted on the wall of the
chamber as shown in Fig. 1. Typical dimensions are shown in Fig. 2.
2-phase hybrid pulse motors with bipolar stator-windings and Sm-Co
magnets mounted on the rotor are used. Every stator-coil is sealed
by a stainless steel can to eliminate outgassing. Lead wires with
fluorocarbon polymer coverings are used for the same purpose
(Fig. 3). Vacuum-Compatibility is guaranteed up to 10^{-7} Torr with
a leak-rate less than $5*10^{-9}$ TLS. Their step angles/length at a

Type	Torque/Thrust	Revolution /Speed	optional configu- ration (Fig.1)
Axial gap pulse motor	0.5~350kgf-cm (intermediate value appox. 5kgf-cm steps)	0.1~ 100r.p.m.	Yes
Radial gap pulse motor	0.3~4kgf-cm (intermediate value appox. 1kgf-cm steps)	0.5~ 600r.p.m.	No
Linear pulse motor	1~4kgf (intermediate value appox. 1kgf steps)	50~ 400mm/sec	Yes
AC servo motor	1~150kgf-cm (intermediate value appox. 5kgf-cm steps)	100~ 1850r.p.m.	No

Pemissible Temperature(Bakable Temp.) : 155℃,   Vacuum Compatibilty : 10^{-7} Torr

Table 1 : YASKAWA Vacuum-compatible Motor Series

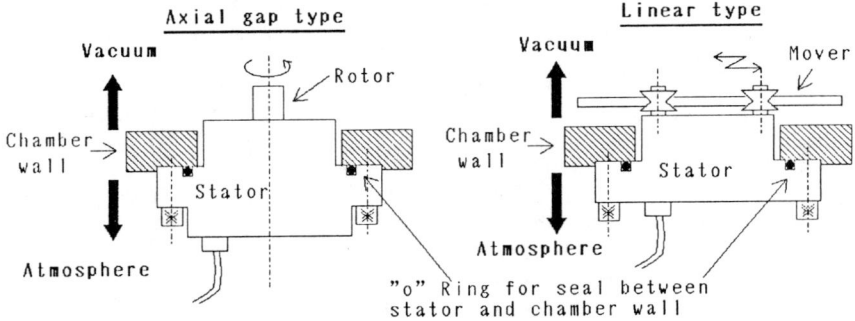

Fig. 1 Optional configuration

full-step drive are 1°, 1.8°, and 0.5mm for axial gap, radial gap, and linear, respectively. Each step is driven through sinusoidal or trapezoidal micro stepping, resolutionally divided by 1024 for smooth motion.

In addition, vacuum-compatible AC servo motor types are available for higher speed applications (Table 1).

DRY LUBRICATION

Dry lubrication is one of the important technologies required for a contamination-free environment in high-vacuum and for high reliability. Particle generation is minimized through the use of dry lubricants and labyrinth seals for bearings in order to maintain cleanliness. The dry lubricants originally developed by YASKAWA in cooperation with a bearing manufacturer in Japan are summarized in Fig. 4 according to the kinds of bearings, rollers and guides on which they are used.

In general, surfaces of bearings are coated or sputtered with

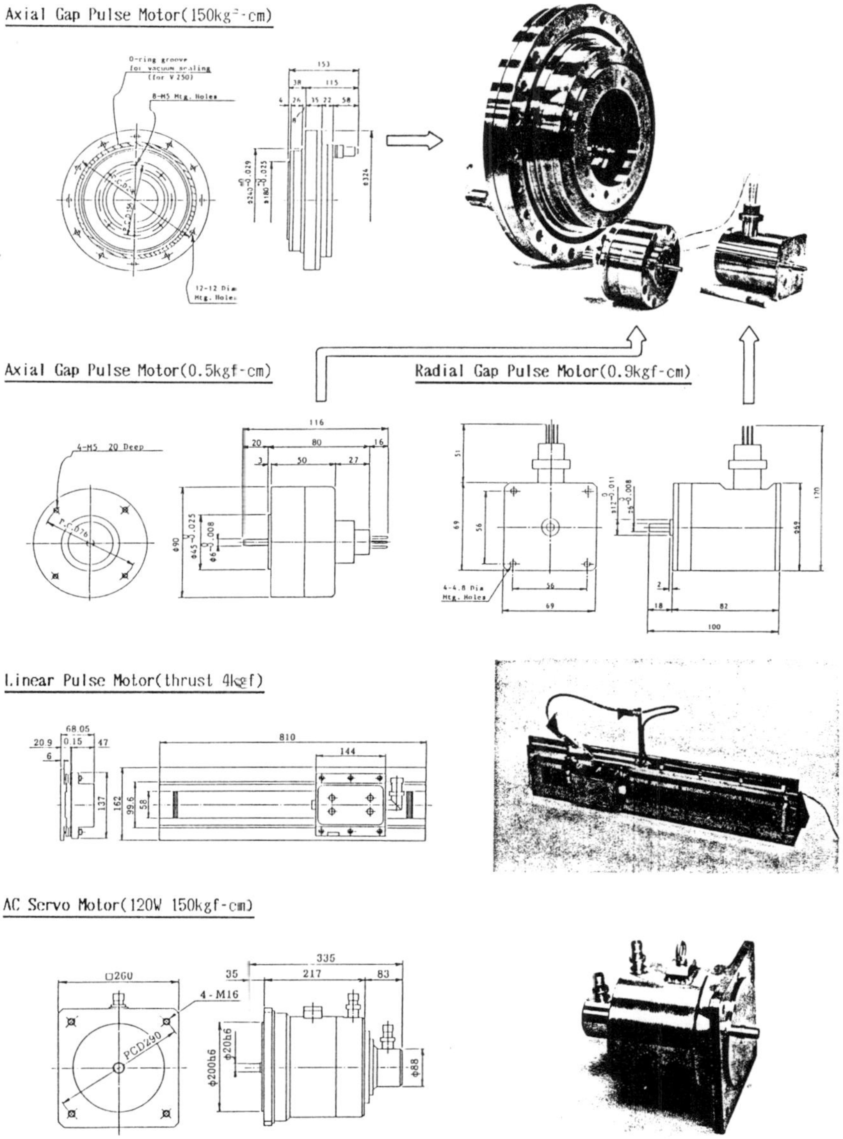

Axial Gap Pulse Motor(150kg²·cm)

Axial Gap Pulse Motor(0.5kgf·cm)   Radial Gap Pulse Motor(0.9kgf·cm)

Linear Pulse Motor(thrust 4kgf)

AC Servo Motor(120W 150kgf·cm)

Fig. 2 YASKAWA Vacuum-compatible Motors (typical examples)

Stator coil coated with
high-thermal insulation
polyimide

3%Si-steel rotor with
Ni-plating

Epoxy molding resin
with low outgas and
high-thermal conductivity

Sm-Co magnet with
Ni-plating

3%Si-steel stator
(high permeability)

Crossroller bearing
with dry lubricant

Labyrinth seal
(minimizing
of particle
from bearing)

Stainless steel housing
(AISI304 low-level
outgas steel)

Thrust bearing
with dry lubricant

Hermetic connector
(sealing outgas)

Stainless steel
can seal
(non-magnetic)

Thermal conduction

Chamber wall

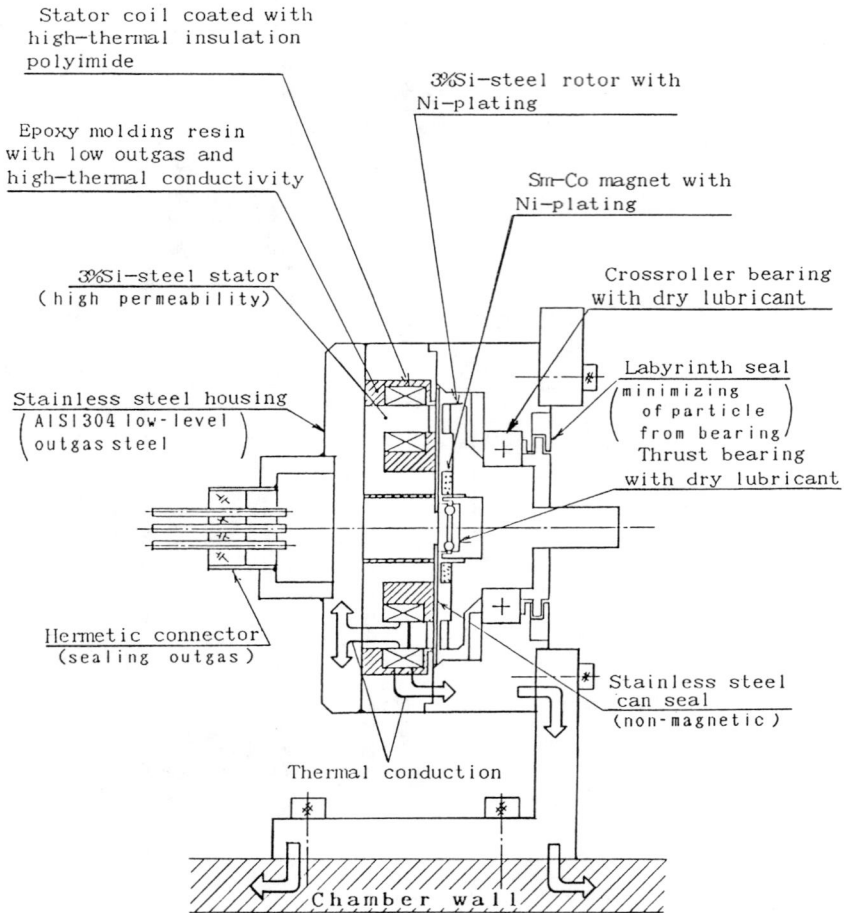

Fig. 3 Detail of YASKAWA's Vacuum-compatible Motor (axial gap type)

Classification	Dry Lubrication Method	Configuration
Cross roller	Outer ring ⎤ Inner ring ⎬>WS₂ Roller ⎦ ⎧ Surface process ⎨ by DICRONITE Inc. ⎩ in USA Roller and Ball : Sintered alloy	
Thrust	Outer ring ⎤ Inner ring ⎬ Ball ⎦ Sputtered MoS₂ Retainer : Sintered alloy	
Ball	same as above	
Linear guide	Truck rail ⎤ Casing ⎬ Ball ⎦ Burnished MoS₂	
Ball screw	Screw ⎤ Nut ⎬ Ball ⎦ Burnished MoS₂	
V roller	Out ring : Sputtered MoS₂ Carriage : Coated PTFE	
Support roller	Same as the thrust bearing Outring : Burnished MoS₂	

Fig. 4 Dry Lubrication for Vacuum-compatible Motors and Robots

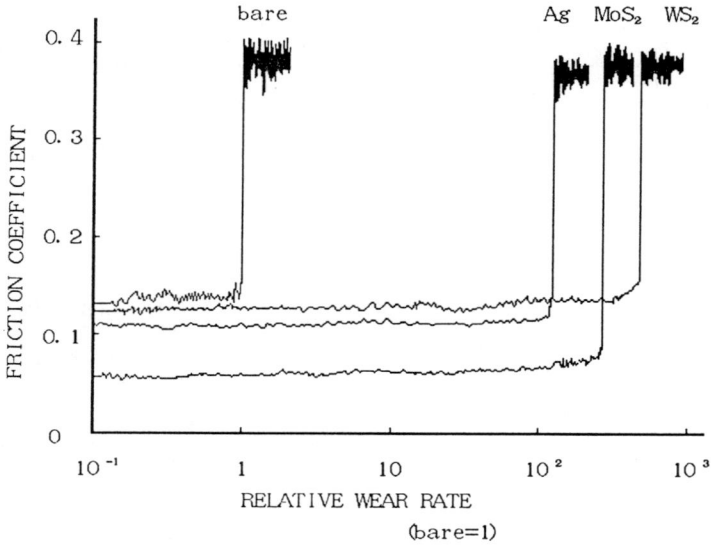

Fig. 5-(a) Wear Test Results in High Vacuum

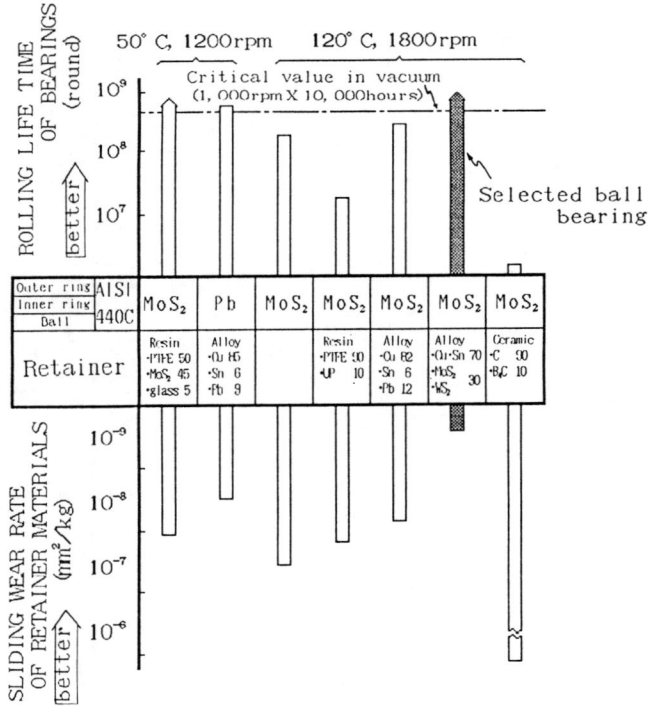

Fig. 5-(b) Endurance Test of Ball Bearings in High Vacuum

MoS_2 or WS_2 for durability. Wear test results are shown in Fig. 5-(a). The thickness of the thin films is 0.5 μm (sputtering) or 5 μm (burnishing). The retainers of all bearings are made of self-lubricating sintered alloy (Cu-Sn 70% and WS_2-MoS_2 30% manufactured by TOSHIBA TUNGALOY CO., LTD.) because of its low friction and good wear resistance. As a result of evaluation tests in high vacuum, YASKAWA's specified ball bearings are guaranteed up to 10,000 hours at 1000 r.p.m., and 120°C (forced temperature of bearing), as indicated in Fig. 5-(b).

Two problems to be solved for the use of cross-roller bearings in vacuum are : proper usage of dry lubrications and heavy thrust loads.

For the dry lubrications, we developed a bearing configuration so that sintered alloy rollers and balls are aligned alternately between metallic rollers, and the retainer is removed, as shown in Fig. 4 (under patent application). The balls decrease friction loss and wear, and the rollers provide smooth transfer of lubricants.

Three-dimensional forces on the bearings cause deterioration. A heavy thrust load may be especially damaging to the bearing. We have developed a new type of cross-roller bearing additionally equipped with dry-lubricated thrust bearings, shown in Fig. 3 (under patent application). This thrust bearing is used for sustaining the heavy thrust load. For further reduction of particles, shield-type ball bearings and labyrinth sealing mechanisms for cross roller bearings are used. The combination of dry lubricants and sealed constructions leads to high performance and reliability.

VACUUM-COMPATIBLE ROBOT

YASKAWA manufactures three types of vacuum-compatible robots, horizontally articulated (Fig. 6-(a)), frog leg (Fig. 6-(b)) and cylindrical types (Fig. 6-(c) and (d)). Stainless steels (AISI304) and Al alloys are mainly utilized for high rigidity, high thermal conductivity to the chamber wall, and minimization of outgassing. Practical design considerations for better thermal conduction from vacuum to atmosphere are important for acquiring high machine accuracy and long endurance. Because backlash is essentially eliminated when using direct drive, the absolute accuracy becomes comparable to the repeatability. The accuracy depends on the position detector's resolution. The SCARF robot consists of a θ-axis (axial gap), Z-axis (radial gap) and R-axis (linear type), as specified in Fig. 6-(c). In general, robots which use an overhanging structure have inherently low natural frequencies and low damping factors because of their insufficient stiffness of support mechanisms. Fig. 7 shows the SCARF robot's modal analysis of vibration. The first-order eigen value changes between 6.5Hz and 9Hz (typically 8.5Hz) due to the inertia change corresponding closely with the position of the R-axis. To decrease the resonant vibration of the θ-axis during its low speed operation, we applied a closed-loop control method via the pulse motors of the SCARF robot. When a pulse motor is driven using open-loop control, the range of speed

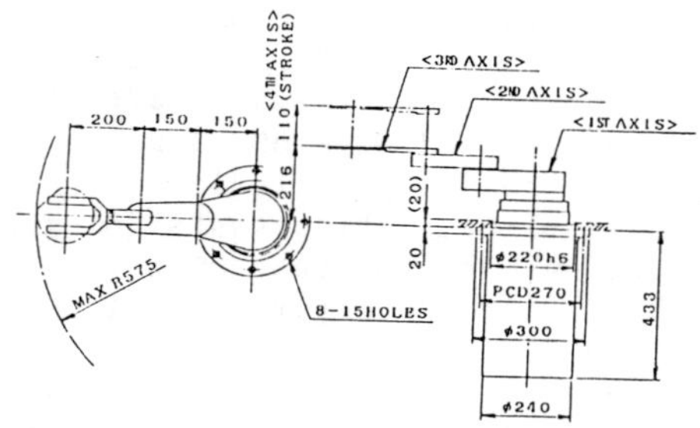

94

	Turning axis(θ)	Virtical axis(Z)	Radial axis(R)
Working range	350 °	120 mm	662 mm
Maximum speed	90 °/sec	60 mm/sec	250 mm/sec
Repeatability	±0.03 mm		
Payload	0.4 Kg		
Vacuum Compatibility	10^{-7} Torr		
Bakable temp.	150 ℃		

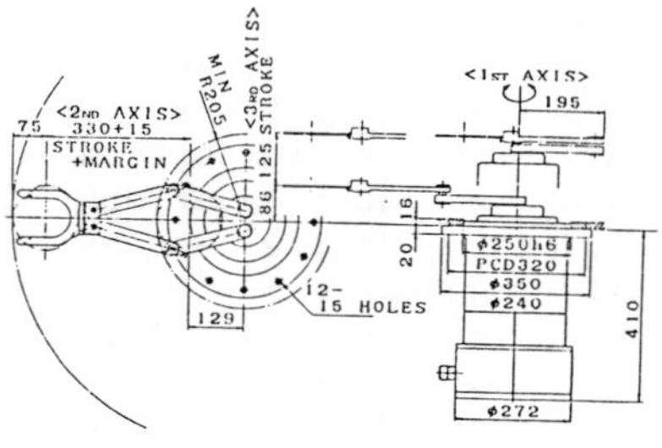

(a) Holizontally Articulated Type
(Payload 0.2kg)

(b) Frog Leg Type
(Payload 0.2kg)

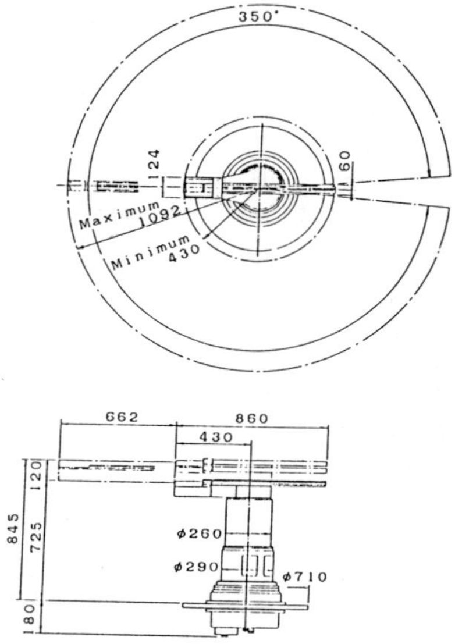

(c) SCARF Robot

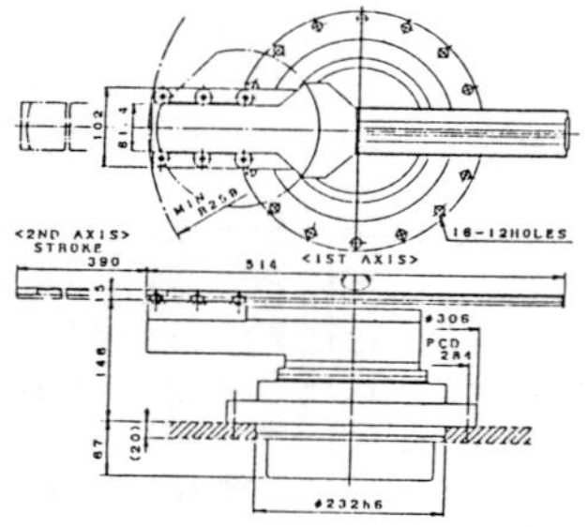

(d) 2axes Cylindrical Type
(Payload 0.2kg)

Fig. 6 YASKAWA Vacuum-Compatible Robots

regulation is not so wide. Accordingly, the speed ripples composed
of a number of frequency components include a wide range of resonance frequencies, especially at low speeds. Feedback control of
the pulse motors improves the system dynamics from 0.8mm resonant
amplitude to a maximum of 0.1 ~ 0.2 mm.

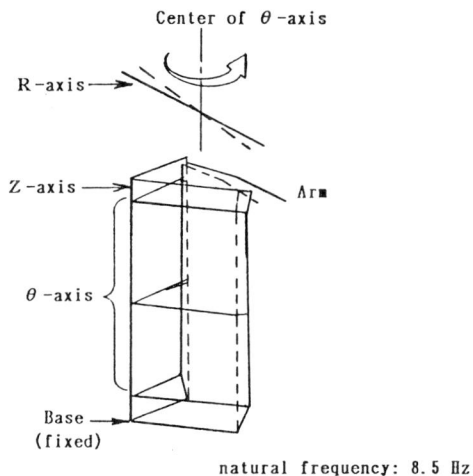

Center of θ-axis

R-axis

Z-axis   Arm

θ-axis

Base
(fixed)

natural frequency: 8.5 Hz

Fig. 7 Modal Analysis of Vibration

CLOSED LOOP CONTROL

A vacuum-compatible magnetoresistive-type encoder originally
developed by YASKAWA is used for position feedback to obtain better
smooth motion, stiffness against load disturbances, high precision
and high acceleration / deceleration characteristics. Fig. 8 shows
the configuration, features and specifications of the encoder used
in the SCARF robot. The encoder can tolerate 150°C. A constant
spatial gap between the magnetic element and the sensor is maintained using ceramic materials for thermal isolation.
The block diagram of the self-positioning function of the
pulse motor is shown in Fig. 9-(a). In the figure the outer solid
line indicates the feed back loop for self-positioning. In our
closed loop control method, the positive feed back (dotted line in
the figure), namely the lead-angle control relative to the rotor
position, is employed to cancel the self positioning loop. As a
result of this torque control-loop, the pulse motor is equivalently
converted to a DC-brushless motor (Fig. 9-(b)). In addition to
this torque control (under patent application), conventional
position and velocity feed back loops are applied for compensation of dynamics, as in the control of DC servo mechanisms.

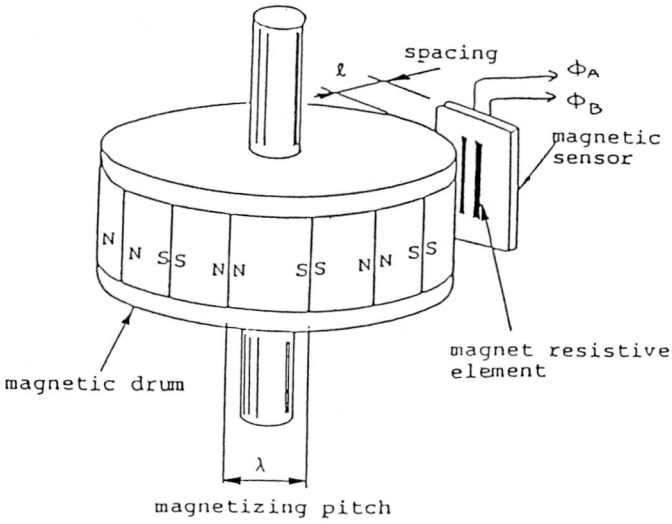

spacing

ϕ_A

ϕ_B

magnetic sensor

magnet resistive element

magnetic drum

λ

magnetizing pitch

Structure of magnetic rotary encoder

Features of Vacuum-compatible Magnetic Encoder

1) Simple and Compact

2) High resistance against mechanical shock

3) Heat-resistance and low outgassing

4) Low thermal drift

	basic pulse repetition rate	dram's diamerer	resolution	
θ axis	4 0 5 OP/R	ϕ 1 5 6	Max	1 2 9, 6 0 OP/R
Z axis	8 1 OP/R	ϕ 3 1	Max	2 5, 9 2 OP/R
R axis	1 2 0 μm/P	—	Min	3 0 μm/P

Fig. 8 Vacuum-compatible Magnetic Encoder

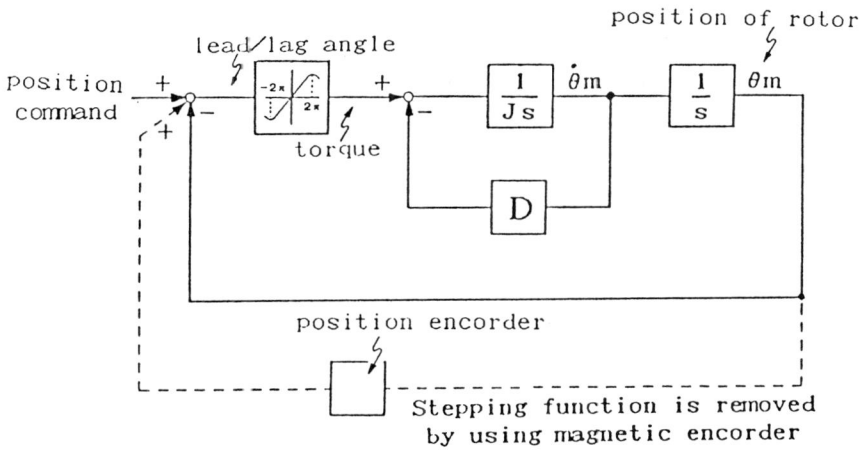

(a) Dynamic Characteristic of Pulse Motor

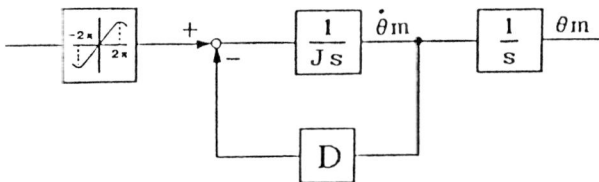

(b) Equivalent Conversion from Pulse Motor to DC brushless Motor

Fig. 9 Torque Control of Pulse Motor

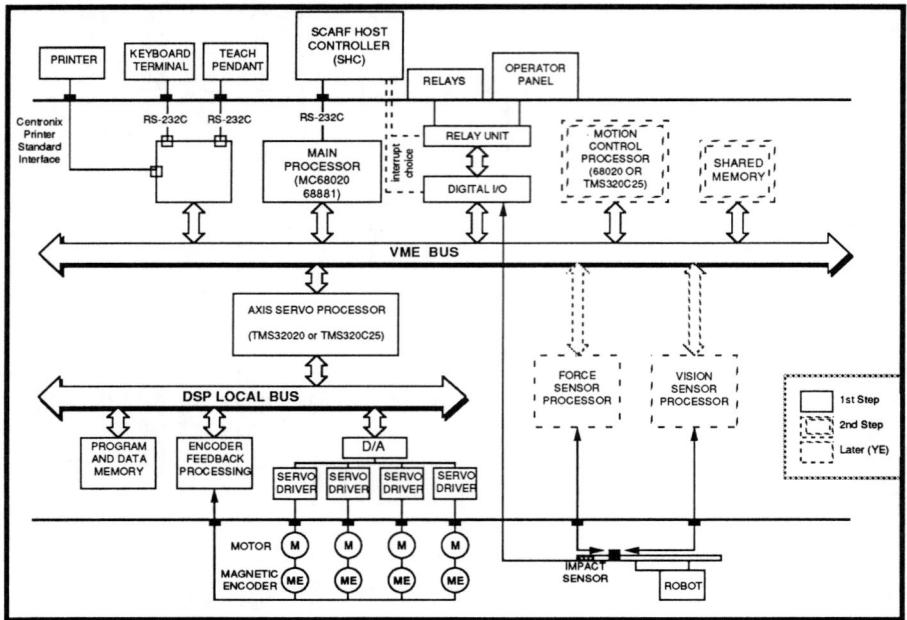

Fig. 10 Architecture of SCARF Robot Controller

For example, the signal issued by the velocity observer is the feed back for the differential compensation of the position loop. These servo controls are processed by DSP (TMS 320C25) software at 4kHz servo cycle.

CONTROL SYSTEM

The robot controller has a multi-processor architecture, with a 32bit main CPU (MC68020) and a DSP. A Pascal-like robot language and offline programming system with simulator enable an operator to program more efficiently. The controller is implemented with a KERMIT-like communication protocol function to communicate with the SHC (SCARF host computer) on a real time OS basis.

FUTURE WORK

Several kinds of evaluation tests will be performed in the high vacuum SCARF chamber. The following subjects are required for advanced robotic, self-contained manufacturing systems.

1. Position compensation of thermal deviation caused by higher ambient and baking temperatures ... Vacuum-compatible visual feedback system.

2. Flexible and highly-functional man-machine system ... Offline programming system with real-time simulator and optimum path generation.

3. High reliability for maintenance-free operation ... Fault tolerance technology.

4. New innovative vacuum-compatible motors and dry lubrication for temperatures to 300°C.

Robot Motion Planning for Self-Contained Manufacturing Systems

B. Paden
University of California, Santa Barbara, Santa Barbara, CA 93106

Alistair Mees
University of Western Austrailia, Nedlands, Australia WA 6009

Mike Fisher
University of Western Austrailia, Nedlands, Australia WA 6009

ABSTRACT

Autonomy is a key requirement of robots used in self-contrained manufacturing systems. This is motivated by the high cost of access to self-contained environments and the awkwardness of programming by teach pendant. We address this requirement in this paper and describe a simple and efficient algorithm for generating a 2^n-tree (generalized quad-tree) representation of the free configuration space for a manipulator moving in a workspace with obstacles. This algorithm is based on the existence of uniform bounds on the Jacobians relating the differential motions of points on the manipulator to differential joint motions. We also describe how this representation can be searched to generate a collision-free path and optimized with dynamic constraints to produce an executable trajectory.

INTRODUCTION

Robots working in self-contained manufacturing cells are difficult to access and program. For example, the UCSB SCARF robotic vacuum workcell for semiconductor processing must be vented and then pumped down every time an operator accesses the cell. Furthermore, visibility into the vacuum chamber is limited to a few viewports which occupy positions where processing equipment could be interfaced to the cell. Consequently, we are motivated to reduce human interaction with the cell and increase the intelligence or autonomy of the cell controller. We can do this by modelling the geometry of the cell and the robot and developing algorithms for autonomously planning collision-free motions in the SCARF system.

In this paper we address the problem of autonomous motion planning and describe a simple and efficient algorithm for generating a 2^n-tree (generalized quad-tree) representation of the free configuration space for a manipulator moving in a workspace with obstacles. This algorithm is based on the existence of uniform bounds on the Jacobians relating the differential motions of points on the manipulator to differential joint motions. We also describe how this representation can be searched to generate a collision-free path and optimized with dynamic constraints to produce an executable trajectory.

Consider the trajectory planning problem of moving a manipulator from a source configuration, p, to a goal configuration, q, in a workspace containing fixed obstacles. A solution to this problem is a trajectory of joint displacements (a curve parameterized by time) which moves the manipulator from the source to destination without violating some set of constraints. This set may include noncollision with obstacles, dynamics and actuator constraints, and sometimes smoothness constraints. Although this problem is well-posed, its "optimal" solution is intractible analytically, and very expensive numerically as the search space is infinite dimensional.

The common approach to this problem is to attempt only a sub-optimal solution which can be found by decomposing the trajectory planning problem into a sequence of simpler problems. The decomposition we use is

1)   Generate a representation of free configuration space (called freespace).

2)   Find a simple collision-free, polygonal path from source to goal.

3)   Tune this path by removing unnecessary segments.

4)   Reparameterize the polygonal path with time and optimize taking into account dynamics and actuator constraints.

A primary contribution of this paper is an extremely simple and efficient algorithm for generating a 2^n-tree (generalized quad-tree) freespace representation for an open kinematic chain manipulator. This scheme requires only distance calculations from the manipulator to the obstacle set and a uniform bound on a set of manipulator Jacobians. We describe how this representation can be searched for a polygonal path from source to destination, and how this path can be parameterized by time and then optimized to provide a complete solution to the trajectory planning problem. There has been considerable research effort invested in this problem already and for comparison we review related algorithms here.

Path planning based on the concept of the free configuration space of a manipulator has been proposed by several researchers. Udupa [1] appears to have been the first to do so and applied these ideas to the Scheinman Arm (he used the boom tip to represent the state of the manipulator). His analysis was quite specific to this manipulator however. Lozano-Perez [2], and Brooks and Lozano-Perez [3] have proposed more general schemes. In [2] a representation of the freespace is calculated using the notion of slice projection. The method of calculation is well matched to the chain structure of open kinematic chain manipulators. The drawback of the representation is that it is computed based on a prior choice of quantization, and in order to increase the resolution in a particular region of the configuration space a large fraction of the representation must be recomputed. Also, prior to finding a path the freespace representation based on slice projection must be processed to identify coherent regions of freespace. (This only has to be done once for a fixed set of obstacles however).

In [3] a freespace representation based on rectangular cells is described for a polygon moving amongst polygonal obstacles which makes efficient use of memory. When rotation is allowed the notion of slice projection must be used to generate a simple representation of freespace. Brooks [4] describes a path planning scheme based on a generalized cone representation of freespace. Although this representation is more compact it is not simple to generate. Faverjon [5] presents a simple and elegant method of generating an oct-tree representation for a particular robot manipulator. He takes advantage of the specific structure of the manipulator for generating this representation, which means the algorithm will be efficient.

Shiller and Dubowsky [6] attack the whole problem of trajectory planning (roughly sub problems 1-4 above). They emphasize the optimization aspects of the problem and only use a very simple representation of the set of free-manipulator-configurations (workspace is quantized into a uniform grid). A branch and bound technique is used to find the optimal trajectory among a cleverly indexed set of trajectories.

Gouzenes [7] shows how the free-configuration space of a manipulator can be decomposed into a tree which reflects the chain structure of the manipulator. He also describes a representation of freespace based on the uniform quantization of the manipulator configuration space which may require excessive computation and memory. Related results are obtained by Kant and Zucher [8] who address the decomposition of trajectory planning into path planning and time scaling. Shwartz and Sharir [9] deal with fundamental complexity issues in motion planning. Donald [15] uses analytic representations of configuration space for motion planning which are promising, but have not been proven for motion planning involving kinematic chains.

Our scheme is based on 2^n-tree representation of freespace and is generated in a top-down fashion as in Faverjon's scheme. However, our approach is more general and applies to all open kinematic chain manipulators. We also generalize some ideas of Cully and Kempf [13] to estimate the size of the collision-free neighborhood surrounding a collision-free configuration of a manipulator. Other researchers have used 2^n-trees to represent free-space as well, Hayward [14] does this but constructs the representation in a bottom-top fashion which is necessarily slow. 2^n-trees are also useful for collision-detection in workspace, Herman [16], Arimoto [17].

The outline of this paper is as follows. Section 2 describes our algorithm, for the "top-down" generation of a 2^n-tree representation of freespace. Section 3 shows how this representation can be transformed to an adjacency graph which can be searched for a rough polygonal path. It is also shown how this path can be "tuned" to produce a simple polygonal path from source to goal. Section 4 discusses the time parameterization of this path and its optimization to produce an executable trajectory. Our conclusions are made in Section 5.

2.   **Freespace Generation Algorithm**

For an n degree-of-freedom manipulator operating in a workspace with obstacles, we represent the configuration space by a 2^n-tree. The leaves of this tree are labeled "freespace", "obstacle", or "not sure or mixed", and represent hypercubes of various sizes in the configuration space. The primary reason we choose this representation is that the tree structure reflects the recursive algorithm we use for testing if a hypercube is free. Other nice things about the 2^n-tree are (1) the adjacency graph which connects the centers of adjacent free hypercubes lies entirely within the freespace ; (2) nodes in this adjacency graph represent "chunks" of freespace and essentially all shape and connectivity information is contained in the adjacency graph; this means that we can find a path with good rough shape at the graph search level; and (3) it is easy to vary the resolution of the representation over the configuration space, or to increase the resolution locally by adding to (not recomputing) the existing representation. Representation of freespace by more general convex polyhedra can save memory, but the corresponding increase in software complexity is only warranted in the case where very high resolution is required.

Figures 1 and 3 illustrate our method of representing freespace for a two-link planar manipulator. Figure 1 depicts the initial and final configurations of the manipulator, p and q respectively. For these configurations M(p) and M(q) represent the set in the plane occupied by the manipulator. Figure 3 is the corresponding quad-tree representation of freespace generated by our algorithm.

Our method for generating this 2^n-tree representation is based on a simple observation. If β corresponds to a collision free configuration, then there is a neighborhood of β which is also free. The size of this region depends on the distance between the manipulator and the obstacles. More explicitly, let

β = manipulator joint coordinate vector

$P(\beta)$ = arbitrary point on manipulator whose coordinates depend on β

O = subset of R^3 representing the obstacle set

$M(\beta)$ = the configuration dependent subset of R^3 representing the set displaced by the manipulator

$\|\Delta\beta\|_\infty = \max_i | \Delta\beta_i |$

$\|\Delta\beta\|_2$ = Euclidean norm on R^n

$d(S_1, S_2)$ = the "distance" (possibly negative!) between the two sets S_1 and S_2 in R^n defined by

$$d(S_1, S_2) = \begin{cases} \min_{\substack{x \in S_1 \\ y \in S_2}} \|x-y\|_2 & \text{if } S_1 \cap S_2 = \varnothing \\ -\max\left(\max_{x \in S_1} \min_{y \in S_2^c} \|x-y\|_2, \max_{y \in S_2} \min_{x \in S_1^c} \|x-y\|_2 \right) & \text{if } S_1 \cap S_2 \neq \varnothing \end{cases}$$

Moreover, suppose

$$\left\| \frac{dP(\beta)}{d\beta} (\Delta\beta) \right\|_2 \leq B \|\Delta\beta\|_\infty \qquad (2.1)$$

for some $B \in R$ and all points $P(\beta)$ on the manipulator. (Physically, (2.1) is a uniform bound on the Jacobians of all points on the manipulator. If the sum of the generalized joint velocities is unity, then no point on the manipulator moves faster than B.) If β' is a free configuration then the hypercube

$$\left\{ \beta \mid \|\beta - \beta'\|_\infty < \frac{d(M(\beta'), O)}{B} \right\}$$

is also freespace. If β' is not free then

$$\left\{ \beta \mid \|\beta - \beta'\|_\infty < \frac{-d(M(\beta'), O)}{B} \right\}$$

is not free (i.e., this hypercube is contained in the so-called configuration space obstacle.)

The existence of the bound (2.1) for a manipulator is clearly important. In Heinzinger and Paden [11] bounds of this type are shown to exist for all open kinematic chain manipulators. For the two-link manipulator in Figure 1, having two unit-length links, B=2. If we had chosen to measure β_2 with respect to the first link, B would be 3. We see that care must be taken in choosing joint coordinates so that the bound B is not too loose. A good rule of thumb is to choose the units of the joint angles differently and such that the sensitivity of the gripper motion to joint displacements is roughly the same for each joint. It is important to note that the bound (2.1) is valid for large displacements not only infinitesimals. The exploitation of this fact is a key component of our freespace generation algorithm which is described as follows.

Given a manipulator whose configuration space is a hypercube in R^n (eg. $[0,2\pi]^n$ for an nR manipulator‡). The corresponding set-valued function $M(\beta)$, and resolution r (dimension of smallest desired hypercube in the 2^n-tree), execute the following algorithm for the node representing the entire hypercube of freespace.

Freesquare:

1)   Use (2.1) with β equal to the center point of the hypercube to determine if the hypercube is "free", "not free", or "not sure or mixed".

   If free, return (FREE)

   If not free, return (NOT FREE)

   Else...

2)   If the hypercube has dimension equal to r then return (TOO SMALL)

3)   If the hypercube is "not sure or mixed" subdivide the hypercube evenly into 2^n hypercubes and call Freesquare recursively. If all are free, return (FREE).

   If all are not free, return (NOT FREE)

   Else

4)   Create 2^n children of the present node and label them accordingly. (Figure 3 was generated by drawing the free children at this step.)

END.

This algorithm generates a 2^n-tree whose FREE leaves form a conservative estimate of freespace. Those points β which are in freespace but are not represented in the free leaves have the property that $d(M(\beta),O) < Br$. Thus, for sufficiently small r the approximation error can be made as small as desired.

‡This configuration space is actually an n-torus, but this topology is recovered in the adjacency graph.

If, after the 2^n-tree is generated, a higher resolution is required we simply call FREESPACE with the new resolution
for each leaf labelled TOO SMALL. There is no need to recompute existing parts of the tree.

The attraction of this algorithm is its simplicity. It is essentialy a numerical algorithm for computing freespace since only the differential properties of the manipulator are used. It is true that the scheme will perform an "excess" of the simple freespace tests as shown in Figure 2. However, the alternative is to do fewer complicated tests. It is possible that a little can be gained in computation time, but the expense is much more complicated software.

The distance calculation accounts for most of the freespace computation and there are existing algorithms for this if the manipulator links and the obstacles are modelled simply (e.g. as a union of convex polyhdra) [12]. On the surface, it appears that for O modelled as m, say, convex polyhedra, and $M(\beta)$ modelled as n convex polyhedra that mn distance computations are required. This is true for nodes near the root of the tree, but further down in the tree where the nodes represent smaller hypercubes many link-obstacle interactions become inactive and need not be computed. In fact, many leaves will be determined free with a single distance calculation between a link and obstacle which are close to each other for the particular configuration.

3.   **Finding Paths**

If one point p in the representation of freespace is reachable from another point q, it is not, in general, hard to find a path that joins them while avoiding configuration space obstacles. Since the hypercubes in the 2^n-tree are convex, straight-line paths from p and q to the centers of the squares, (S_p and S_q), containing them are collision-free. Further, the adjacency graph consisting of the centers of squares (nodes) and line segments (arcs) connecting centers of adjacent squares can be searched for a path from S_p to S_q.

It is natural to try to select a path that is optimal according to some criterion such as transit time, energy expenditure, or length in joint space. As explained earlier, we do not try to do so immediately. At this stage we solve a simpler problem: we look for a piecewise linear path containing the minimum number of segments. Besides simplicity, this criterion favors paths that steer clear of obstacles and pass through large open regions. This gives us room for smoothing the path to get one which is better dynamically. Such a path is the shortest path in the network obtained by giving all arcs in the adjacency graph unit length. By giving all arcs the same length, we can also use a simple shortest path algorithm which runs in O(#nodes) time instead of the O(#nodes)log(#nodes) required if arcs have different lengths. The algorithm we implemented is the so-called "brushfire" algorithm outlined below (A* could also be used).
Polygonal-path (p,q):

Let S_p and S_q be the squares containing p and q respectively.

Label S_q with its predecessor (null) and distance to itself (zero), $(\emptyset, 0)$.

Set $L = \{S_p\}$. (L will be a first-in first-out queue).

While $(L \neq \emptyset)$ do
{

    remove the first element s from L.
    for each square n joined by an arc to s, and not previously
    labelled: {label n with $(s, \alpha+1)$ where s has label (m, α).
    append n to L.
    if $n = S_q$, return (p, a, b, ..., m, n) with cost $\alpha +1$, where m
    is the predecessor of n, a of b, and so on
    }

}

    An example path computed by this algorithm for a particular p and q is shown in Figure 3 together with the terminal segments connecting the centers of S_p and S_q to p and q, respectively. This algorithm examines each arc at most twice, and since our network has #arcs bounded by a multiple of #nodes, it terminates in a time bounded by O(#nodes) as claimed.

    By inspecting Figure 3, we see that the path generated still has a relatively large number of segments. In fact, it is easy to shorten this path and reduce the number of changes of direction by connecting vertices which are "visible" to each other. Such an improved path is shown in Figure 4.

    Formally, p and q are visible to each other if the line segment $\overline{pq}$ is contained in the representation of freespace. To verify if p and q are visible to each other we execute the following:

    visible (p,q):
    S_p: = square containing p.
    S_q: = square containing q.

while S_p is free do

{

if $S_p = S_q$, return (TRUE)
else
let r be the point where $\overline{pq}$ (See Fig. 5) intersects the boundary of S_p.

S_r: = square adjacent to Sp containing r.
p: = r
S_p: = S_r
}
Return (False)

    We have appealed to genericity in the reassignment of S_p; for example, in two dimensions we have assumed $\overline{pq}$ does not go through the corner of a square. In practice, we simply check this condition and assign S_p accordingly. In order to tune-up the initial path (Figure 3) we use the following algorithm.

Tune-path [p,a,b,...,m,n,q]:
      If cost is 1, return;
      else
      define S_p and S_q as usual;
      Let $r = S_q$, t = predecessor of S_q

      while $p \notin t$
{

      If predecessor of t is visible from r, replace by its predecessor.
      otherwise, r: = t, t: = predecessor of t.

}
End;

The application of this algorithm to the path in Figure 3 yields the simple path of Figure 4.

4.   Smoothing and Optimizing the Path

The methods of the previous section generate a polygonal path through freespace. In this section this path is time-scaled and optimized to produce an executable trajectory--a solution to the trajectory planning problem.

It is possible to calculate smooth robot trajectories which will follow the path of Figure 4. These trajectories necessarily speed up and then slow down along each segment such that the velocities at the vertices are zero. Thus, despite the roughness of the path it is possible to parameterize it smoothly by time. This smooth curve serves as an initial feasible path for a minimum time optimization algorithm. Such an optimization can be computed using existing optimal control software such as MISER (Goh & Teo, 1987). Unfortunately, this path cannot at present be computed in real time. It could, however, be implemented by robots which perform repetitive tasks.

For optimization we choose a convenient set of coordinates for manipulation in Figure 1 defined by $\theta_1 = \beta$, $\theta_2 = \beta_2 - \beta_1$ (ie., we measure the joint two displacement relative to link 1). For the purpose of example we assume zero gravity, unit length links, and unit mass at the distal end of each link. If F_1 and F_2 are the joint torques then the dynamics are

$$F_1 = \ddot{\theta}_1(3 + 2\cos\theta_2) + \ddot{\theta}_2(1 + \cos\theta_2)$$
$$- \dot{\theta}_2^2 \sin\theta_2 - 2\dot{\theta}_1\dot{\theta}_2 \sin\theta_2,$$

$$F_2 = \ddot{\theta}_1(1 + \cos\theta_2) + \ddot{\theta}_2 + \dot{\theta}_1^2 \sin\theta_2. \qquad (4.1)$$

Each joint has a motor with operating characteristics determined by the equations

$$F_j = K_j I_j, \qquad\qquad j = 1, 2, \qquad\qquad (4.2)$$

$$V_j = R_j I_j + K_j \dot{\theta}_j, \qquad j = 1, 2 \qquad (4.3)$$

where I_j and V_j are, respectively, the current and voltage of the jth motor and K_1, K_2, R_1 and R_2 are constants defining the characteristics of the motors. The K_j are the back emf constants of the DC motors and the R_j are the armature resistances. We will assume that the currents and voltages for each motor can only take values within some operating limits and so we have the constraints

$$|I_j| \leq \alpha_j \quad \text{and} \quad |V_j| \leq \beta_j \quad \text{for} \quad j = 1,2, \qquad (4.4)$$

where the α_j and β_j are known constants. These constraints represent realistic amplifier constraints. Since we desire a relatively smooth trajectory we shall specify that the jerk is bounded. For simplicity of the optimization the dynamics of the robot trajectory are given by

$$\frac{d\theta_j^3}{dt^3} = u_j(t), \quad \text{where} \quad |u_j(t)| \leq \gamma_j, \quad \text{for } j = 1, 2, \qquad (4.5)$$

where the γ_j are constants. In this formulation the manipulator dynamics (4.4) are viewed as constraints. The advantage of taking (4.5) as the dynamics is that our optimization algorithm will generate a piecewise cubic joint trajectory.

If the constraints (4.4) are ignored, a minimum time trajectory which tracks a given polygonal path in joint space can be easily calculated. It is well known from Optimal Control Theory that a time optimal control for the system (4.5) is a bang-bang control with two switches. This results in the optimal trajectory being composed of piecewise cubic functions of θ_1 and θ_2. For the three segment polygonal path of the example, the minimum times for the three segments, with γ_1 and γ_2 both chosen as 1, are 4.69, 4.02 and 3.27 giving a total trajectory time of 11.98 seconds. This trajectory can, of course, violate the constraints (4.4). A simple algorithm could however be devised which would, if necessary, decrease the bounds γ_1 and γ_2 on the controls so that these constraints are satisfied. These calculations could all easily be accomplished in real time.

We now discuss the calculation of a smooth path which moves the robot from the given initial point to the given terminal point in minimum time. This problem can be formulated as a minimum time optimal control problem in which the system dynamics are described by equations (4.5) and there are state constraints given by equations (4.1-4.4). The final ingredients in this problem are the constraints imposed by the obstacles. With the obstacle constraints included, this becomes a very difficult computational problem to solve. We have found that the MISER optimal control software can successfully handle this problem in the case of convex obstacles with smooth boundaries if a good starting trajectory is used to initiate the computation. Such a trajectory is available in the form of the polygonal path generated by the methods of the previous sections. The procedure will be outlined in the context of the following example.

Example: Consider the example of Figure 1, that is a two link planar robot with two circular obstacles in the workspace. Let the obstacles be centered at the points Q^k and have radii r^k for $k = 1,2$. Let P_1 and P_2 be the coordinates, in workspace, of the endpoints of the robot links and let the origin be coincident with the base of the first link. Define the functions φ_1^k and φ_2^k by the equations

$$\varphi_1^k = \left(Q^k\right)^T P_1$$

and

$$\varphi_1^k = \left(Q^k - P_1\right)^T (P_2 - P_1) \quad \text{for } k=1,2. \quad (4.6)$$

The squares of the distances of the two robot links from the centers of each circle are now given by

$$\left(d_1^k\right)^2 = \begin{cases} \left(Q^k\right)^T Q^k & \text{if } \varphi_1^k \le 0, \\ \left(Q^k\right)^T Q^k - \left(\varphi_1^k\right)^2 & \text{if } 0 < \varphi_1^k < 1, \\ \left(Q^k - P_1\right)^T \left(Q^k - P_1\right) & \text{if } \varphi_1^k \ge 1, \end{cases} \quad (4.7)$$

$$\left(d_2^k\right)^2 = \begin{cases} \left(Q^k - P_1\right)^T \left(Q^k - P_1\right) & \text{if } \varphi_2^k \le 0, \\ \left(Q^k - P_1\right)^T \left(Q^k - P_1\right) - \left(\varphi_2^k\right)^2 & \text{if } 0 < \varphi_2^k < 1, \\ \left(Q^k - P_2\right)^T \left(Q^k - P_2\right) & \text{if } \varphi_2^k \ge 1. \end{cases} \quad (4.8)$$

The obstacle constraints can now be expressed as the equations

$$\left(d_1^k\right)^2 \ge \left(r^k\right)^2 \quad \text{and} \quad \left(d_2^k\right)^2 \ge (r^k)^2 \quad \text{for } k = 1, 2, \quad (4.9)$$

which have to be satisfied over all of the trajectory.

Any computational procedure requires an initial guess for the controls $u(t)$. As men- tioned previously, because of the difficult nature of this problem it is essential to have a good initial guess. This is provided by the polygonal trajectory generated previously. The control parameterization procedure used in MISER partitions the time interval into subintervals of equal length and approximates the controls by parameters which are constant on each subinterval. We therefore need to compute a set of piecewise constant controls which will generate our initial polygonal trajectory to use as the initial guess for the computational procedure. Since we are constrained by the software to equal subintervals of time, the minimum time trajectory mentioned earlier which tracks the polygonal trajectory is unsuitable (switching times are not simultaneous for each point). A tracking trajectory can however be obtained using constant subintervals of time as described in the following paragraph.

Let $\theta^0, \theta^1, ..., \theta^m$ be the position vectors, in joint space, of the vertices of an m-segment polygonal path. Consider the qth segment, where $1 \le q \le m$. A piecewise constant control for which the system (4.5) generates this trajectory is

$$u(t) = (\theta^q - \theta^{q-1})\, \sigma(t), \qquad t \in [0,T], \qquad (4.10)$$

where

$$\sigma(t) = \left(\frac{3}{T}\right)^3 \begin{cases} 1 & t \in [0, T/3], \\ -2 & t \in [T/3, 2T/3], \\ 1 & t \in [2T/3, T], \end{cases} \qquad (4.11)$$

and T is the time associated with the qth segment. Since each component of u(t) satisfies $|u_j(t)| \le \gamma_j$, the minimum time taken for the qth segment is given by

$$3 \max_{j=1,2} \left\{ \frac{2}{\gamma_j} \left| \theta_j^q - \theta_j^{q-1} \right| \right\}^{1/3} \qquad (4.12)$$

We now require all segments to have equal time so we define

$$T = 3 \max_{q=1,...,m} \left\{ \max_{j=1,2} \left\{ \frac{2}{\gamma_j} \left| \theta_j^q - \theta_j^{q-1} \right| \right\}^{1/3} \right\} \qquad (4.13)$$

For the complete trajectory, u(t) is now a piecewise constant control, that is, the trajectory consists of piecewise cubic functions of the joint angles, defined on 3m subintervals of time each of length T/3. The total time for the whole trajectory is mT.

The minimum time optimal control problem for system (4.5) with the constraints (4.4) and (4.9) can now be solved using the MISER software. One would expect that the optimal trajectory will just touch one or more of the obstacles. For the examples we considered this was in fact the case. From a practical viewpoint we would prefer a trajectory which remained a reasonable distance away from the obstacles. This can be obtained by first obtaining a minimum time trajectory and then using this trajectory as the initial guess for a fixed time optimal control problem which minimizes the objective function

$$J = \int_0^T \sum_{k=1}^2 (r^k)^2 \left\{ \frac{1}{\left(d_1^k\right)^2} + \frac{1}{\left(d_2^k\right)^2} \right\} dt \qquad (4.14)$$

where the time T for this problem is chosen to be slightly larger than the optimal time for the previous minimum time problem. The solution to this problem should be a trajectory which is forced further away from the obstacles. The larger we choose the value of T the more freedom the trajectory has to move away from the obstacles.

The results from the optimization applied to the path of Figure 4 is shown in Figure 6 where we have taken the parameter values in Equations (4.2) and (4.3) as $K_1 = K_2 = 1$ and $R_1 = R_2 = 1$. The bounds on the currents and voltages as defined in Equations (4.4) have the values $\alpha_1 = \alpha_2 = 2$ and $\beta_1 = \beta_2 = 2$ and the bounds on the jerk (control) as defined in Equation (4.5) are $\gamma_1 = \gamma_2 = 1$. The two obstacles together with a strobed version of the trajectory are shown in Figure 7. The trajectory used to initiate the optimal control software MISER consists of 9 equal time subintervals with a total time of 16.75 seconds. The smoothed time optimal trajectory, which is not illustrated, just touches the smaller of the two obstacles and takes 6.69 seconds. Finally, this trajectory was used to initiate the fixed time optimal control problem which minimizes (4.14) with the total time set at 6.9 seconds. The trajectory resulting from the solution to this problem is shown, firstly in joint space in Figure 6 and secondly in work space in Figure 7.

Conclusion

We have described a general method for generating a freespace representation for any manipulator with the uniform bound in equation (2.1). Furthermore, we have shown how this representation can be searched to find a polygonal path connecting source to destination which is tuned and then optimized to solve the trajectory planning problem. This is a solution to autonomous planning in seof-contained manufacturing systems.

The contribution of this paper is the simple generation of the freespace representation which uses only a distance function and a uniform bound on Jacobians of the manipulator. There have been previous attacks on the integration of path-planning and optimization [6], however the discretization of the control problem used in MISER seems to be a good way to reduce the dimension of the search to a reasonable number as well.

It is important to point out that this method of trajectory generation is applicable to a large number of mechanical problems--all we need is a finite dimensional configurations pace, the bound B, and a distance function to apply the method. For example, we could easily solve the problem of moving a polygon admist polygonal obstacles using this method.

We have not discussed self collision of the robot. The incorporation of this into the algorithm using a weaker bound on the minimum joint space distance to collision is straightforward. This is needed since collisions can occur between links which are both moving.

References

[1]   S.M. Udupa, "Collision detection and avoidance in computer controlled manipulators," Proc. Int. Joint Conf. on AI, MIT, Cambridge, MA, Aug. 1977, pp. 737-748.

[2]   T. Lozano-Perez, "A simple motion-planning algorithm for general robot manipulators," IEEE Journal of Robotics and Automation, Vol. RA-3, No. 3, June

1987, pp. 224-238.

[3]   R.A. Brooks and T. Lozano-Perez, "A Subdivision algorithm in configuration space for findpath with rotation," IEEE Trans. on Systems, Man, and Cybernetics, Vol. SMC-15, No. 2, March/April 1985, pp. 224-233.

[4]   R.A. Brooks, "Solving the find-path problem by good representation of freespace," IEEE Trans. Systems, Man and Cybernetics, Vol. SMC-13, No. 3, March, pp. 190-197, 1983.

[5]   B. Faverjon, "Obstacle avoidance using an octree in the configuration space of a manipulator," Proc. of the IEEE Int. Conf. on Robotcs and Automation, pp. 504-511, Atlanta, GA, March 1984.

[6]   Z. Shiller and S. Dubowsky, "Global time optimal motions of robotic manipulators in the presence of obstacles," Proc. IEEE Conf. on Robotics and Automation, Philadelphia, PA, 1988, pp. 370-375.

[7]   L. Gouzenes, "Strategies for solving collision-free trajectories problems for mobile and manipulator robots," The Int. Journal of Robotics Research, Vol. 3, No. 4, pp. 51-65, Winter 1984.

[8]   K. Kant and S. Zucker, "Toward efficient planning: the path-velocity decomposition," The Int. Journal of Robotics Research, Vol. 5, No 3, pp. 72-89, Fall 1986.

[9]   J.J. Schwartz and M. Sharir, "On the piano mover's problem: III. Coordinating the motion of several independent bodies: the special case of circular bodies moving amidst polygonal barriers," Int. Journal of Robotics Research, Vol. 2, No. 3, Fall 1983.

[10]   G. Heinzinger and B. Paden, "Bounds on the Derivatives of the Forward Kinematic Map," UCSB Mechanical Engineering Department Memo UCSB-ME-89-4, February 1989.

[11]   E.G. Gilbert, D.W. Johnson and S. Sathiya Keerthi, "A fast procedure for computing the distance between complex objects in three dimensional space," IEEE Journal of Robotics and Automation, Vol. 4, No. 2, pp. 193-203.

[12]   C.J. Goh and K.L. Teo, MISER: An Optimal Control Software, 1987, Applied Research Corporation, National University of Singapore, Kent Ridge, Singapore.

[13]   R.K. Culley and K.G. Kempf, "A Collision Detection Algorithm Based on Velocity and Distance Bounds," IEEE Int. Conf. on Robotics and Automation, 1986, pp. 1065-1069.

[14]   V. Hayward, "Fast Collision-detection Scheme by Recursive Decomposition of a Manipulator Workspace," IEEE Int. Conf. on Robotics and Automation, 1986, pp. 1044-1048.

[15]   B. Donald, "On Motion Planning with Six Degrees of Freedom: Solving the Intersection Problems in Configuration Space," IEEE Int. Conf. on Robotics and Automation, 1985, pp. 536-541.

[16]   M. Herman, "Fast, Three-Dimensional, Collision-Free Motion Planning," IEEE Int. Conf. on Robotics and Automation, 1986, pp. 1056-1063.

[17]   S. Arimoto, H. Noborio, S. Fukuda, and A. Noda, "A Feasible Approach to Automatic Planning of Collision-Free Robot Motions," Robotics Research: 4th Int. Symposium, R. Bolles and B. Roth, eds.

114

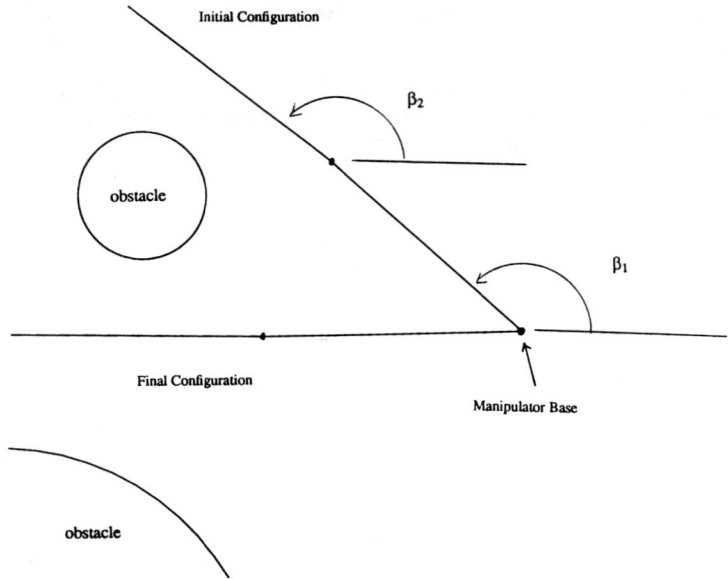

Figure 1. Two Degree-of-Freedom Manipulator with Circular Obstacles

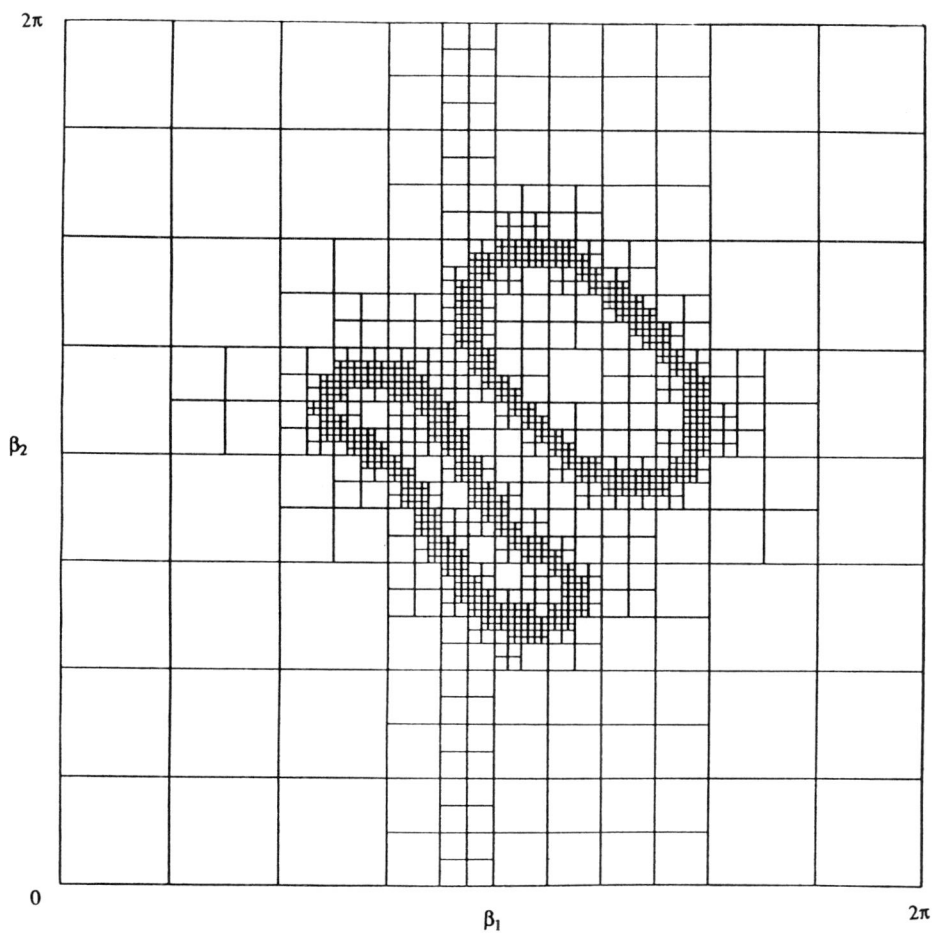

Figure 2. "One Test Per Square"

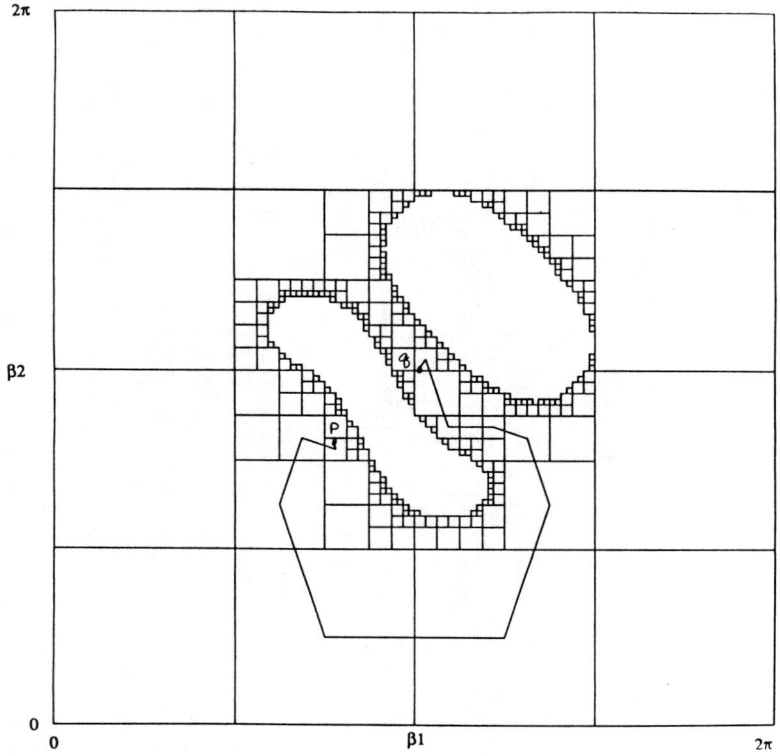

Figure 3. Quad-Tree Representation of Free Configuration space
with Collision-Free Path

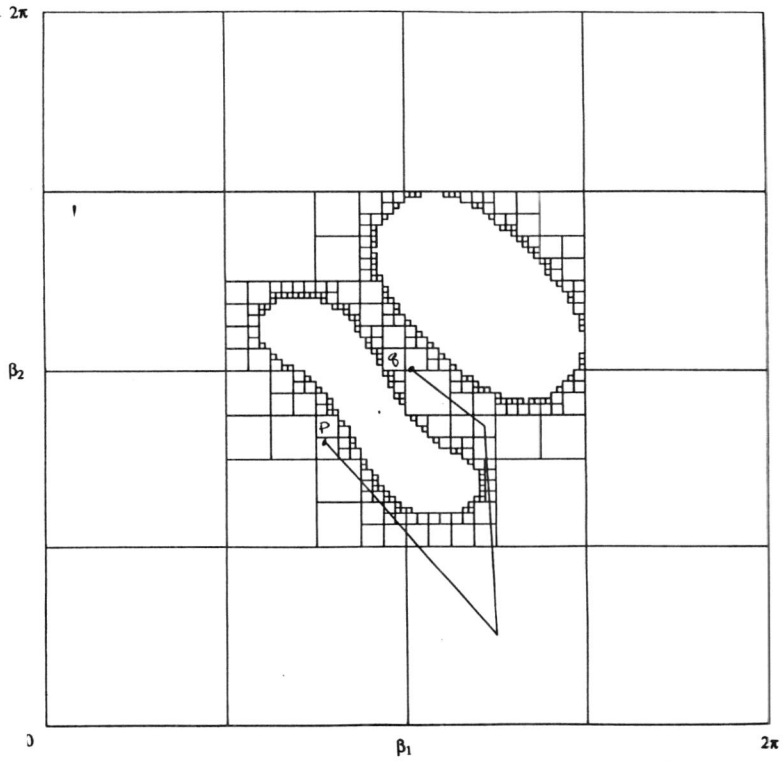

Figure 4. Simplified Polygonal Path

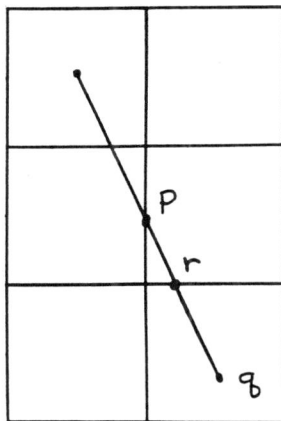

Figure 5. "Ray Tracing" through Quad-Tree

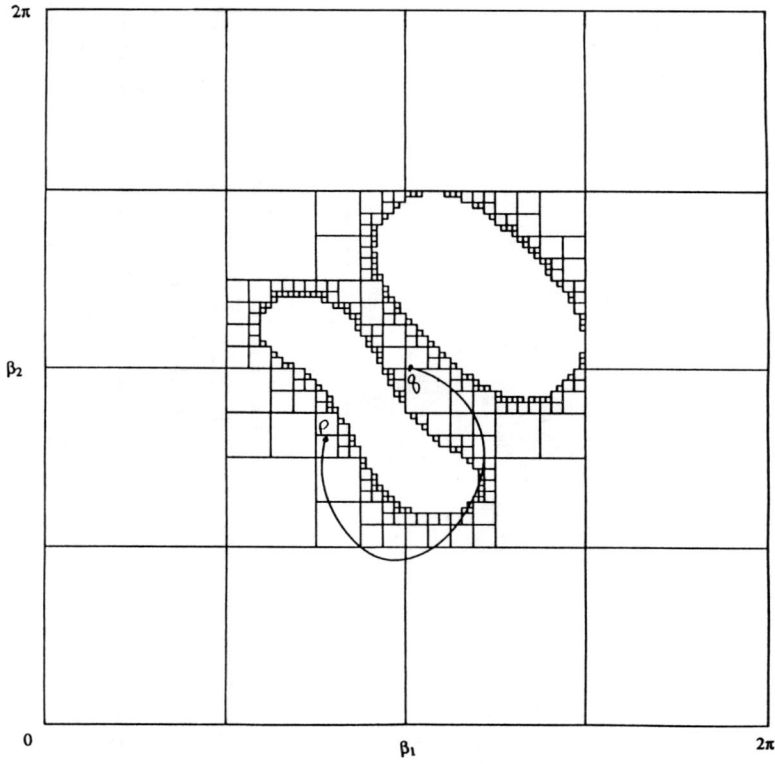

Figure 6. Optimized path superimposed on the (conservative) representation of freespace.

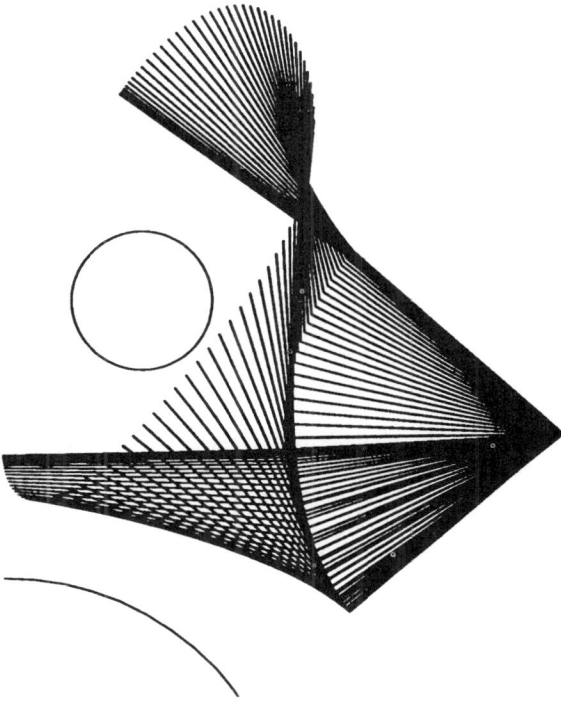

Figure 7. Optimized Robot Motion

THE DESIGN, FABRICATION, AND ASSEMBLY OF AN ADVANCED VACUUM ROBOTICS SYSTEM FOR SPACE PAYLOAD CALIBRATION

Neil P. Reid and Michael Peck

Space Sciences Laboratory, University of California, Berkeley, Ca. 94720

ABSTRACT

The Large Tank Manipulator (LTM) is one of the key components of the calibration facility at the Space Sciences Laboratory, University of California at Berkeley. The facility has been built to calibrate the NASA Extreme Ultraviolet Explorer (EUVE) satellite. The robotics system features four axes of movement, with 0.76 m of linear motion (horizontal and vertical) and ± 20 degrees of movement of rotary motion (pitch and yaw). The LTM is designed to manipulate payloads of up to 450 kg in a high-vacuum environment (1×10^{-6} Torr). The system, located inside the largest of the calibration facility's three vacuum chambers, is accessed from a class 10,000 clean room. The LTM will calibrate each of the four telescopes on the *EUVE* satellite with respect to a fixed beam line of UV light, between 44 and 2600 Å, generated by a monochromator.

OVERVIEW OF LTM SYSTEM

The Large Tank Manipulator (LTM) is the cornerstone of the EUV calibration facility at the Space Sciences Laboratory, University of California at Berkeley.[1] The system is located inside a large, 5 m × 3 m vacuum chamber, which opens to a class 10,000 clean room (Fig. 1). The LTM's primary function is to calibrate the four telescopes which make up the EUVE, a NASA Explorer payload scheduled for launch in the Fall of 1991 on a Delta II rocket.[2] The system will calibrate each of the four EUVE telescopes by manipulating them with respect to a fixed EUV beam line generated by various light sources coupled to a grazing incidence monochromator at various wavelengths between 44 and 2600 Å.

The monochromator and EUV light source combination generates a photon beam which will be reflected at grazing-incidence by telescope assemblies before being picked up by microchannel plate detectors.[3,4]

To accommodate the largest of the four space telescopes, the Deep Survey Spectrometer,[5] the LTM is designed to handle loads of 454 kg with a safety factor of 3.5. Movement accuracy is 5.3 μm for the horizontal and vertical axes, 5" on the pitch axis, and 0.5" on the yaw axis.

The robotic motion system is composed of two major subsystems, the LTM itself (see Fig. 2), which has two major subsystems, and a rollout assembly on which the robot is stored when outside the vacuum chamber. The two major systems of the LTM are the vertical stage and the three-axis carriage. The three-axis carriage comprises the horizontal, pitch, and yaw axes and is located within the vertical stage.

The entire LTM can be removed from the chamber onto the portable rollout assembly for payload mounting and ease of servicing. The rollout is an extension of the rails inside the chamber on which the robot travels longitudinally. The rollout is attached to the chamber only when the main chamber door is open. The unit is otherwise disassembled while the LTM is in operation, thereby minimizing the need for storage space and maximizing the amount of floor space in the large clean room.

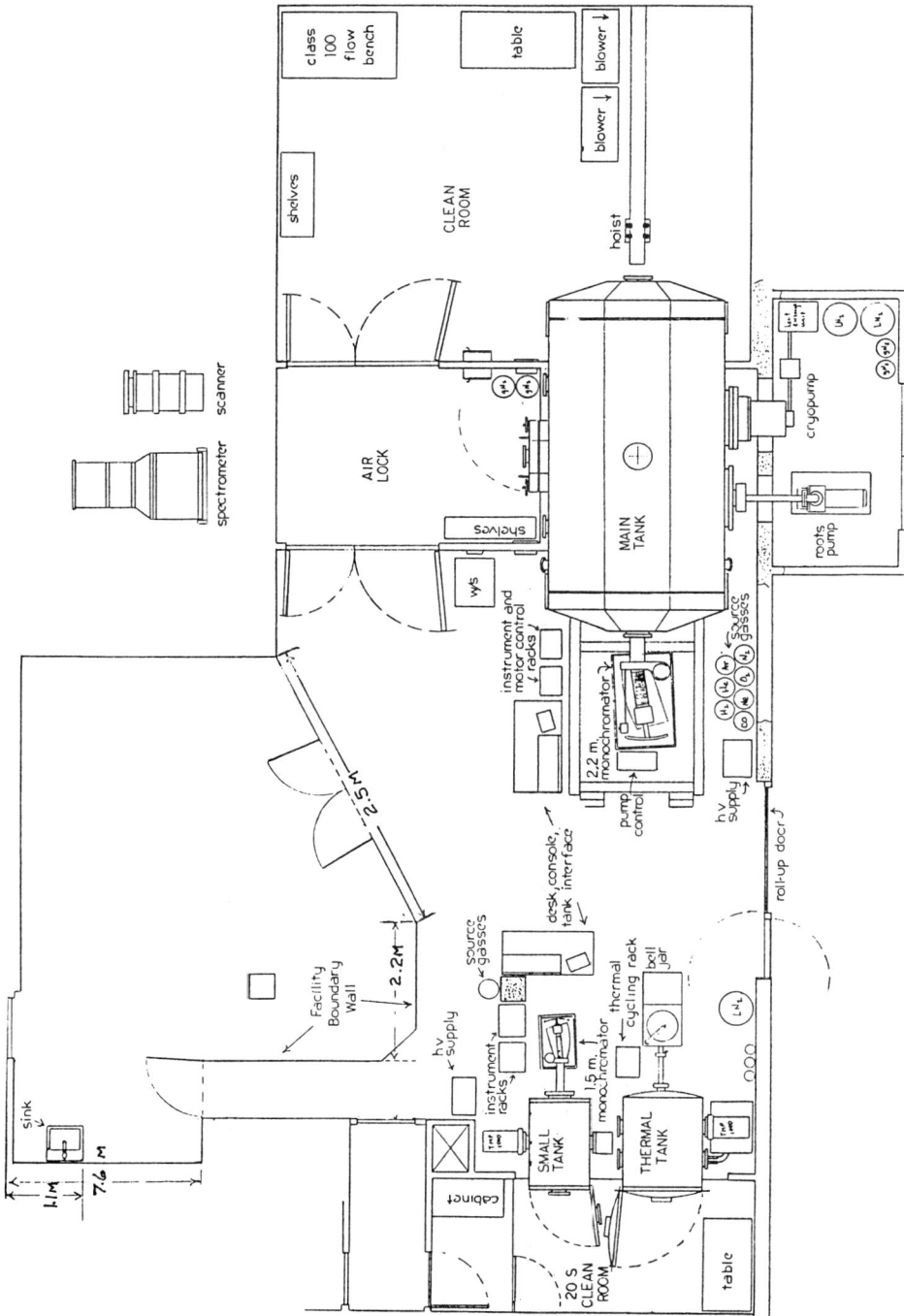

Figure 1. EUVE Calibration Facility

Figure 2. EUVE Payload (assembled flight configuration shown)

Control electronics are used to operate five high-resolution stepper motors: two motors for the vertical stage, and one motor each for the horizontal, pitch, and yaw axes. The various stages for the robot are actuated in part by leadscrews that are precision-ground, mild steel threaded rods. The leadscrews have zero-backlash, ball bearing–mounted nuts that rotate freely about the rods. The size and quantity of the ball bearings in the nuts control the amount of backlash in the leadscrew. The horizontal, pitch, and yaw leadscrews are 19 mm in diameter, while the vertical stage utilizes 25.4 mm diameter leadscrews. The pitch, yaw, and horizontal axes have one leadscrew each, and there is a leadscrew at each of the four corners of the vertical stage (Fig. 3).

Optical rotary encoders are located at one end of each of the leadscrews, with the exception of the vertical stage, which has encoders on two of the four leadscrews. The control electronics (Fig. 4) include two manual control panels, one of which is a hand-held unit that can be carried into the chamber for relative location of payloads with respect to a laser beam at atmospheric pressure. It is also used for servicing the LTM when on the rollout assembly. The other control unit is placed in the main control panel outside the clean room. The control system has an interface with a Sun MicroSystems minicomputer, which is used to operate the control software that autolocates beams on the instruments.

The drive system is actuated by precision leadscrew assemblies and stepper motors on all axes. The yaw axis also features a zero backlash 90:1 harmonic drive. The motors are fitted with failsafe brakes that must be powered to release. If there were a power outage at the facility, the system would lock into place without danger to person-nel in the chamber, the flight hardware, or facility. The brake system also has a zero backlash feature.

All components have been surface-treated and/or cleaned to the same level of cleanliness as the optics cavity hardware in each of the four telescopes. The cleanliness level is MIL-STD-1246B particle level 200 with a maximum of 0.2 mg non-volatile residue (NVR) per square foot.[6]

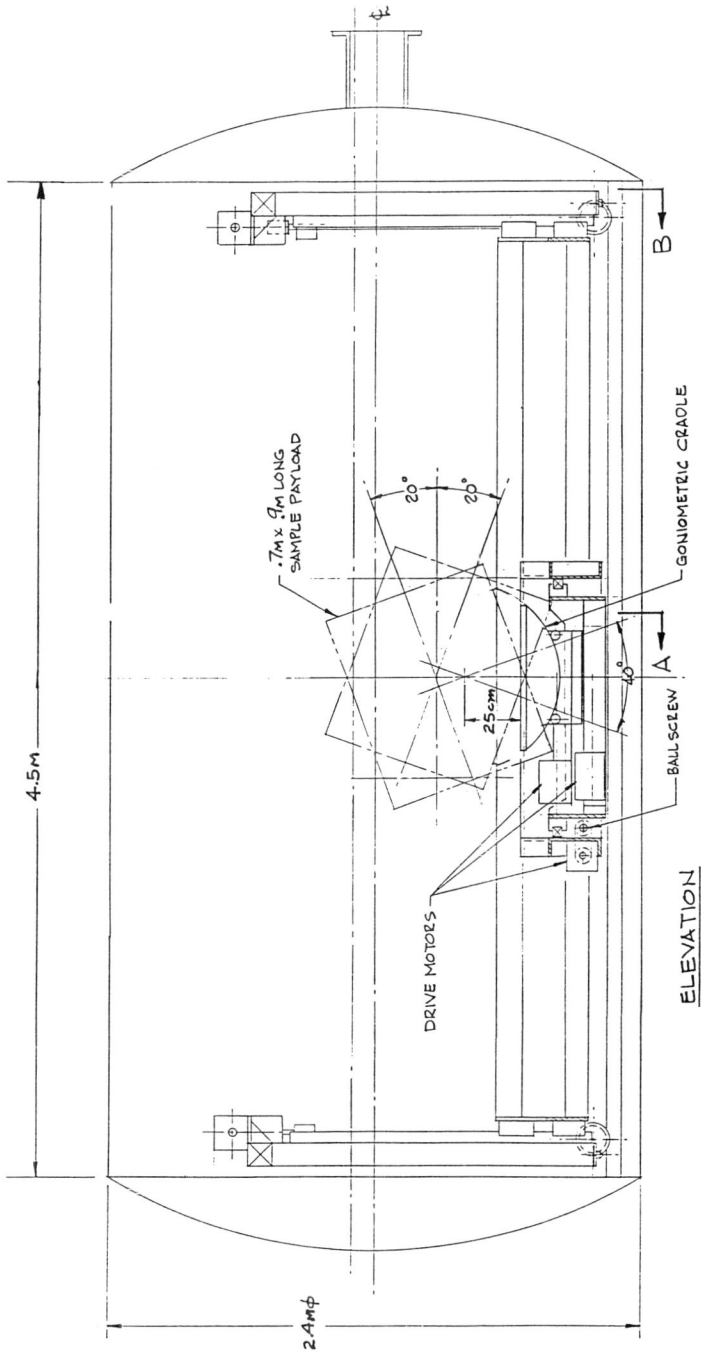

Figure 3a. LTM (side view)

124

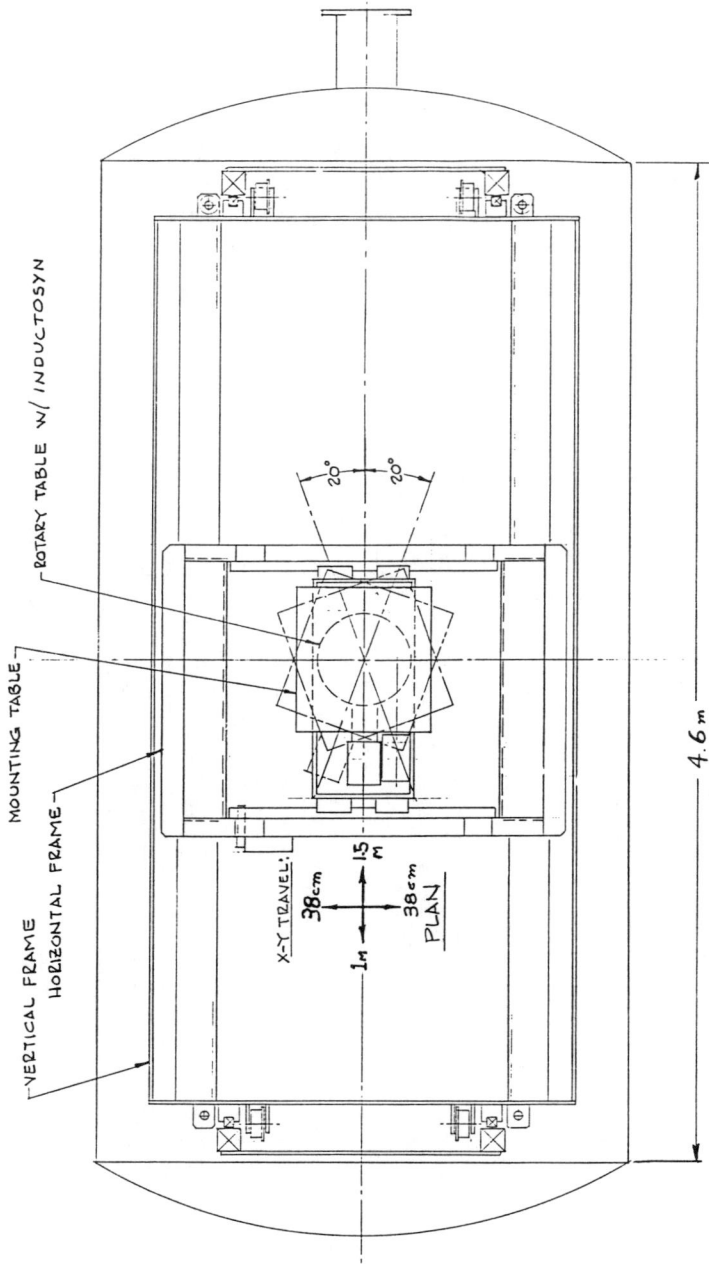

Figure 3*b*. LTM (top view)

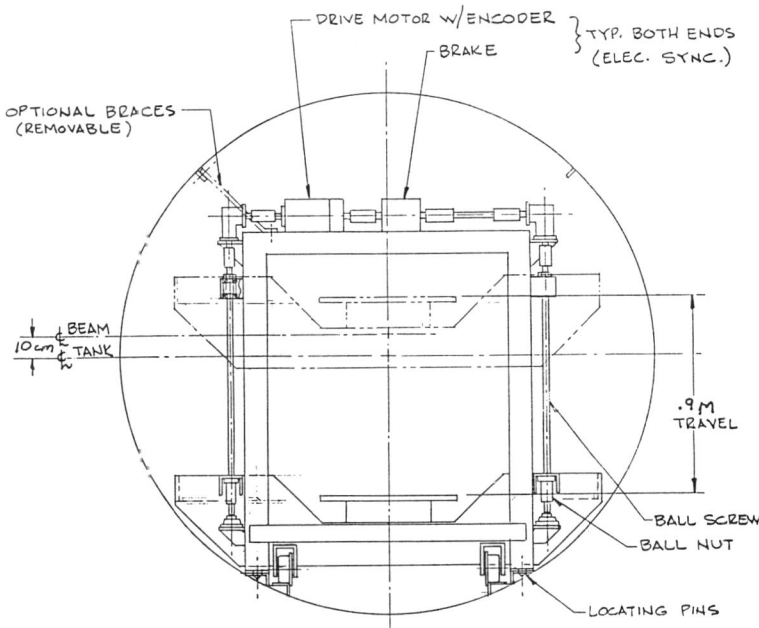

Figure 3c. LTM (end view)

FUNCTIONAL REQUIREMENTS

The functional requirements for the LTM were set by the EUVE project scientists.[7] Primarily, the requirements pertain to the manipulative resolution of the four axes. The requirements were set at 0.10 mm absolute accuracy on the vertical and horizontal axes, 25″ on the pitch axis, and 1″ on the yaw axis.

It was also required that the vertical axis have a minimum of 0.72 m of travel, with the horizontal axis having a minimum of 0.76 m of travel. The system was designed to have 0.80 m of travel on both axes. Both pitch and yaw axes required a minimum of 20° of rotation, which was achieved.

The largest of the telescopes to be calibrated on the EUVE project weighs approximately 354 kg, and the project required a minimum weight safety factor of 2. The LTM is capable of manipulating 454 kg with a safety factor of 3.5 in a static mode and 1.75 in a dynamic mode.

The manipulator design has two other important features. It is designed to operate in a very clean mode in order to maintain the contamination budget assigned to the optics cavity of the four telescopes. Furthermore, it is to operate in a high-vacuum environment.

Although there was no hard requirement for electrostatic discharge, it was important to keep electronic noise to a minimum level so as not to affect the detectors or interfere with any spacecraft electronics. Calibration performed on the LTM will be accomplished in a static mode, which is to say that the incident EUV light beams will be used during stationary moments in the manipulative routine. Power consumption at

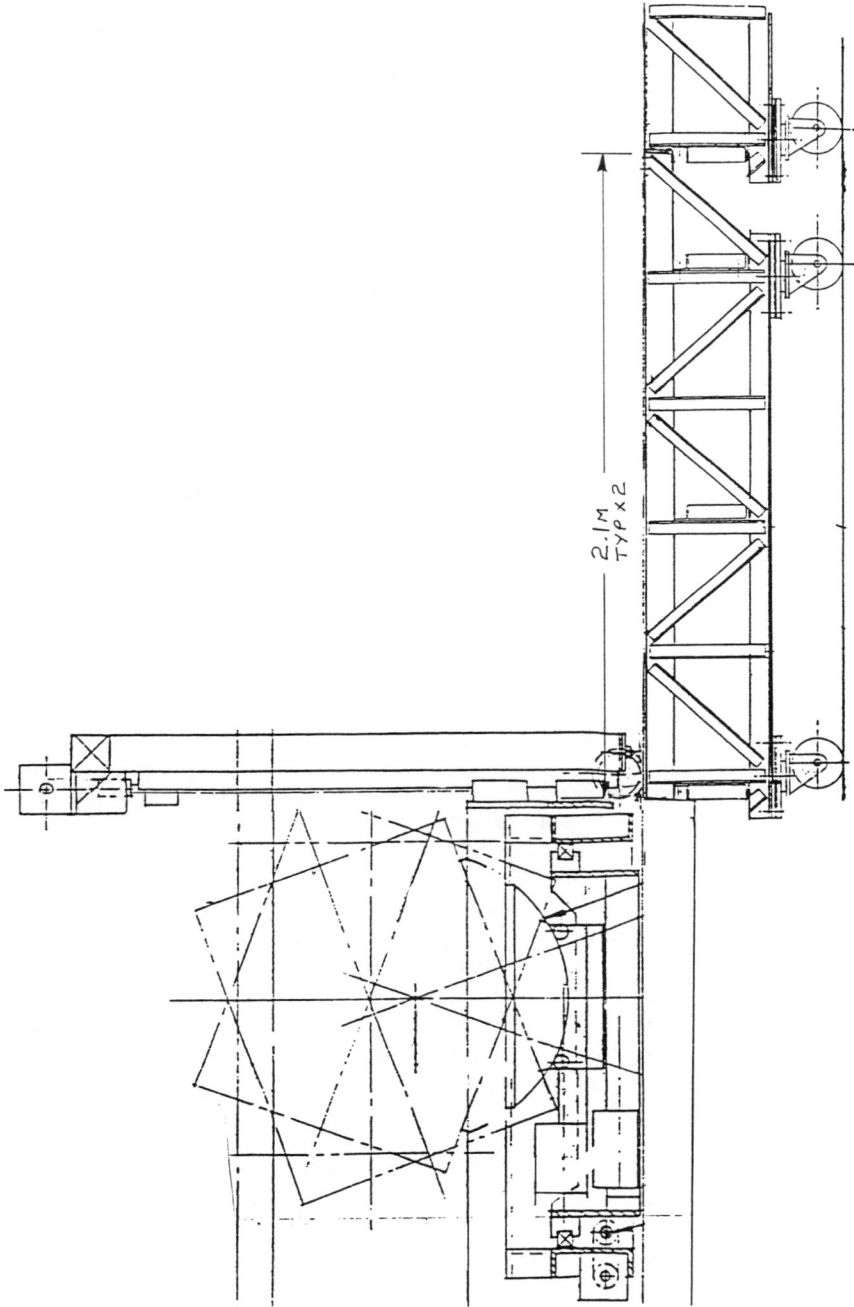

Figure 4. LTM Rollout Assembly (shown attached to LTM)

127

the motors will be approximately 5% of capacity during stationary phases of the calibration routine.

The final configuration of the LTM was established by elimination of a number of possible approaches. The possibility of using a scissors jack assembly was examined, but it was deemed too unstable at any given height. A forklift configuration would limit the payload size when extended from the center of gravity of the manipulator. It was also desirable to be able to move a payload over most of the 4.7 m length of the chamber. The design finally adopted uses a system that has a pair of end frames lifting a large, bed-shaped structure between them. A payload of 454 kg or more could be lifted with sufficient stability, retaining a safety margin for strength.

COMPONENT SELECTION AND FABRICATION OF LTM

The LTM comprises more than 6500 individual components, 80% of which required fabrication. Much of this fabrication was accomplished in the machine shop at the Space Sciences Laboratory. The larger parts, such as end frames, bed ends, and main channels, were fabricated by an outside vendor because component size prohibited in-house fabrication. The plan was to weld and/or machine all components as required and then perform a full trial assembly of the instrument prior to surface-treating and precision-cleaning. This procedure would allow for any necessary fitup-machining prior to surface-treating. The surface-treating of the components included the lubrication of certain moving components with Dicronite,* which is a modified tungsten disulfide (see section on lubrication). The final process prior to clean assembly was to have an outside vendor clean all parts to the level stated in the Overview section.

After the LTM had successfully completed its initial fitup and trial run (see section "LTM Trial Assembly"), we had to disassemble the unit completely and pack it carefully into 13 crates in order to send the robot to various vendors for surface treating, lubrication, and precision-cleaning. The gross weight of this operation was in excess of 2268 kg.

The instrument is made of approximately 60% A–36 mild steel plated with 25 μm of nickel; 20% 6061–T6 aluminum treated with alodine 1200; and 15% A–286 stainless steel that was passivated. The remaining 5% of the LTM consists of vacuum-compatible nonmetals such as urethane and teflon, which received no surface treatment. The nonmetal materials used on the LTM were tested for outgassing before the LTM was used with flight hardware.

The positioning accuracy of the motors is the same on all axes. However, the yaw axis, the primary axis on the LTM, requires a greater degree of mechanical accuracy. This accuracy was achieved through the use of an inductosyn, an encoder that features 0.2″ resolution and 1″ accuracy. The yaw axis also differs from the other axes in that the encoder is attached directly to the axis rather than being attached to one end of a leadscrew.

After interferometry tests, it was determined that the LTM was able to achieve 12 μm of mechanical accuracy on the vertical and horizontal axis, 5″ on the pitch axis, and 0.5″ on the yaw axis.

---

* Registered trademark.

LTM TRIAL ASSEMBLY

The LTM assembly strategy took into account that there are basically two types of assembly, standard and clean assembly. Several issues are pertinent to each type of assembly. The issues germane to both approaches are safety, organization, the manipulation of heavy components, lubrication, fabrication, qualifications of personnel, and assembly environments. Project policies restrict the use of solvents such as MEK and Trichlor 1,1,1 in the clean room because their vapors can potentially damage high-efficiency particulate air (HEPA) filters. However, there was occasion to use 1,1,1 trichlorethane (inhibited), methylethylketone (MEK), and Freon* TF (by Du Pont) during the assembly of the LTM. Some of the components weighed over 318 kg and therefore presented a potential handling hazard to technicians. Consequently, great care was exercised in the manipulation of the parts.

Organization was handled through configuration control, which is essential whenever an assembly has thousands of components, all of which must be tracked during the many phases of the effort. In this project, every part was catalogued and double-checked against a manifest prior to packing of crates. In many cases, for example with the ball bearing assemblies that were custom fit into the various leadscrews, it was critical that the integrity of the assemblies be maintained. The ball bearing assemblies were double-bagged, and the bags were attached to the appropriate assemblies. Identification tags were placed between the second and third bags (the third bag being the outermost), and all components that should not be mixed with similar-looking components were processed individually and carefully monitored at all times to prevent accidental integration.

The author contacted each of the vendors before the surface-treating/lubrication and precision-cleaning phase of the project, and very detailed meetings were conducted at the project site. During the meetings, the vendors were given copies of the overall project plan and a detailed inspection of the robot. Because the precision-cleaning of the LTM involved every component, two representatives were called to the project site before the LTM was disassembled. This vendor (Astropak of Downey, CA 90241) was given a highly detailed briefing of the robot. Approximately 100 photographs were taken by the vendor so that they would be aware of the scope and details of their task and so that they would be prepared for the number of parts.

The author also went to the vendor sites to oversee the repacking and final inventory of the components prior to shipment. As a result of this overall plan, not a single component of even the smallest size was lost. The final result of the cleaning phase was that the cleanliness of the parts was in conformance with the requirements of the project, and this phase was completed on schedule and on budget. This indicates that the efforts made at the start of this phase paid off.

LUBRICATION

One of the key areas that must be addressed with any dynamic mechanical system in a vacuum is the issue of lubrication. The assembly of ultra-clean parts can be difficult to accomplish safely without galling, and therefore a lubricant is necessary to facilitate fitup of the components in addition to performing standard lubricative functions on

---

* Registered trademark.

components that are mechanically cycled. High-vacuum lubricants must be low in out-gassing for space optics programs. In addition, the EUVE project requires that they must not contaminate the optics cavity components of the spacecraft or any other flight hardware. During fabrication of the LTM, several lubricants were used.

Dicronite was used initially on the leadscrews and on the ball and linear bearings. This material, which uses air as a carrier and adheres to the substrates by mechanical interlock, is a modified tungsten disulfide and is applied nominally at a thickness of 0.5 μm. With a coefficient of friction of 0.25, it has approximately one-half the coefficient of graphite at 400,000 psi and has an operational temperature range of −188 C to 538 C. Dicronite can be fully removed only by removing the substrate itself.

In the final analysis, it was established that Dicronite was not a good lubricant for our application because there were repeated problems with gear boxes operating at vacuum. Further, Dicronite provides little or no protection from metal corrosion even at the 50% average humidity of the clean room. Gear teeth were chipping under nominal loads to the point where individual teeth would wear completely off of the gear shafts. This phenomenon occurred on all four vertical-stage gear boxes at similar rates and almost as fast as if there was no lubricant at all. When Braycote 602* was substituted and applied to the replacement gears, the wear on the worm gears of the vertical-stage right-angle drive gears was reduced significantly, until the grease was displaced by the sliding action of the worm gear. At this point, the failure mode repeated. To solve the problem, a replacement gear box has been designed with bevel gears. This decision was based on the success of the bevel gear assemblies in other LTM drive boxes that had had Braycote 602 applied.

It would appear that Dicronite does not work on substrates such as gear surfaces: these substrates are not smooth enough to enable the Dicronite to cover the surface completely and adequately. On surfaces such as ball bearings, which have a typical finish of 4 μm, there were problems with the Dicronite binding the races. The technicians on the LTM project removed excess Dicronite on three separate occasions on the same lead-screws to improve the rotation of the nuts. The removal of excess Dicronite is a difficult task. This lubricant does not come off readily by hand, and it did not respond well to removal with any of the solvents approved for use on the EUVE project (see section on lubricants).

The second type of lubricant used was Braycote 601* and Braycote 602. Braycote 601 was applied to linear bearings, circular bearings, and leadscrews because of its anticorrosion additive. Braycote 602 was used inside various gear drives that are components on the vertical stage. These two lubricants are common high-vacuum lubricants and are highly effective on gear surfaces. Both types of Braycote will lose less than 0.7% of their weight at 232 C over 30 hours at the chamber base pressure used during the calibration exercises. The vapor pressure of this lubricant is less than 5×10^{-12} Torr at 20 C and less than 5×10^{-9} Torr at 100 C. Because the environmental conditions inside the chamber are pressures of 1×10^{-6} Torr at ambient temperatures, these lubricants appeared to be quite acceptable. The contaminant partial pressures were given final approval by the EUVE contamination control engineer, who used a residual gas analyzer (RGA) and witness plates during the initial LTM vacuum pumpdown.

---

* Registered trademark.

The third lubricant was molydisulfide. This lubricant was applied after a slurry utilizing Freon was made the carrier. The slurry was mixed at 1 part moly to 20 parts Freon TF; this ratio proved to be the least amount of lubricant necessary to prevent galling on the fasteners and yet not introduce any more lubricant than necessary to the assembly. Threaded fasteners and/or inserts of similar metals which have been precision-cleaned and not lubricated have a great propensity for galling, to the point where they can be removed only by being broken. Stainless fasteners that attach to other stainless components have the highest tendency to gall. Almost 90% of nonlubricated stainless fasteners galled and had to be broken for removal. After lubrication, no failures occurred.

The slurry is kept in a small container, the male threads (typically) are dipped into the mixture, and the excess lubricant is wicked off back into the container. The slurry is of a correct ratio when it discolors the fastener only slightly. More lubricant than this is excessive, and either the amount of molydisulfide should be reduced with respect to the Freon TF carrier and/or the excess should be removed from the fastener by carefully allowing the slurry to drip back into the container. If the technician performing this task allows the fastener to touch the inside of a wet container with the original slurry, the excess lubricant easily wicks off. When no more lubricant wicks off, the correct amount is on the fastener. The container holding the slurry should be covered when not in use, because Freon evaporates readily. Hardware with excess lubricant is highly susceptible to cross-contamination, and it takes a surprisingly small amount of time or excess lubricant before lubricant is spread a long distance over a clean facility. It is therefore imperative for technicians to change gloves and, in some cases, entire clean suits after lubricating fasteners or other components in a clean facility. Molydisulfide particulates during the installation and removal of fasteners and can also contaminate hardware with airborne particles. The appropriate technique for installing and removing fasteners lubricated with molydisulfide is to hold a vacuum hose close to the threads during installation and removal.

LTM CONTROL SYSTEM

The LTM manipulative operations are based on the Parker Compumotor AX Model 32* stepper motor controllers and is written in Compumotor command language. Figure 5 illustrates the circuit diagrams for the control system. Command entry is via Model 32 programmable ASCII terminals or via serial port from the host computer. User-friendliness and a substantial saving of time are achieved by programming all standard LTM operations into the 16 function buttons. This also reduces the potential for jamming the system because of typographical errors entered when commanding the system. The programmable functions for each of the function keys includes axis select, run up (or down), jog up (or down), go to absolute position, stop, kill-emergency stop and reset, go to low power, and go home.

The fully self-contained motor controllers drive a wide range of motor sizes, operate closed loop with encoders, and are controlled via an RS-232 loop with up to eight motor drivers. The AX driver has optically isolated outputs that are used on the LTM for brake control and stall indication as well as driver coordination.

---

* Registered trademark.

131

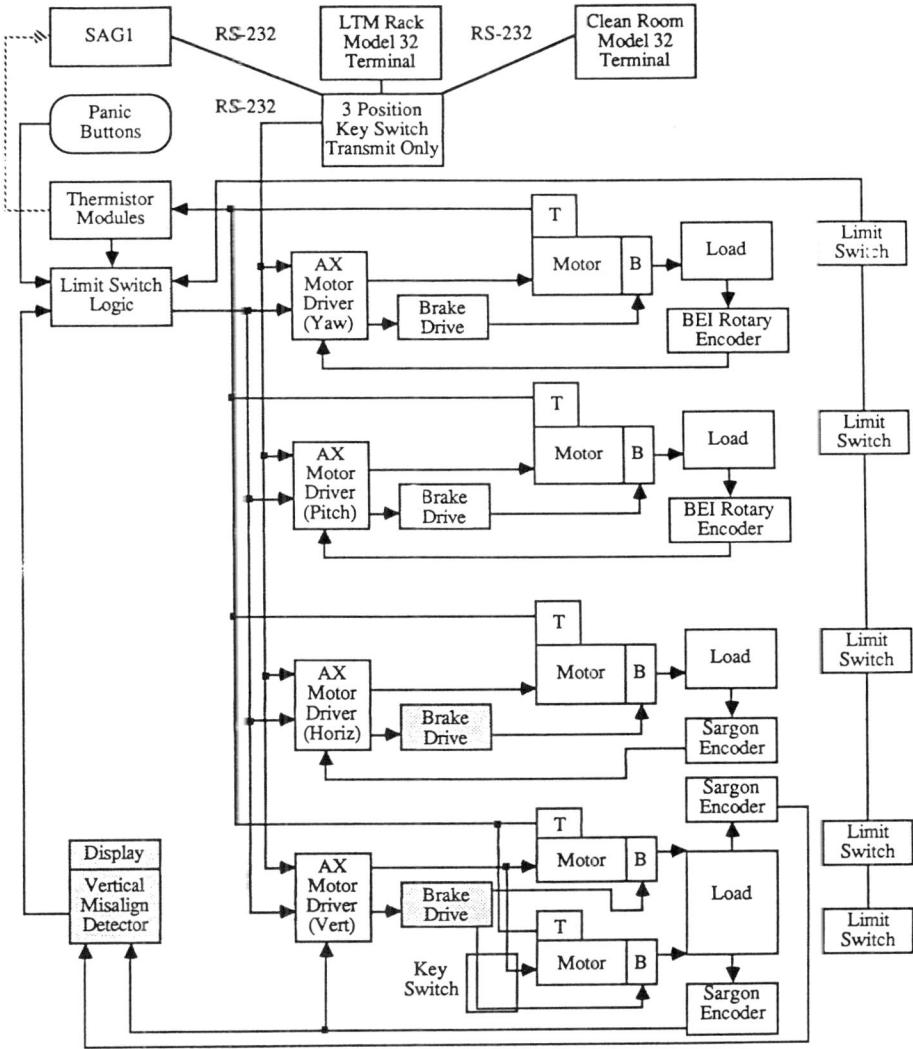

Figure 5. LTM Electrical System Schematic

The system has five motor drivers. The LTM uses two drivers in tandem for the two vertical-stage motors and three separate drivers to operate the pitch, yaw, and horizontal axes. Programmable sequences in the AX drivers are used for drive initialization and axis motions. Each driver is programmed to initialize on power-up with the proper encoder resolution and function operations and with the brake engaged and motor power off. Other programmed sequences achieve unit motion appropriate for each axis, such as one degree for pitch and yaw and one inch for vertical and horizontal. One function button on the motor control keypad can then achieve one unit JOG by issuing the command to execute the standard sequence number, i.e., XR2 (sequence for JOG-n).

The entire setup for the AX drivers and for the programmable terminals resides in a single source file on the Sun minicomputer and is downloaded via special software into the system. This achieves documentation and configuration control in one place.

A Thermal Monitoring System* (TMS) from Analog Devices, an important feature on all five stepper motors, has current temperature and alarm units which are mounted in the main control panel outside the clean room. The units give 0–100 C readings with an audible warning at 60 C and power removal at 80 C. Stepper motor heat management while at vacuum is accomplished by three methods: automatic motor current reduction to one-eighth in the AX driver, a brake driver circuit that supplies one-fourth voltage for brake hold and full voltage for brake pull, and software in the function buttons and computer that automatically actuates the brake and powers down the motor when it is not in use.

A diagnostic display panel is incorporated into the main operator console above the Model 32 terminal. This panel displays axis limits, home switch ("home" is the very middle of each axis' travel), drive power, motor power, brake position, and stall indication.

CONTAMINATION CONTROL

Ideally, one should fabricate components intended for high-vacuum environments in a manner that precludes the use of nonvacuum-compatible materials such as machining oils, greases, and visible contamination. However, real-world situations tend to make this principle difficult and often expensive to adhere to completely. A good example is welded components that necessitate fabrication in an environment that is not clean. In the case of the LTM, the baseline plan was to fabricate parts in standard machine and weld shop environments and have each component cleaned by an outside vendor before final assembly in the clean room. This approach was satisfactory for almost all components of the LTM. Some components, however, required further processing and evaluation.

One of the prime considerations was how to minimize the probability of the stepper motors' overheating while the optics cavities were exposed during the calibration exercise; overheating the motors could cause outgassing. The original approach included a separate vacuum pumping system on the motors in the event that they overheated while in use. This system proved to be ungainly and expensive in terms of maintenance and potential failure modes.

---

* Registered trademark.

Empire Magnetics (Petaluma, CA 94952) was contracted to improve the motors by integrating high-vacuum–compatible materials and components that would take greater thermal loading. They also installed lower outgassing windings and the TMS. The surface area of each motor where it attaches to the LTM was rechecked to ensure an adequate thermal path. Motor assemblies were improved by increasing thermal conductivity from their stainless steel motor casings to the LTM structure. This was done by installing strips of copper around the casings until the copper made solid contact with the aluminum housings in which the motor assemblies operate. Thermal radiation from the motors was also improved by removing material that inhibited the radiative path.

The LTM was monitored at vacuum with a quadrupole contamination system and NVR plates installed in the chamber to determine what was outgassing from the robot. Mostly light oils and water outgassed, which is normal in this kind of scenario, and it was determined that the LTM met the contamination requirements.

Virtual leaks can pose a serious contamination problem if they trap nonvacuum-compatible materials such as heavy oils or welding flux. Interestingly enough, one of the best detectors for contaminants in a potential leak area is the human nose. If something smells like oil or contamination, it often is. Threaded fasteners can be an area of concern in terms of virtual leaks. The LTM was baselined to have all through-holes. Where this was not practical, blind holes and/or the fasteners were vented to allow the trapped gasses to escape at a maximum rate.

FINAL ASSEMBLY

After the last of the major components arrived from a precision-cleaning operation, the final assembly was initiated. Because some of the components are almost 6 m long and the anteroom for the clean room is about 3 m long, some of the conventional clean room practices were temporarily relaxed in order to move the large pieces into the clean room. The parts arrived from the vendor triple-bagged, which is the project standard for clean components. The vertical-stage beams, bend ends, and end frames were loaded one at a time onto a low dolly. Three teams of technicians were organized: one to move the parts to the anteroom, a second set of technicians with clean gloves and smocks on in the anteroom, and a third set of technicians in full clean suits who took the parts from the anteroom into the clean room.

As each part arrived into the anteroom, the outer bag was peeled off. The second bag was removed in the clean room and the part located at a predestined spot on the floor inside the clean room. After the main structural components were inside the clean room, assembly began.

The rollout assembly was the first to be put together. The vertical-stage main frames were attached next, then the bed ends, and, lastly, the end frames. The major structural component assembly was completed in approximately two weeks, and from there the leadscrews and other items were added. The final systems to undergo final assembly were the electrical and monitoring systems, such as encoders and thermal monitors. The total final assembly, prior to debugging, required approximately two and one-half months.

FINAL CALIBRATION AND TEST

Two final tests were scheduled before delivery of the LTM to the calibration group. The first was an interferometry test to confirm the positioning accuracy of the robot, and the second a proofload test of the system.[8]

Laser Interferometry

We used a Hewlett-Packard 5528A Laser Measurement System[9] which utilizes a two-frequency laser and polarizing optics. The laser head is a source of two coaxial, linearly polarized, monochromatic light beams. One is polarized parallel to the mounting feet of the head and the other is perpendicular to the head. Their optical frequencies differ by approximately 2 MHz, or approximately 4 parts in 10^{-9} of the average optical frequency.

All of the measurements are made by converting a physical motion, such as travel along the beam axis, into changes of optical path length. In the interferometer, a polarizing beam splitter separates the two beams. Beam 1 is directed into the variable path of the interferometer, while beam 2 is deflected into the fixed path. Beam 2 strikes a reflector (a cube corner), which returns the beam parallel to its original direction, but with an offset. Beam 1 strikes a movable cube corner, and both beams return to the beam splitter where they recombine as a single coaxial beam. This combined beam returns to a counter, and the frequency difference between the two components is measured by the optical receiver.

If beam 1 strikes a cube corner that is moving, the beam returns at a different frequency, as a result of the Doppler effect. Since the type of interferometry performed on the LTM measures relative motion or changes in position, not absolute distance, measurements are begun at arbitrary points along the particular lead screw being measured. Typically, one of the ends of each lead screw was chosen arbitrarily, and the motion control system was programmed to cycle each axis completely from one end to the other over a period of approximately ten hours. Plots generated by the HP system were analyzed to determine the resolution of each axis in terms of mechanical accuracy and address repeatability.

The interferometry test was performed in the identical manner during final assembly as it was performed during the trial assembly. The test revealed that the LTM did not perform at the same level after clean assembly as it did during its trial assembly. This was due in part to the application of Dicronite on the pitch leadscrew and bearings. After the leadscrew and bearings were replaced and lubricated with Braycote 601 and a newly designed bearing block was integrated, the interferometry analysis revealed an improvement of a factor of 5 in accuracy over the initial clean assembly results.

Proofloading

The second and final test performed on the unit was a proofload test, to ensure that the LTM would support the weight of the largest of the telescopes it was designed to calibrate. A total of 907 kg of clean-bagged lead bricks was used, mounted on a 12.7 mm thick aluminum plate. This plate was bolted to the main table of the LTM, and the test load was manipulated by each axis of the robot. Visual inspections were performed on the welds before and after the proofloading, as well as on the main structural components, to determine whether or not any permanent deflecture was sustained by the mechanical system. The test was passed without any problems or measurable deformation.

INTEGRATION INTO VACUUM CHAMBER

The physical size of the manipulator with respect to the vacuum chamber precluded assembly inside the chamber. Therefore, the clean assembly took place on the rollout assembly, which is a device onto which the LTM can be rolled from the chamber for ease of servicing as well as payload mating and demating. The rollout assembly also makes possible maneuvering the LTM around the clean room as required to facilitate projects not associated with EUVE which require the clean room. Because the LTM uses about one-half of the entire clean room floor while on the rollout assembly, this became an important issue. The rollout is a truss assembly with a pair of rails that mate to the rails inside the chamber. The rollout attaches to the chamber only during the integration and removal of the LTM.

Safety specifications indicated in NASA Handbook NHB5300.4 specify that "no single point failure can cause loss of life, loss of mission, or major damage to hardware or facilities. No two combinations of failures can cause injury to personnel, damage to hardware or facilities." Therefore, special precautions were implemented during the design phase of the rollout assembly to eliminate the possibility of cantilevering or toppling the LTM while it is on the rollout assembly. The problem was solved by establishing a very wide tracking footprint and by designing each end of the rollout so that the wheels are located directly under the connecting point between the assembly and the chamber.

In a worst-case scenario, a technician can forget to connect the rollout assembly to the chamber, move the LTM onto the assembly, and not topple the LTM/rollout assembly. The footprint of the wheels was also placed wide enough that 25 technicians, each weighing 91 kg, can hang on one side of the LTM, with a 454 kg payload situated all the way to the same side of the LTM, and yet the entire assembly will not topple. Since there are not 25 technicians on the EUVE project, there can never be 25 individuals with simultaneous access to the room. The design was found to be safe.

In spite of weighing 1678 kg, the LTM can be moved easily with one person inside the chamber or on the rollout assembly, because of the lack of rolling resistance between the nickel-plated mild steel wheels of the LTM and the metal rails on the rollout and inside the chamber. Each LTM wheel has an independent integral locking device, a screw mechanism that binds directly on the wheel. A pair of hydraulic shock absorbers at the end of the rollout assembly stops the robot in the event of excess velocity. The probability of excess velocity during LTM movement exists since the amount of rolling resistance to overcome is minimal; however, only trained personnel handle the LTM.

One of the first tasks performed after installation of the robot in the chamber was to determine the time required to establish a base pressure of 1×10^{-6} Torr. This test helped determine the total outgassing level and whether or not there were any virtual leak problems in the LTM. The vacuum pumpdown characteristics of the chamber were tested prior to the installation of the LTM and were considered to be controlled variables.

Prior to the fabrication of the LTM, a gas load analysis (GLA) was performed, which is a mathematical computation designed to indicate the load placed on a vacuum pumping system. The first step of the analysis was to identify all of the various materials to be used. Next, the total exposed surface area of each material was calculated and its particular outgassing rate established. After totaling all of the robotic surfaces in this manner, the same calculation was performed on the total surface area of the inside of the vacuum chamber that houses the LTM. This included the Viton* O-ring area that seals the doors at each end of the chamber. Next, the pumping capacity of the vacuum system was calculated. The conclusion of the GLA was established by comparing the calculated outgassing rate of all surfaces inside the chamber, including the chamber itself, to the total vacuum pumping capacity. From this, a matrix was assembled that indicated theoretical times and base pressures available.

A GLA does not take into account the presence of excessive outgassing or virtual leaks, however. Virtual leaks are insidious, because they can go undetected until the initial pumpdown. It is estimated that a pocket of trapped gas of only a few cubic centimeters can degrade by a factor of 100 the base pressure in the chamber which houses the LTM. Therefore, it was essential that all virtual leaks be minimized at the design phase and that a close inspection of all welded and fabricated parts ensure that no trapped volumes will be present to degrade the base pressure. Welding vendors were under contractual agreement that they would use only metal inert gas welds. Gas or arc welding methods have greater propensities for occlusions and stress risers, which result from weld splatter and/or incorrect heat settings.

During the initial pumpdown test of the LTM, a base pressure of 5×10^{-6} Torr was achieved after four hours of pumping. This verified the cumulative relationship between the pumping capacity, the outgassing estimates, and the integrity of the chamber as forecasted in the GLA. It can be determined that the closer the theoretical pumpdown rate is to the actual rate, the fewer the qualitative and quantitative virtual leaks are, and the better the vacuum pumpdown performance. The vacuum system at SSL is fairly new; therefore, it can be concluded that there are no significant virtual leaks from the LTM.

ACKNOWLEDGMENTS

I would like to thank Steve Battel, the EUVE Project Manager, for his support and advice in all phases of the project. Very special thanks are in order to Gregori T. Stirling, the LTM lead mechanical engineer, and to Jeff Sather, the lead technician. Thanks also to Dr. Pat Jelinsky, EUVE Instrument Scientist, Dr. Barry Welsh, EUVE Calibration Scientist, David C. Ray, EUVE Contamination Control Engineer, and Roger F. Malina, EUVE Instrument Principal Investigator. Special thanks are due our editorial and secretarial staffs, who are the best. A word of thanks is always in order to the authors' long-time mentor and supporter, Mr. Earl Powell. The author also expresses heartfelt thanks to his wife Wendy, who is ever in support of the author's career and various endeavors. This work was performed under NASA contract NAS5-29298.

REFERENCES

1. Welsh, B., Jelinsky, P., and Malina, R. F., *Proc. SPIE,* **982,** in press.
2. Bowyer, S., *Adv. Space Res.,* **2,** 157 (1983).

* Registered trademark.

3. Lampton, M., *Proc. IAU Colloq.*, **40,** 1 (1976).
4. Martin, C. et al., *Rev. Sci. Instrum.*, **52,** 1967 (1981).
5. Bowyer, S. et al., *Appl. Optics,* **13,** 575 (1974).
6. Ray, D. et al., *Proc. SPIE,* **1118,** in press.
7. Reid, N., Space Sciences Laboratory, University of California at Berkeley, internal document (1986).
8. Powell, E., Assembly and Inspection Travellor for LTM Proofload, Space Sciences Laboratory, University of California at Berkeley, internal document (1985).
9. HP Laser Interferometry Data, *Hewlett-Packard Journal* (1983).

DESIGN CRITERIA FOR MECHANISMS USED IN SPACE

Robert M. Warden, Sr. Aerospace Mechanical Design Engineer
AEC-Able Engineering Company, Inc., Goleta, California

INTRODUCTION

Mechanisms for use in space must satisfy unique requirements compared with terrestial applications. The mechanisms must survive considerable vibration during launch, operate in the vacuum of space with outstanding reliability, yet be of a minimum weight and volume. The purpose of this paper is to give a brief description of some of the considerations that go into designing a mechanism for use in space.

VIBRATION

The structural designs for mechanisms used in space are often dictated by the launch vehicle vibration levels. The rumbling of the rocket motors, the buffeting of the aerodynamic forces and the acoustic pulses are all components of the excitation energy spectrum. To design for these forces requires a characterization of the input energy as a function of frequency.

Each launch vehicle has its own characteristics. On each launch, numerous accelerometers and pressure transducers are mounted throughout the vehicle with emphasis on structural interfaces. Real data is thus generated for various payload weights and configurations, actual wind shears, variations in propulsion effects, etc. The data from the sensors is correlated to generate the excitation energy function for various conditions. Millions of data points are processed to generate the input power distribution as a function of frequency as shown:

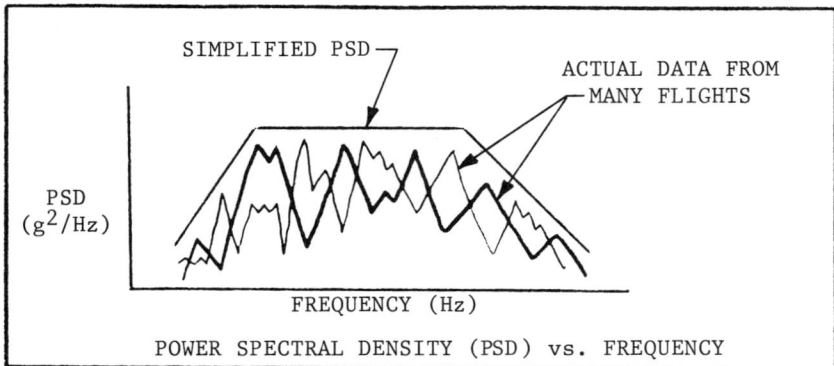

POWER SPECTRAL DENSITY (PSD) vs. FREQUENCY

This power spectral density function (PSD) is normally very ragged with large energy variations between frequencies. To simplify analysis, the PSD is simplified by creating an envelope which is greater than any real data points. Since this simplified PSD exceeds any experimental data and since the experiental data set contains millions of data points, it is normally assumed that the simplified PSD envelope is a three-standard deviation excitation power level distribution. Various techniques are used to predict the standard deviation response of structures to the PSD excitation input.

It is standard practice in the aerospace industry to take the predicted response, which is already based on a worst-case excitation, and multiply by a safety factor of 3 to generate the design load levels. Some components must also have a safety factor of 1.5 in addition to this. In the paranoia following the space shuttle disaster, the PSD has also been increased to the point where some structures must be designed to withstand loads of 50 to 60 g's. In simpler terms, if the shuttle were to crash, killing all life forms aboard, delicate experimental mechanisms aboard will have been designed to still function properly.

When the sources of the PSD are analyzed, it is found that most of the low frequency energy (5 to 200 Hz) comes from structural vibration of the mounting surface, whereas most of the higher frequency energy (200 to 2000 Hz) comes from acoustic excitation while still in the atmosphere. This change in energy source is useful in the testing of large structures because it is very difficult to vibrate a large structure at high frequency. It is becoming standard practice to mechanically vibrate only at lower frequencies and to acoustically test at higher frequencies.

VACUUM

Pressure is not a primary concern for vacuum-compatible mechanisms. Even in the hard vacuum of deep space, pressure differential is less than 15 psi, which usually does not change the way a mechanism operates. It is a good design practice to avoid enclosed volumes or to at least provide vent holes. It is undesirable to have an enclosed volume which is not sealed or vented because in vacuum testing it takes longer to achieve the desired pressure.

The main concern in designing a vacuum-compatible mechanism is outgassing. The generally accepted outgassing values for space are 1% TWL (total weight loss) and 0.1% VCM (volatile condensible material). Materials which exceed these values require special permission to use. The main problem with outgassing is contamination. If a substance outgasses from one part, some of it may condense on another part. Sensitive optical equipment is particularly susceptible to contamination.

There are several quirks to the outgassing problem. Nylon, for example, has low outgassing values, but it is hydroscopic. The water vapor absorbed by the nylon will outgas in a vacuum and may condense on a sensitive instrument nearby.

Graphite brushes in D.C. motors rely on water vapor in the air for lubrication. If the water vapor is removed by outgassing in a vacuum, the graphite becomes abrasive and literally grinds the motor to a stop. To solve this problem, special brush material is used or a "brushless" motor is substituted.

Lubrication is a serious problem in vacuum. Most wet lubricants such as oil and grease are not stable in a vacuum and will simply evaporate away. This is a double problem because not only is the mechanism without needed lubrication, but the oil may condense elsewhere and contaminate another part.

FRICTION

Friction is one of the many concerns for a mechanism designer. First, reducing friction is desirable to reduce force. For example, a smaller motor can be used in a more efficient system. Second, reducing friction prolongs life. Bearings, for example, will last much longer with proper lubrication. Finally, consistency of operation is usually achieved when friction is reduced.

Lubricants to reduce friction usually fall into one of three categories. The first are wet lubes such as oil and grease. The second are dry lubes such as dry film coatings. And the third are surface treatments or material selection.

Oils and greases are able to carry the highest load, but they migrate, so they have to be replenished after extended use. Dry lubes generally do not survive high loads well but work better than oils for aluminum-on-aluminum applications. Dry lubes may produce debris which can contaminate other systems.

By far the most preferred method is compatible-material selection. Rubbing parts of the same alloy usually have high friction and galling problems. Aluminum-on-aluminum is one of the worst combinations. An aluminum hinge with a steel hinge pin, however, needs little or no lube in most applications. Brass is occasionally used with steel to prevent galling. Another option is to anodize one part. Anodized aluminum on bare aluminum is usually acceptable.

There are some recently developed processes which provide excellent surface lubrication. One of these involves "co-depositing" Teflon with hard anodize on aluminum. The result is a surface which is both hard and slippery.

MATERIALS

Materials used to build space mechanisms must satisfy numerous requirements. They must be lightweight, easy to machine, resistant to stress-corrosion cracking, inexpensive, low outgassing, strong, stiff, stable at high and low temperatures, and corrosion-resistant.

Aluminum is the most common material used to build space mechanisms. Not all alloys are acceptable, however. Some alloys and tempers are susceptible to stress-corrosion cracking. 6061-T6 is easy to obtain and satisfies all the requirements. Fasteners are usually made of 300 series stainless steel (18-8) which is relatively weak, but it is corrosion-resistant.

For higher-strength requirements, 7075-T6 aluminum is used, but it must be stress-relieved to -T73 to prevent stress-corrosion cracking. 15-5 PH steel is used where high strength and/or stiffness is required.

STRESS-CORROSION CRACKING

Stress-corrosion cracking is a material failure which happens when the material is under tensile stress in a corrosive environment. The actual cracks are microscopic and often the material appears normal. The corrosion occurs in the grain of the material and is accentuated or accelerated when the material is under tensile or shear stress.

Certain materials are more susceptible to stress-corrosion cracking than others. Most aluminum alloys are resistant but the high-strength alloys used in aerospace are susceptible at certain tempers and must be stress-relieved, which makes the alloy slightly weaker. Protective finishes do not appear to have any preventative effect.

The reason stress-corrosion cracking is a concern for flight mechanisms is that the highest stress occurs during the vibration of launch and most launch facilities are near the ocean. This combination has the potential of catastrophic failure which could easily averted by judicious material selection.

ATOMIC OXYGEN

Atomic oxygen (O) is the main corrosive component of the thin atmosphere of low-earth orbits. Although the concentration is very low, it is very reactive, especially when impacted at 5 mile/sec. orbital speeds.

Exposure tests on the space shuttle (STS-5 and -8) have shown that some materials are more reactive than others. Three metals which were particularly affected are: carbon, silver, and osmium. Metal oxides were non-reactive. Organic materials such as Kapton and Mylar were highly reactive, but Teflon (TFE & FEP) was not measurably reactive.

These results are important because many solar panels have a Kapton backing and dipole antennae are usually silver plated. Ignoring the effects of atomic oxygen could have catastrophic results on low-earth-orbit satellites such as the space station.

HYDROGEN EMBRITTLEMENT

Hydrogen embrittlement is rarely a problem in current mechanism design because it is now better understood and precautions are routinely taken to prevent this effect.

It occurs mainly in metals which have been heat-treated or plated and involves hydrogen at high temperature or high pressure. The hydrogen permeates the metal surface and reacts to impurities to form other gasses which cannot escape. In this way, surface stress is built up which makes the material brittle. (This is something like the effect of water getting into small cracks, then freezing and expanding, causing larger cracks.)

To prevent this effect, strict procedures for heat-treating and plating have been developed which must be followed for parts to be used on space mechanisms. One material of note is 440C stainless steel which is commonly used for ball bearings. This metal is highly susceptible to hydrogen embrittlement if not properly heat-treated.

RELIABILITY

An incredible amount of time, energy and money goes into each launch into space. A failure of any particular component could cause a failure of the entire mission. It is therefore of utmost importance for the system to be reliable.

Reliability based on the past performance of a quantity of units is a simple problem in statistics. The reliability of an unflown one-of-a-kind unit, however, is nearly impossible to accurately predict. To increase the reliability of a mechanism for use in space, several factors are considered.

Simplicity of design is a good property of any mechanism, particularly for those used in space. A system with fewer parts or a more direct load path offers many advantages over a more complex system of equal function. Analysis of a simpler system is easier and usually more accurate. Fabrication and assembly are usually done with fewer errors.

Flight history is a good justification for using an existing design but is not always accepted on current flight programs. Some materials such as magnesium and nylon have extensive flight history but can no longer be used because of potential fire hazard. Welding has been used on nearly all of the early programs, but new restrictions make this process almost impossible to get approved. Modification of an existing design is a potential source of failure if the ramifications are not thoroughly examined.

Proven designs are always preferable, if not in exact detail at least in concept. A successful flight operation yields one data point in favor of an existing design. A designer must be wary, however, of the "It worked before, it will work again" attitude, especially if any changes are incorporated. The best results usually occur when an existing design is used as a guide rather than as a rule in making a new design. In this way, the complete design is thoroughly thought out.

Redundancy is one way of providing for unexpected failures. The usual goal is for no single point failures. Systems are frequently built to use either of two motors. If one motor fails, the other can be used. Telemetry switches are usually installed in pairs to give two indications of location. The problem with this is the case where the switch indications are different. Fortunately, the customer usually dictates the quantity and function of the switches. Structural redundancy is the reason many space systems, such as the Space Station, are four-sided. One leg of the truss can be damaged or removed, and the system retains some structural integrity.

Analysis is used to size structural elements. By using finite element models, accurate load levels and paths can be calculated to determine the required size of a structure.

Safety factors are routinely added to predicted loads to cover unknown or potential conditions. Unrealistic designs, however, can result from adding safety factors to safety factors.

Testing is the best way to demonstrate the reliability of a system. A development unit is usually made to prove out a concept and to refine the design. A qualification unit is made to undergo extensive testing to prove out the design. The actual flight unit should be exactly like the qualification unit but tested to lower levels.

The following is a list of typical tests performed on a unit destined for operation in space:

Structural (strength and stiffness, bending and torsion)
Vibration (sinusoidal, random, and acoustic)
Vacuum (operation, thermal)
Life (cycles to failure)
Thermal (high and low temperature)
Operation (high and low voltage)
Operation (redundant motor)

The matrix of test variations often becomes excessive, and the danger exists of wearing out the unit before all the tests are completed. Arbitrary safety factors are often introduced to overtest the unit. Careful selection of test conditions and test sequence is an important part in proving reliability.

Materials Selection Guide

Aluminum

ALLOY-TEMPER	YIELD STRENGTH (psi)	COMMENTS
6061-T6XXX	36,000 PSI	Acceptable in any form
7075-73X	55,000	Must be stress relieved
5056 H32	28,000	Solid rivets
5052 H32	22,000	Bent sheet metal shapes

Steel

ALLOY	YIELD STRENGTH (psi)	COMMENTS
303 S	30,000	Easiest to machine
302/304	30,000	Cold formed parts
300, 18/8	30,000	Generic fasteners, any form
440 C*	300,000	Ball bearings
410-416*	190,000	Dowel pins
15-5 ph 1025	145,000	Highest strength

*Normally requires material usage agreement from the customer.

Fiberglass

Type	YIELD STRENGTH (psi)	DENSITY (lb/in.^{3})
S-2 Unidirectional	280,000	0.075
G-10 Laminate	15,000	0.075

Spring Wire

TYPE	G 10^6 (psi)	E 10^6 (psi)	ALLOWABLE STRESS (psi)	COMMENTS	DENSITY (lb/in.^{3})
302	10.5	28	55,000	Least expensive (Stock)	0.28
Elgiloy	11.0	29.5	160,000	Non-Magnetic	0.30
MP35N	11.7	34.0	158,000	High-Strength	0.30
BeCu	7.0	18.5	75,000	Non-Magnetic	

Plastic

TYPE	YIELD STRENGTH (psi)	TEMP (°F)	COMMENTS	DENSITY (lb/in.^{3})
Delrin	10,000	-68 to +250	General Purpose	0.051
AF Delrin	7,000	-68 to +250	Teflon Added	0.055
Vespel SP1	12,500	-80 to +500	General Purpose	0.052
Vespel SP3	8,200	-80 to +500	Molydisulfide Added	0.058

Adhesives

TYPE	DESCRIPTION
EA 934 NA	High Viscosity
EA 956	Low Viscosity
EA 9394	High Viscosity High Strength
Solithane 113/300	Thread Locking Compound
Stycast 1095/9	Potting Compound

Lubricants

TYPE	PRODUCT OR MANUFACTURER	COMMENTS
Wet	Bray Oil 815 Bray Grease 601	
Dry	Everlube 620 Everlube 620C	Slightly Conductive Non-Conductive
Surface	Tiodize Hardtuff X-20 Anadite Anotef II	

Protective Processes

TYPE	STANDARD	COMMENTS
Chemfilm	MIL-C-5541	Conductive (Aluminum)
Anodize	MIL-A-8625	Non-Conductive (Aluminum)
Passivate	QQ-P-35	Conductive (Stainless Steel

CONCEPTS AND REQUIREMENTS FOR SEMICONDUCTOR MULTIPROCESS INTEGRATION IN VACUUM

Brian Hardegen
Brooks Automation Inc.
1 Executive Park Drive
N. Billerica, MA, 01862
USA

ABSTRACT

The requirements for front end process automation in the semiconductor industry have led to the development of modular, isolation transport systems. Such equipment enables batch load locking as well as serial processing and Scanning Electron Microscope inspection of wafers.

As multiprocess integration in vacuum gains acceptance in the semiconductor industry, the concept of space saving, high throughput networks must be considered. The successful implementation of such networks is, to a large extent, contingent upon the efficiency, cleanliness, and reliability of the wafer transport system(s).

Examples of vacuum process integration are shown, and a concept for high throughput networking by means of modular isolation transport systems with redundant wafer routing, is presented. A comprehensive reliability study on a vacuum robot is also reviewed.

1.0 OVERVIEW

Front end semiconductor manufacturing technology has evolved rapidly from largely human controlled and operated processes, to highly integrated systems involving computer control of transport automation and of process parameters. As in most industries, the motivation for such evolution is economic, with a goal of maximum yield at minimum manufacturing cost. Fabrication technology has also been driven by advancements in device density and performance.

Photo-lithography remains the most widely used means of pattern generation in 1989. While the associated emulsion formation, exposure, and development processes are performed in ambient conditions, liquid immersion is no longer required in the majority of front end processes. Device constituent film deposition and removal is largely done in a low pressure isolated environment. Since the majority of non-lithography related processes involve isolation, the load lock has become one of the most commonly used mechanisms in the semiconductor front end facility. Though conditions vary from one process to the next, and in many cases, from one equipment manufacturer to the next, the common requirement for vacuum isolation is shared by most process tools. Successive iterations of vacuum pumping and venting to atmosphere are required for each wafer or batch of wafers. These functions are inefficient with respect to time, energy and space consumption. They also provide opportunities for undesirable contamination of the product between steps, and preclude the achievement of certain device properties which are desirable for performance.

Between 1984 and 1988, both **intraprocess** and **interprocess** automation have been established as effective means to increase semiconductor product yield in the front end by means of contamination control and efficiency improvement.

This paper focuses upon the concerns of the semiconductor front end manufacturing facility, and more specifically, the means for addressing the requirements of contamination and process control in an efficient way, particularly for those processes involving isolation. Since isolation systems must involve automated wafer handling, this paper also covers in some depth, the subject of in-vacuum wafer transport mechanisms.

2.0 APPLICATIONS FOR ISOLATION PROCESSING

Semiconductor front end processes which presently involve isolation, broadly categorized, include the following:

Film Deposition and Rapid Thermal Processing

"Dry Etch" (Plasma)

Ion Implant

Electron Beam Lithography

Scanning Electron Microscopy (Inspection)

New processes involving isolation, the potential of which are not yet fully realized in the industry include:

Surface Planarization

Ion Beam Lithography

3.0 MULTIPROCESS INTEGRATION

A new concept has recently emerged which further improves manufacturing efficiency by partially consolidating the automation requirement and greatly reducing opportunities for contamination. This concept has become known as **vacuum multiprocess integration**, and involves the consolidation of more than one isolation process module in a general envelope which is exclusive of atmosphere. Ideally, a common wafer handling system is employed in such a system. The preferred configuration appears to be radial, with a single, vacuum compatible transport module in the center of the system.

3.1 Disadvantages

The only disadvantages of this type of equipment are that successful operation becomes fully dependent upon the reliability of the central handling module, and the expansion of the system is restricted by the limitations to the radial "reach" of the handling device. The system throughput is also limited by the speed of the central handler unless a dual end effector/exchange mechanism is integrated. There is clearly a level of expansion of a "single wheel" system beyond which diminishing returns would be realized.

3.2 History

The early semiconductor equipment involving multiprocess integration was not radial in configuration, and generally involved wafer transport equipment which was in part, resident in the process areas. While such equipment may have indeed provided high throughput, it did not necessarily offer the reliability or flexibility of a radially configured system like those which are currently available.

3.3 Examples of Multiple Chamber Systems with a Radial Handler

As mentioned previously, the preferred means of wafer handling for contemporary multiprocessing equipment is the vacuum compatible robot, housed within a centrally located chamber. It is desirable but not essential that the central chamber volume be minimized since the surrounding chambers, and in particular, those which serve as load locks, may be isolated by slot valves.

For historical reference, a concept sketch (figure 1) shows what was probably the first multiple vacuum process system with a central, pick and place type robotic handler. Substrata are transferred between successive deposition cycles in different chambers by the central handler, all without exposure to atmosphere. This system was constructed in 1984 and remains in operation in 1989.

One current example of a central handler in a multi-task application is that of the NanoQuest Scanning Electron Microscope (figure 2). The SEM column and a vacuum wafer aligner are attached directly to a 5 sided central chamber. Three Vacuum Cassette Elevators are also positioned around the central chamber and may be selectively isolated by slot valves. Respective elevator chambers may be alternately vented for cassette exchange, and subsequently pumped down for equalization and service. These vent and pump cycles do not significantly affect system throughput due to the fact that the central handler may randomly access and return wafers to/from a single cassette.

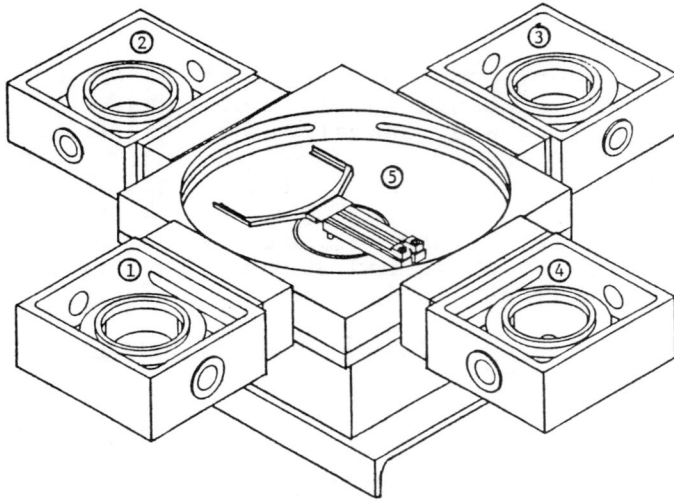

1.   LOAD LOCK AND PROCESS CHAMBER

2, 3 & 4.   PROCESS CHAMBERS

5.   MODULAR VACUUM TRANSPORT MECHANISM
     AND CHAMBER

Figure 1 - Outline of Multiple Process Deposition System

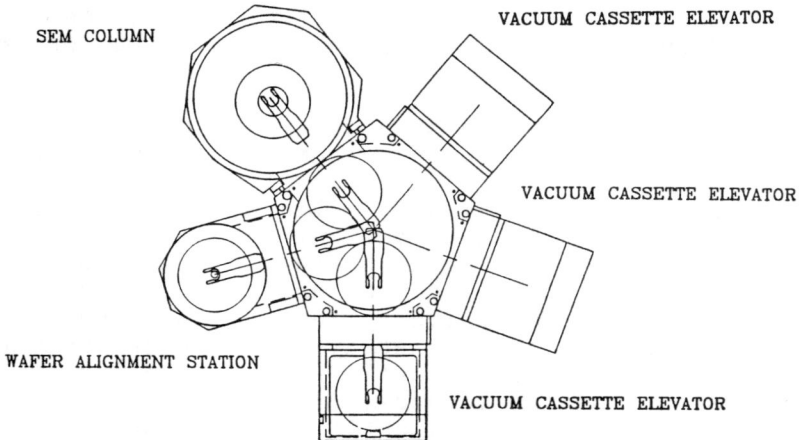

SEM COLUMN

VACUUM CASSETTE ELEVATOR

VACUUM CASSETTE ELEVATOR

WAFER ALIGNMENT STATION

VACUUM CASSETTE ELEVATOR

Figure 2 - Nanolab Model SR600 Automated Scanning Electron Microscope Inspection System (Courtesy NanoQuest)

Another hypothetical example involving a central robotic handler shows a multiprocessing system of "generic" form, with two Vacuum Cassette Elevators facing a clean loading area, and with three process chambers (figure 3). This system offers the flexibility of serial or parallel processing. A station in the sixth radial position provides a cooling and/or staging area for the wafers leaving the respective processes. Throughput in a system such as this one is clearly dependent upon both the speed of the central handler, and upon the time periods required for each respective process.

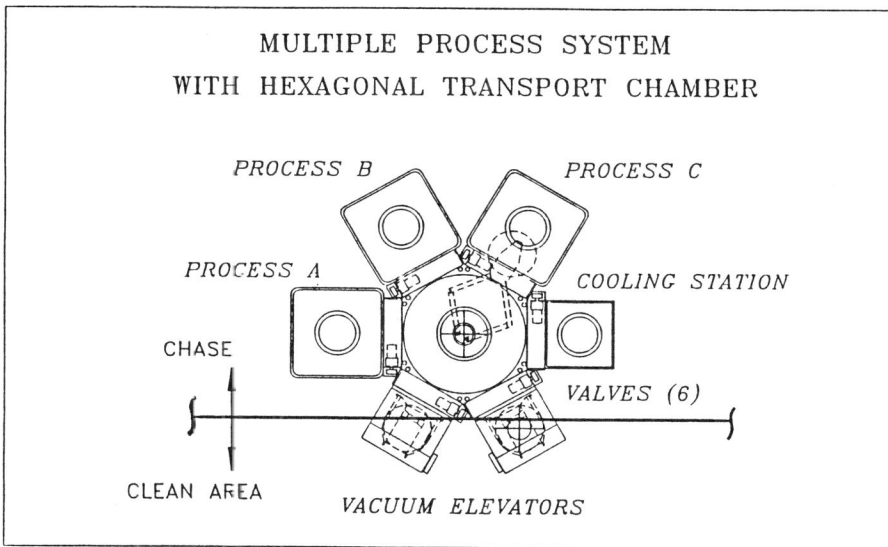

MULTIPLE PROCESS SYSTEM
WITH HEXAGONAL TRANSPORT CHAMBER

PROCESS B   PROCESS C

PROCESS A   COOLING STATION

CHASE

VALVES (6)

CLEAN AREA   VACUUM ELEVATORS

Figure 3

An alternative configuration for a fully automated and isolated process involves two wafer handling systems bridged by a vacuum Wafer Aligner (figure 4). The wafer aligner module serves as both a wafer staging and wafer pre-alignment station. This system architecture allows input wafers to be introduced into alternate load locks, separate from those which processed wafers are removed from, all without delay due to venting or pumping.

The process chamber and dual transport chambers
remain in continuous isolation.

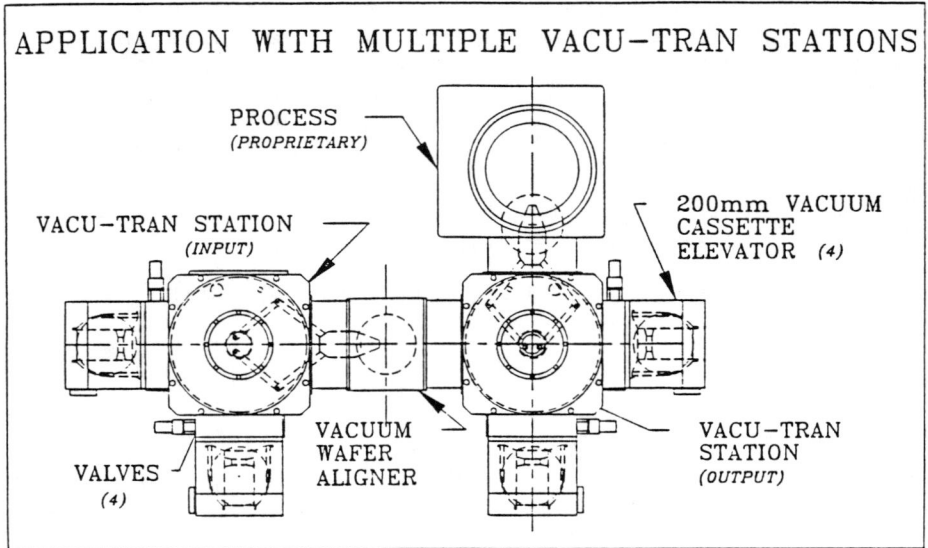

Figure 4

Vacuum Process Integration is clearly a new trend
in 1989, and it is probable that this concept
shall be utilized extensively in the 1990's for
front end micro-electronics manufacturing.

4.0   THE VACUUM COMPATIBLE ROBOT AS CENTRAL
HANDLER

The axes of motion required for simple, in-vacuum
wafer handling are: Radial "R", Rotational "θ",
and Vertical "Z". Additional axes of motion may
be required for wafer retention and for subsequent
rotation or inversion.

4.1 Isolation Mechanism Compatibility:

The challenge of reliable mechanism performance in
a vacuum has thus far been addressed in 2 ways:

a)   TOTAL VACUUM COMPATIBILITY;
     mechanisms are fully vacuum compatible, and
     are constructed of non-outgassing and
     corrosion resistant materials, with
     sufficient means for conductive cooling of
     motors and other heat producing devices where
     necessary.

b)   ISOLATION FEEDTHROUGH;
     conventional mechanisms operating in
     atmosphere are coupled through a mechanical
     or electro-mechanical sealed feedthrough to
     the isolated region, all to another
     functional mechanism which is fully vacuum
     compatible.

There are advantages and disadvantages associated
with each of these approaches.

The robot which is entirely vacuum compatible
operates without the friction or drag associated
with a sealed mechanical feedthrough, and without
the forces due to differential (atmospheric)
pressure. Performance may consequently be
achieved without sacrifice in power efficiency.

The robot in which the drive mechanism is isolated
from the vacuum chamber may be built from lower
cost conventional materials, and may be more
readily accessed for adjustment and/or
maintenance. Standard lubricants may be used, and
the cooling of motors and actuators may also be
conventional. Particulate generated by bearings
and dynamic electrical contacts are not introduced
to the isolation chamber, the volume of which may
be minimized.

4.2   The Vacu-Tran^{TM} Robot:

The vacuum compatible robot is at the center of
the Integrated System. As previously indicated,
reliability is essential to the performance of the
system built around it.

The Vacu-Tran^{TM} is a robot designed specifically
for wafer handling in isolation. It was
originally introduced in 1984. Axes of motion are
R (radial), Θ (rotational), and Z, (vertical),
enabling retrieval from, and replacement to
peripheral devices such as wafer storage,

alignment, or process stations. (Reference figure
5.)

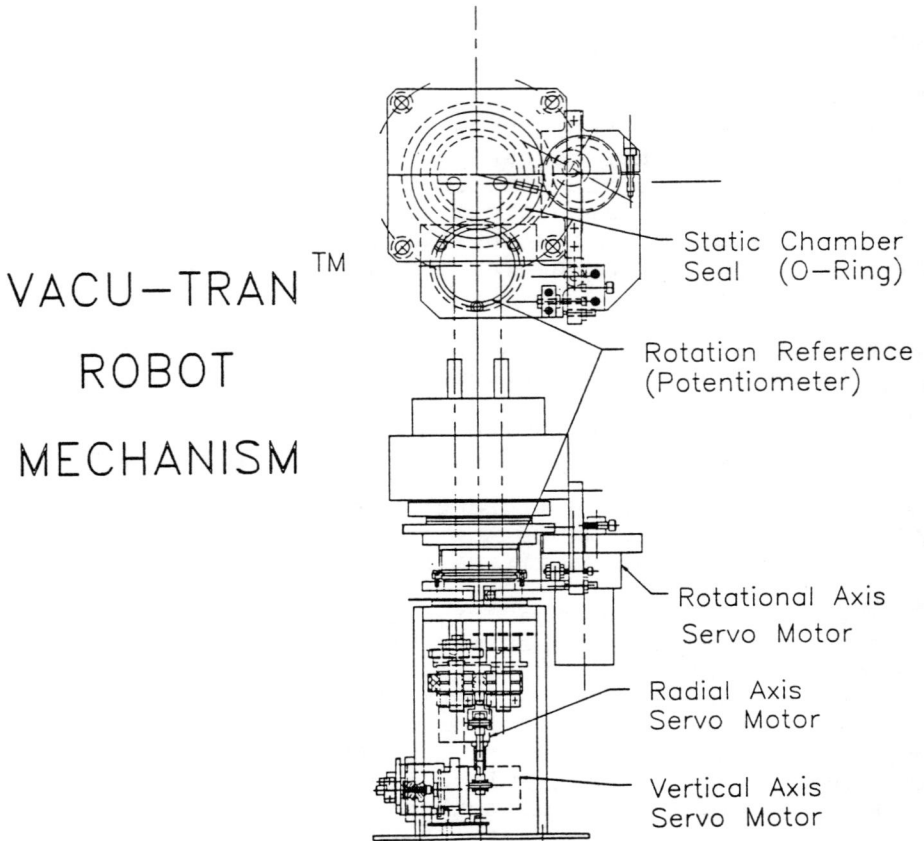

VACU–TRAN^{TM}

ROBOT

MECHANISM

Static Chamber
Seal (O–Ring)

Rotation Reference
(Potentiometer)

Rotational Axis
Servo Motor

Radial Axis
Servo Motor

Vertical Axis
Servo Motor

Figure 5

4.21 Patented Arm Mechanism

Operating in isolation is the patented "Frog Arm"
mechanism.   The arm consists of complimentary 2
bar linkage, with bearings at the elbow and wrist
joints.   These bearings are lubricated with the
vacuum compatible compound Krytox[R].   The end
effector is generally passive, and may be of
virtually any shape, as required for the
application.   The velocity profile of the end
effector provides optimum acceleration and
deceleration as a function of the linkage, and

reliability is assured by the simplicity of the design.

Since the end effector is passive, and in most forms, does not contact the wafer edge, the potential for contamination is minimal. Active mechanisms do not pass directly over (or under) the wafer surface, even during retrieval or replacement at a cassette load lock.

4.22 Feed Through Assembly

The proprietary seal and bearing assembly provides for both suspension and isolation of the functional robot arm mechanism.

Dynamic isolation is provided by 3 pairs of dual thermoplastic "C" seals. The space between the respective seals may be differentially pumped to a pressure $\leq 5 \times 10^{-4}$ Torr, thus eliminating the direct interface between the high vacuum and atmosphere. The pressure difference and consequent potential leakage between the differentially pumped space and the robot chamber is minimized. The dynamic seal leak rate in real operating conditions is $\leq 5 \times 10^{-8}$ Torr-litres/second.

Combination rotational/axial bearings suspend the complimentary shoulder shafts. The rotating turret is supported by high capacity angular contact bearings. In each case the bearings are located in atmosphere, below the seal sub-assemblies.

4.23 Servo-mechanisms

The 3 axes of motion of the Vacu-tran^{TM} are driven by independent DC gear motors.

Both the Z (vertical) and the R (radial) motion are actuated by relatively simple and highly repeatable dual position mechanisms. Sinusoidal velocity profiling is defined by the respective mechanical linkages as opposed to a complicated and potentially unreliable control system.

The Θ (rotational) axis operates in a closed loop, with absolute position reference and infinite resolution provided by a military grade, precision potentiometer.

4.24 Controller

Input to and output from the control PC board is effective in real time, with discrete signals for each function or event. Velocities are independently adjustable, and user selectable motion interlocks are provided. Motor current limit sensing in the R and θ axes provides for safety and diagnostics.

Sequencing of robot functions is not included in the driver card, and must be provided by an external control device.

4.3 Reliability Testing

Comprehensive reliability testing is necessary to establish the longevity of a product. A facility for the testing of the Vacu-Tran^{TM} under realistic operating conditions is shown schematically in figure 6.

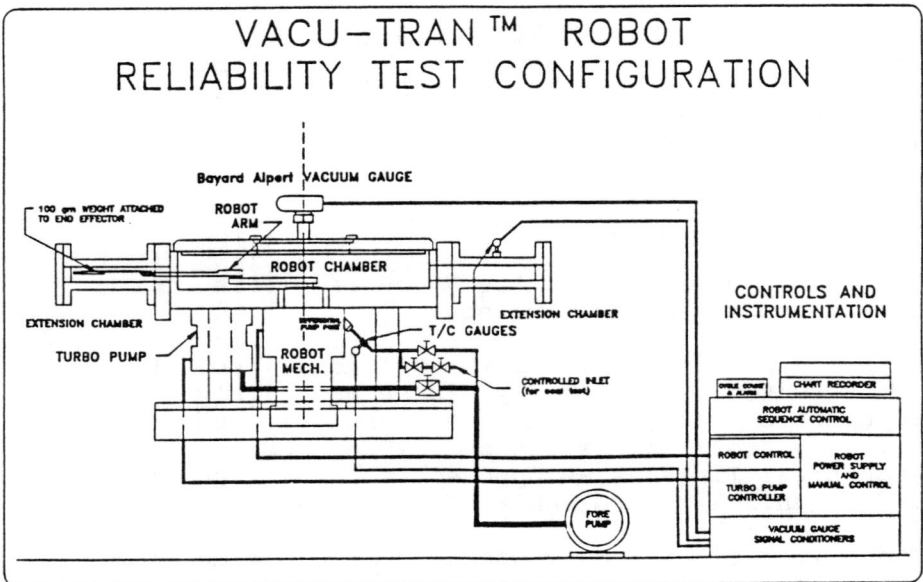

Figure 6

The testing involves repeated cycling of the robot in high vacuum, with a 100 gm weight attached to the end effector, simulating a load greater than that of a 200 mm wafer (which is approximately 65 gm). The sequence emulates a real application, and involves 2 each "pick and place" functions, with $180\frac{1}{2}$ rotation both to and from the origin. The duty cycle is effectively 100%, with the robot in motion during 17 seconds of a 20 second cycle.

The parameters which are monitored continuously include:

a) chamber pressure
b) rotational axis servo motor current
c) radial axis servo motor current
d) cycle count

The parameters which are monitored periodically include:

e) rotational positioning repeatability
f) cycle time
g) relative leak rate of the upper seal
h) differential pump port pressure

Testing of the Vacu-Tran[TM] has thus far proven reliable service in excess of the rated MTF of 200 hours at 100% duty cycle (or 2000 hours at 10% duty cycle). Continued testing is planned for the next generation Vacu-Tran[TM] robot.

5.0 ISOLATION NETWORK CONCEPT

Some imagination is required to provide a model wherein the radial multiprocess integration concept may be expanded efficiently and without restrictions. The hexagonal network, when modelled, appears conceptually to be both feasible and space efficient. This concept would address many of the aforementioned disadvantages of a multiprocess system with "single wheel", linear, or hybrid architecture, while creating new challenges which provide numerous opportunities for innovation.

A front end isolation network concept is shown in
figure 7. An orthogonally configured cluster of
photolithography related stations is shown for the
purpose of comparison. Dimensions shown are based
upon current, realistic dimensions. The hexagonal
configuration is clearly space efficient, and the
ratio of process to transport modules is slightly
greater than that of the orthogonal system, as
shown.

The hexagonal network model includes a combination
of transport and process modules with identical
outer form. Transport modules are identified with
the letter "T". Other devices such as cassette
load locks, low current ion implant stations,
wafer alignment modules ("A"), wafer inspection
stations, and wafer inversion stations are located
peripherally because their form is not consistent
with that of the "beehive" network.

Note that the modules which operate in isolation
do not require an ultra clean environment. The
cassette I/O (load locks), as well as the wet and
lithography related processes would necessitate
the expense of a clean room.

Wafer alignment is necessary for wafer
identification and inspection, and is preferred
for consistent in-process evaluation. Wafer
inversion is preferred for some film deposition
processes wherein the process by-products are a
potential contamination source.

The hexagonal network concept as shown provides
for various non-process functions. Wafer
alignment and metrology modules are peripheral in
location, but remain in isolation, and may serve
any part of the system as required. The wafer
inversion stations are located near the load
locks, and thus provide the option of wafers being
placed into individual carriers and subsequently
re-inserted into cassettes.

The hexagonal isolation network as shown is 260
inches wide, encompassing 11 modules. The center
distance is 24 inches, and the inscribed chamber
diameter is 20.75 inches. Isolation slot valves
separate each hexagonal module, and are shown at 3
inch depth.

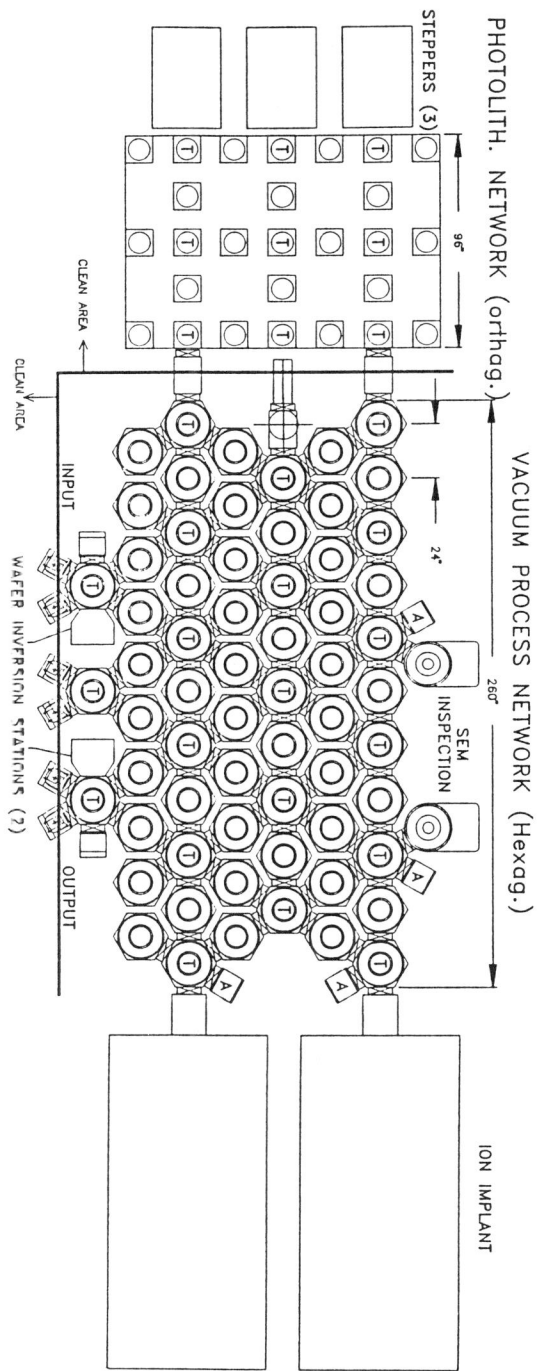

Figure 7 - Isolation Network Concept

Process related thermal conditions may necessitate
the inclusion of a single convolution bellows at
each interface to accommodate the dimensional
differences resulting from differential expansion
of modules.

5.1 Advantages of Front End Isolation Network

The hexagonal isolation network, when compared to
the single wheel, linear, or hybrid architecture,
provides significant advantages to the prospective
(user) device manufacturer.

   a)   space efficiency is optimum

   b)   clean space requirement is minimized

   c)   interprocess product batch transfer is
         minimized

   d)   product routing is flexible, enabling:

            -    serial or parallel processing
                 without re-configuration
            -    optimum throughput
            -    reduced dependency upon the
                 reliability of any single transport
                 or process module

5.2 Requirements for Isolation Process Network
Implementation

The isolation network concept as shown would
represent a very large investment. Considerable
effort would be required for the development of
new technology, the refinement of conceptual
technology, and the integration of existing
technology toward the successful implementation of
a comprehensive, network type manufacturing
facility.

The following entities are seen as some of the
requirements for the implementation of an
isolation process network. The list is
conceptual, and perhaps incomplete. Each item is
generally categorized as either:

- **existing technology** (E),
  that which is already implemented in a
  semiconductor front end manufacturing
  facility

- **conceptual technology** (C), or
  that which already exists in non
  semiconductor related industry, or exists on
  a smaller scale in a semiconductor related
  industry, or is assumed to be in an R&D
  phase.

- a **requirement** which remains to be addressed
  (R),
  that which is an obstacle to network
  implementation in 1989.

5.21 Equipment

- **Vacuum Compatible Robotic Handler   (E, C)**
  Both linear handling systems and R/θ/Z robots
  presently exist. Some experimentation with
  magnetic levitation systems for wafer
  carriers is in progress.

- **Cassette Load Lock   (E)**
  This device is most often a single axis
  cassette elevator.

- **Vacuum Wafer Alignment   (E)**
  This capability is presently available in a
  unit which does not involve edge or top
  surface contact with the wafer.

- **Vacuum Wafer Inversion Station   (C)**
  This device would, in concept, enable the
  individual wafers to be gently inverted
  (180°) without edge clamping. Wafers could
  subsequently be either retrieved, or placed
  into a carrier disc.

- **Laser Marking System   (C)**
  Laser marking systems do presently exist, and
  should be easily implemented in a vacuum
  provided the marking beam is directed upward.
  The only other potentially limiting
  considerations are thermal.

- **Wafer Characterization Equipment** (C)
Alpha-numeric and bar code reading equipment
is presently used in atmosphere, and should
be easily adapted to vacuum.

- **Multi-Wafer End Effector (for vacuum handling
module)** (C)
The ability of a single vacuum handler to
support more than one wafer offers a means of
significantly increasing the throughput of a
multiprocess network. Such a device would
also be space efficient by potentially
eliminating the need for a peripheral wafer
holding station.

- **Vacuum Surface Metrology Equipment** (E, C)
Scanning Electron Microscopy is presently
used for direct inspection of wafer surfaces.
Other non-contact measurement systems
(particularly those which are optical) should
be adaptable to vacuum.

- **Fully Modular Equipment Design** (E, C, R)
Handling modules should be autonomous, with
transport equipment being ideally non-
resident in the process modules. Wafer track
and levitation systems are not easily adapted
to this requirement.

5.22 Utilities (E)

Those items such as power, air, purge gasses, and
cooling water, which might be required by more
than one module, could be connected from a common
distribution point.

5.23 Equipment Access (C)

Horizontal access is not an option for modules
which would be "imbedded" within a network. It is
therefore likely that the wafer plane in a network
would be elevated so as to enable passage below
the system. Pumping equipment, utilities, and
process chemical I/O could be accessible and
removable from the bottom side, while handling and
process equipment could be removable from the top
side. Process control and support equipment could
be suspended above the respective modules without
preventing the top side
removability/replaceability of functional

equipment. The hexagonal network would very likely require more vertical space than a conventional semiconductor assembly facility.

5.24 Contamination Limits (C)

A goal of < .003 particles/cm^2 (at a size $\geq$ 0.5μm) per process/handling cycle represents approximately 1 particle per 200mm diameter wafer, at the indicated size. Particle density at smaller sizes (which could affect product yield) may be assumed greater than the number indicated. The size of 0.5μm is referenced for the purpose of measurability.

With respect to handling equipment and slot valves, this goal appears achievable with existing technology. Considerable effort may be necessary to ensure that such a limit is not exceeded in certain isolation processes.

5.25 Equipment Reliability Rate (C)

A goal of > 5000 hour MTF at 30% duty cycle is not unrealistic, and perhaps represents a point of diminishing return with respect to initial and ongoing costs, respectively.

Reliability remains an important issue in the multiprocess network concept. However, due to the option for redundant process modules and wafer re-routing, reliability is not necessarily a gating item as in the case with a "single wheel" cluster system.

5.26 System Controls

- **Distributed Intelligence Control Network (C)** This concept provides for localized control of regional process, transport, or pumping modules, and reduces the communication and computation burden of the central controller (master or host). Distributed tasks should be those which are autonomous by nature, and also those which are more efficiently controlled at the local level. Centralized control tasks should be all which are not handled locally, such as traffic management, recovery from interruption, wafer tracking, and summarized data storage.

- **Shared Isolation Valve Control (Process/Transport Modules) (C)**
This concept is important for safety considerations. The local, contiguous transport and process controllers and the central host should all have access to valve status. Each device should, on a priority basis, also be able to enable a particular valve in the event of unplanned circumstances. The contiguous transport module controller should determine valve direction based upon the safe clearance of the handling system.

- **Comprehensive, Centralized Traffic Management Software (R)**
The task of system management would be particularly complicated, and would require considerable development effort. The particular tasks of system optimization, recovery, and safety would perhaps be most challenging.

  Other industries including petrochemical, and air and rail traffic control, have successfully addressed the complex requirements which are in some ways similar to those of the multiprocess network.

- **Centralized Wafer Tracking (C)**
This particular task involves direct interface with wafer sensing, marking, and reading modules, as well as the associated central "book keeping" function.

5.27 Safety Requirements

- **Comprehensive Test and Diagnostic Routines (R)**
Both local and centrally controlled routines at various levels could be executed during preventive maintenance, before start-up, and otherwise, at random intervals.

- **Contamination Interlocks (R)**
This safety feature is required in both the local and centralized control systems. The interlock could provide for the detection of a potentially dangerous gas in an unsafe

location. The response could include a
containment process, by means of valve
closure, and a notification of operating
personnel.

- **Equipment and Process Interlocks (E)**
Little explanation is required for this
category of safety feature. One example of
an equipment interlock would be the
prevention of valve closure onto a transport
module arm.

- **Redundant Sensing For:**

    Substrate Presence of Absence (E, C)
    Wafer sensing should be provided in
    process and transport modules as well as
    in isolation valves. Sensing is also
    useful in the load locks, and on the end
    effector of the handling mechanisms.

    Internal Pressure (E)
    This parameter must be monitored within
    individual chambers to ensure the
    appropriate vacuum level and to reduce
    the potential for cross contamination.

    Presence of Hazardous Gas (E, C)
    Instruments with the capability of low
    concentration gas detection are
    presently available. Specific gas
    detection instrumentation is less
    expensive than that which has analysis
    capability. The input from multiple
    detection modules of a residual gas
    analyzer may be multiplexed to a common
    signal conditioner.

- **Emergency Power (E)**
A disruption due to a power failure would
have considerable impact upon a multiprocess
network. A fast changeover to a back-up
power source could eliminate the need for a
complicated recovery process.

5.28 General Requirements

- **Compatibility of Interfaces (R)**
This particular issue could prove to be the
greatest obstacle to the successful

implementation of multiprocess networks. The magnitude of a network practically precludes the possibility of a single equipment vendor. Adaptation may be an option in some cases, but standardization and subsequent interchangeability is necessary for the following interfaces:
>   **Mechanical,**
>   **Utility/Pumping,**
>   **Sensing,** and
>   **Controls**

- **Standardized Process and Transport Chamber Configuration** **(R)**
  This is clearly a requirement for the hexagonal network shown in figure 7, though non-standard chamber configurations may be positioned around the periphery of the network. Internal chamber configuration does not necessarily need to conform to the outer dimensions.

- **Well Defined Process Parameters** **(C)**
  Experimentation with a particular process module may necessitate the disruption of product flow in the network. Process definition is most easily performed outside of the network.

6.0   CONCLUSION

Vacuum Multiprocess Integration Systems have
evolved rapidly in the past 6 years.   The
application of such systems in front end
microelectronics manufacturing facilities is very
likely to increase in the near future, with a
larger scale of integration and reduced dependence
upon human input.

The device which appears to have been most
instrumental in the development of vacuum
multiprocess technology is the radial type, vacuum
compatible wafer handler.   The reliability of the
wafer handler remains fundamental to the
productivity of an integrated processing system.

It is likely that semiconductor manufacturing
technology shall continue to be one of the most
significant applications for vacuum compatible
automation equipment.

AIP Conference Proceedings

		L.C. Number	ISBN
No. 1	Feedback and Dynamic Control of Plasmas – 1970	70-141596	0-88318-100-2
No. 2	Particles and Fields – 1971 (Rochester)	71-184662	0-88318-101-0
No. 3	Thermal Expansion – 1971 (Corning)	72-76970	0-88318-102-9
No. 4	Superconductivity in d- and f-Band Metals (Rochester, 1971)	74-18879	0-88318-103-7
No. 5	Magnetism and Magnetic Materials – 1971 (2 parts) (Chicago)	59-2468	0-88318-104-5
No. 6	Particle Physics (Irvine, 1971)	72-81239	0-88318-105-3
No. 7	Exploring the History of Nuclear Physics – 1972	72-81883	0-88318-106-1
No. 8	Experimental Meson Spectroscopy –1972	72-88226	0-88318-107-X
No. 9	Cyclotrons – 1972 (Vancouver)	72-92798	0-88318-108-8
No. 10	Magnetism and Magnetic Materials – 1972	72-623469	0-88318-109-6
No. 11	Transport Phenomena – 1973 (Brown University Conference)	73-80682	0-88318-110-X
No. 12	Experiments on High Energy Particle Collisions – 1973 (Vanderbilt Conference)	73-81705	0-88318-111–8
No. 13	π-π Scattering – 1973 (Tallahassee Conference)	73-81704	0-88318-112-6
No. 14	Particles and Fields – 1973 (APS/DPF Berkeley)	73-91923	0-88318-113-4
No. 15	High Energy Collisions – 1973 (Stony Brook)	73-92324	0-88318-114-2
No. 16	Causality and Physical Theories (Wayne State University, 1973)	73-93420	0-88318-115-0
No. 17	Thermal Expansion – 1973 (Lake of the Ozarks)	73-94415	0-88318-116-9
No. 18	Magnetism and Magnetic Materials – 1973 (2 parts) (Boston)	59-2468	0-88318-117-7
No. 19	Physics and the Energy Problem – 1974 (APS Chicago)	73-94416	0-88318-118-5
No. 20	Tetrahedrally Bonded Amorphous Semiconductors (Yorktown Heights, 1974)	74-80145	0-88318-119-3
No. 21	Experimental Meson Spectroscopy – 1974 (Boston)	74-82628	0-88318-120-7
No. 22	Neutrinos – 1974 (Philadelphia)	74-82413	0-88318-121-5
No. 23	Particles and Fields – 1974 (APS/DPF Williamsburg)	74-27575	0-88318-122-3
No. 24	Magnetism and Magnetic Materials – 1974 (20th Annual Conference, San Francisco)	75-2647	0-88318-123-1
No. 25	Efficient Use of Energy (The APS Studies on the Technical Aspects of the More Efficient Use of Energy)	75-18227	0-88318-124-X

No. 97 The Interaction Between Medium Energy
Nucleons in Nuclei – 1982 (Indiana University)   83-70649   0-88318-196-7

No. 98 Particles and Fields – 1982
(APS/DPF University of Maryland)   83-70807   0-88318-197-5

No. 99 Neutrino Mass and Gauge Structure
of Weak Interactions (Telemark, 1982)   83-71072   0-88318-198-3

No. 100 Excimer Lasers – 1983
(OSA, Lake Tahoe, Nevada)   83-71437   0-88318-199-1

No. 101 Positron-Electron Pairs in Astrophysics
(Goddard Space Flight Center, 1983)   83-71926   0-88318-200-9

No. 102 Intense Medium Energy Sources
of Strangeness (UC-Sant Cruz, 1983)   83-72261   0-88318-201-7

No. 103 Quantum Fluids and Solids – 1983
(Sanibel Island, Florida)   83-72440   0-88318-202-5

No. 104 Physics, Technology and the Nuclear Arms Race
(APS Baltimore –1983)   83-72533   0-88318-203-3

No. 105 Physics of High Energy Particle Accelerators
(SLAC Summer School, 1982)   83-72986   0-88318-304-8

No. 106 Predictability of Fluid Motions
(La Jolla Institute, 1983)   83-73641   0-88318-305-6

No. 107 Physics and Chemistry of Porous Media
(Schlumberger-Doll Research, 1983)   83-73640   0-88318-306-4

No. 108 The Time Projection Chamber
(TRIUMF, Vancouver, 1983)   83-83445   0-88318-307-2

No. 109 Random Walks and Their Applications in the
Physical and Biological Sciences
(NBS/La Jolla Institute, 1982)   84-70208   0-88318-308-0

No. 110 Hadron Substructure in Nuclear Physics
(Indiana University, 1983)   84-70165   0-88318-309-9

No. 111 Production and Neutralization of Negative Ions
and Beams (3rd Int'l Symposium, Brookhaven,
1983)   84-70379   0-88318-310-2

No. 112 Particles and Fields – 1983
(APS/DPF, Blacksburg, VA)   84-70378   0-88318-311-0

No. 113 Experimental Meson Spectroscopy – 1983
(Seventh International Conference, Brookhaven)   84-70910   0-88318-312-9

No. 114 Low Energy Tests of Conservation Laws in
Particle Physics (Blacksburg, VA, 1983)   84-71157   0-88318-313-7

No. 115 High Energy Transients in Astrophysics
(Santa Cruz, CA, 1983)   84-71205   0-88318-314-5

No. 116 Problems in Unification and Supergravity
(La Jolla Institute 1983)   84-71246   0-88318-315-3

No. 117 Polarized Proton Ion Sources
(TRIUMF, Vancouver, 1983)   84-71235   0-88318-316-1